Statistics for Library and Information Services

A Primer for Using Open Source R Software for Accessibility and Visualization

ALON FRIEDMAN

D0075374

ROWMAN & LITTLEFIELD
Lanham • Boulder • New York • London

Published by Rowman & Littlefield
A wholly owned subsidiary of The Rowman & Littlefield Publishing Group, Inc.
4501 Forbes Boulevard, Suite 200, Lanham, Maryland 20706
www.rowman.com

Unit A, Whitacre Mews, 26-34 Stannary Street, London SE11 4AB

British Library Cataloguing in Publication Information Available

Library of Congress Cataloging-in-Publication Data

Friedman, Alon, 1966–
  Statistics for library and information services : a primer for using open source R software for accessibility and visualization / Alon Friedman.
    pages cm
  Includes bibliographical references and index.
  ISBN 978-1-4422-4992-9 (hardcover : alk. paper) — ISBN 978-1-4422-4993-6 (ebook)
  1. Information science—Statistical methods. 2. Library statistics. 3. R (Computer program language) 4. Information visualization. I. Title.
  Z669.8.F75 2016
  020.72'7—dc23
                                                          2015020574

Printed in the United States of America

Contents

List of Figures   vii

Acknowledgments   xi

Preface   xiiii

PART I: INTRODUCTION TO STATISTICS

1   Introduction   3
2   Research Design   13
3   Data (Types and Collection Methods)   29
4   How to Run R   45

PART II: MAKING SENSE OF STATISTICS

5   Descriptive Statistics   67
6   Bivariate Statistics   79
7   Probability Theory   89
8   Random Variables and Probability Distributions   105
9   Sampling   123
10   Confidence Interval Estimation   149
11   Fundamentals of Hypothesis Testing   171
12   Correlation and Regression   189
13   Analysis of Variances and Chi-Square Tests   205
14   Time Series and Predictive Analytics   235

PART III: VISUALIZATION IN R

15   Visualization Display   257
16   Advanced Visualization Display   277
17   Applying Visualization to Statistics Analysis   299

APPENDIX A   Statistics Formula Sheet   315

APPENDIX B   Z Score Table   319

APPENDIX C   Useful R Commands   323

References   341

Index   345

About the Author   355

List of Figures

1.1	Descriptive versus Inferential Statistics	5
1.2	Population versus Sample	6
1.3	Deposit Slip Made by Post Office Saving Bank 1869	8
1.4	Open Source R Table	9
2.1	The Research Process	16
4.1	The R's Console	46
4.2	Excel Save Window	60
4.3	R Display of the Data	61
4.4	Google Publish Window	62
5.1	Symmetrical Distribution	71
5.2	Negative Skewed Distribution	72
5.3	Positive Skewed Distribution	72
5.4	The First Histogram Using R	76
6.1	Positive, Negative, and No Correlation	81
6.2	Computing Pearson's	83
6.3	The Plotting of Our Pearson's	85
6.4	The Monotonic Relationships in Spearman's Correlation	86

7.1	Illustration of Probability	91
8.1	Dostoyevsky's *Humiliated and Insulted*	108
8.2	Book Distribution	109
8.3	Binomial Distribution	113
8.4	Books Read by Volunteers	116
8.5	The Common Bell Curve	117
8.6	The Distribution Percentages of a Bell Curve	118
9.1	Population and Sample	124
9.2	Histogram	137
9.3	Fitting the Normal Curve to the Histogram	138
10.1	Populations May Contain Any Number of Samples which Approximate, but May Vary Somewhat From, the Values of the Entire Population	150
10.2	Illustration of the Point Estimate's Relationship to the Confidence Interval	151
10.3	Illustration of a Confidence Level	155
10.4	The t Distribution Compared to the Standard Distribution	158
10.5	Confidence Level and t Distribution	159
10.6	Distributions of Means for Repeated Samples	162
11.1	Two-Tailed Hypothesis	178
11.2	Plot X and Y under t Distribution	183
12.1	The Pearson Product-Moment Correlation under Three Conditions	191
12.2	Scatterplots of Sample Correlations, Note Positive and Negative Values	193
12.3	The Z Score and Its Values	195
12.4	Eight Least Square Regression Formula	196
12.5	Regression Analysis and Student Borrowing Habits	197
12.6	High School and College Student Habits Use of the Library	197
12.7		198
12.8	R Scatterplot of High School vs. College Library Borrowing	202

14.1   The Number of Books Borrowed from the Library   238

14.2   Long Term Upward   239

14.3   Downward Movement   239

14.4   Linear Line Graph of the Old Numbers of Years   243

15.1   Minard's Napoleon Invasion of Russia of 1812   258

15.2   Plot Made with "Mtcars" Dataset   260

15.3   Example of a Hexadecimal Color   261

15.4   Part of the List of Colors Command   262

15.5   The Rainbow Palette   263

15.6   The Heat Palette   263

15.7   The Terrain Palette   264

15.8   The Topo Palette   264

15.9   R Plot PCH Symbols   266

15.10 A Simple Pie   267

15.11 A Pie with Text   268

15.12 A Pie with Color and Text   269

15.13 The Plot of "Cars" Dataset   271

15.14 Cars with Type = "h"   272

15.15 The Histogram of Duration   273

15.16 Using Colors   274

16.1   Example of Line Specified by Slope and Intercept   279

16.2   Example of Color, Fill, and Alpha   281

16.3   Example of Geom Bar   282

16.4   Example of Different Coloring Scales   284

16.5   Example of Coord_Flip()   285

16.6   Example of Stat_Summary   286

16.7   Box Plot with Colors   288

16.8   Scatterplot with One Color   289

16.9   Scatterplot with Multiple Colors   290

16.10   Pareto Chart   291

16.11   Multivariate Data in 2D   293

16.12   Example of Heat Map   294

16.13   USA Map   296

17.1   Bar Graph without Text   302

17.2   Titled and X and Y Axes   302

17.3   Title, Annotations, and Labels Are Used Sparingly   303

17.4   This Figure Holds Three Thousand Data Points Based
        on Student's Scores   304

17.5   Two-Dimensional Graph Arranged by Word Frequencies   304

17.6   The Three Primary Colors   305

17.7   Additive Colors   306

17.8   Subtractive Colors   307

17.9   Subtractive Primaries Mixing Chart   308

17.10   Gridlines Are Not Muted   309

17.11   Gridlines Are Muted   310

17.12   Graph with a Border Line   310

17.13   Without Border   311

17.14   Unnecessary Use of Too Many Tick Marks   311

Acknowledgments

Thank you to editor Charles Harmon and his team for support and help throughout the development of this book. I would also like to thank JoAnn Tebo for her tireless editing efforts and Kevin Hawley for helping with the book's logo. And most importantly, I would like to thank my wife, Colleen Parker, for standing by me and allowing me to pursue this project.

Preface

> These days the statistician is often asked such questions as "Are you a Bayesian?" "Are you a frequentist?" "Are you a data analyst?" "Are you a designer of experiments?" I will argue that the appropriate answer to ALL of these questions can be (and preferably should be) "yes," and that we can see why this is so if we consider the scientific context for what statisticians do.
>
> —George E. P. Box

About This Book

Statistics for Library and Information Services: A Primer for Using Open Source R *Software for Accessibility and Visualization* is designed to provide non-statisticians working in library and information settings with a logical, user-friendly, and step-by-step guide to the concepts of statistical theory and data collection methodologies. It also offers ways to extend to the topics of visualization creation and display so non-statisticians can better conduct statistical analysis and communicate findings.

Special attention is given to statistical methodologies and frameworks, with a focus on understanding both the pragmatic aspect of statistical methodologies and the meaning behind these methodologies as the means for analyzing data as employed by library science professionals. The guide employs open source R software as its main statistical application service, which can be used on Macintosh systems, the Google platform(s), and Microsoft system(s). The visualization aspect of the book is customized and presented as a process that is directly connected to the study of statistical analysis and will provide readers with an understanding of the visual design choices that they can pursue after conducting their statistical analysis. The book is specifically geared for information science students and professionals.

Open source R is a software programming language and software environment for statistical computing and graphics that is available free of charge. R is a programming language that people can customize to meet their needs and that gives users more control than other statistical software applications. Another advantage of R is its ability to run on any platform with any electronic device. R has gained wide acceptance in many fields and different sectors, from governmental institutions to private companies. This book aims to serve a hybrid purpose that covers statistical topics and R software, demonstrating the power of statistical analysis visualization produced in R.

Audience

The target audience for this book consists of information science students and faculty and professionals. The majority of information science departments in the United States offer some basic courses in statistics; many of these courses, however, do not use a standardized textbook but instead borrow those from other fields.

The second target audience for this textbook is information professionals who work in the public and business sectors. These professionals do not have any statistical analysis reference textbooks or software applications to support their daily work activities in the field.

Organization

Statistics for Library and Information Services: A Primer for Using Open Source R Software for Accessibility and Visualization features seventeen chapters, organized into three parts. Each chapter illustrates how to use open source R and contains two subsections emphasizing the statistical model and its visual representation. The statistical model will capture the main statistical formulas/theories covered in each chapter, while the visual representation will address the subject of the types of visualization that are produced from the statistical analysis model covered in that particular chapter.

The book's contents include part I, Introduction to Statistics, which features four chapters. Chapter 1 discusses essential background information. It covers basic terminology and the basic installation of open source R. Chapter 2 develops the process of research and the research hypothesis, helping the student to identify their research question. Chapter 3 examines the types of data and collection methods so that students can determine the type of data they will need to analyze and the effect of that data on the choice of scales of measurement. Chapter 4 introduces the R interface and its command line.

Part II, Making Sense of Statistics, comprises ten chapters. Chapter 5 considers descriptive statistics, including central tendency, variation, shape of distributions, frequencies, and the standard deviation in R. Chapter 6 introduces bivariate analysis, often called one of the simplest forms of analysis that entails the analysis of two variables (denoted as X and Y). Chapter 7 introduces the concept of probability theory and its basic properties, including Z scores. By the end of the chapter, the student will be familiar with conditional and independence, and estimating probability using simulation. Chapter 8 discusses random variables and probability distributions, including discrete and continuous random variables, and both the mean and standard deviation of a random variable. Chapter 9 introduces the ideas of sampling, the central limit theorem, and sampling distributions for proportions.

Chapter 10 takes up confidence intervals in a population, point estimation, large-sample confidence interval in a population, and the population mean. Chapter 11 introduces hypothesis testing of the mean, testing a proportion p, testing with paired difference (dependent sample and independent sample), correlation and coefficient determination, and comparing two populations and treatments. Chapter 12 follows through with correlation and both linear and regression analysis.

Chapter 13 explores inferences using the chi-square distribution, single factor ANOVA, the F test, multiple comparisons, and the Two Factor ANOVA. Chapter 14 introduces the student to nonparametric tests that address distribution that does not fit the normal pattern. Time series and predictive analysis are covered in chapter 14, including probability and non-probability distribution methods. Chapter 15 ends the section with common distribution theories in library science. These are familiar ones which occur frequently in library science including Pareto's law, Benford's law, Lotk's law, and Zipf's law. By the end of the chapter, the student will be using different applied bibliometrics.

Part III, Visualization in R, begins to delve more deeply into visualization. It contains three chapters. Chapter 15 discusses visualization analysis by examining the steps to produce basic visualization, including bar, line, and pie graphs. By the end of the chapter, the student will be able to employ R in order to analyze descriptive statistics distribution. Chapter 16 continues the discussion with display of visualizations by introducing a package called ggplot2 in order to produce more advanced visualization analysis. By the end of the chapter, the student will have clear methodologies and examples of designing more complex visualization. Chapter 17 ends the section by putting the design element and statistics analysis together to produce better visualization. The chapter discusses five major checklists that include supporting text, arrangement, colors, lines, and grabbing the user's attention.

Three appendices summarize several topics. Appendix A provides a summary of all the frequency statistical formulas used throughout this book. Appendix B offers the statistics tables, including Z score and critical values for T-distribution. Appendix C lists the most common commands in R.

Together, these sections provide an excellent working introduction to statistics and R, adding future studies and important employment skills for information science students, faculty, and practitioners. This information will also be an asset to those seeking direction in statistical analysis for business and public sector needs. The visualization skills gained through use of R will be useful for the explanation and presentation of data in various settings.

## PART I

INTRODUCTION TO STATISTICS

CHAPTER 1

Introduction

1.1   What Is Statistics?
1.2   A Short History of Statistics
1.3   Types of Statistics
1.4   Population Versus Sample
1.5   Data and Levels of Measurement
1.6   Introduction to Spreadsheets
1.7   Open Source Software
1.8   How to Install R
1.9   Summary
1.10 Glossary
1.11 References

1.1 What Is Statistics?

The term *statistics* has two traditional meanings that are often used in different contexts. Most often, statistics refers to numerical facts. Under this definition, statistics provides a numerical value for any object/subject/text that we examine. Two good examples of statistics according to this definition would be (A) the number of visitors to the library catalog website each month and (B) how often users rely on Facebook to find out about new events that the library offers.

The second definition of statistics refers to a group of methodologies that provide directions on how to collect, analyze, represent, and interpret data and make better decisions. In this book, we will discuss statistics on the basis of the second definition, in that we will cover the role of statistics that helps us examine the data we collect and provide the interpretations needed to make better decisions. Statistics includes three major functions. The first function covers the data collected, the second involves the methodology used to analyze this data, and the last facilitates the communication of the findings from our analysis to the people around us.

So, why it is so important to learn about statistics? Statistics has become a global tool and language for empirical studies in every field and profession across cultures and languages, expanding at the same rate as the use of computer systems. In the field of library science, statistics will play an important part in how we will measure user impact and demand upon library services.

1.2 A Short History of Statistics

The history of statistics has often been recorded as part of the history of mathematics. The first documentation of mathematics was found in ancient Egypt and Babylonia, and it continued growing in ancient Greece and the rest of the world. Mathematics was transported to different cultures and geographical regions and became a global language throughout the entire world. The historian Thucydides described the method Athenians used to calculate the height of a wall plate they built during 508 BCE. First, they counted the number of bricks in an unplastered section of the wall. Multiplying this value by the height of the bricks used in the wall allowed the Athenians to determine the height of the ladders necessary to scale the walls. The count was repeated several times by a number of different soldiers. Today, this type of counting is called the mode, which stands for the most frequent value that allows us to determine the most likely value of the number of bricks. Statistics is the practice and science of collecting and analyzing numerical data that helps professionals to measure and predict the future requirements of their specific projects.

1.3 Types of Statistics

Statistics has often been divided into two areas of investigation: theoretical and applied. Over time, however, a third classification was developed that includes two types of statistical approaches: descriptive and inferential. Descriptive statistics often deals with organizing, displaying, and describing the entire dataset by using the summary central tendency, frequencies, variation, and shape. Inferential statistics, in contrast, consists of the use of sample results to help make decisions or predictions about the population. We will discuss descriptive statistics in chapter 2 and inferential statistics in chapters 6–8. Figure 1.1 summarizes the two different statistical approaches.

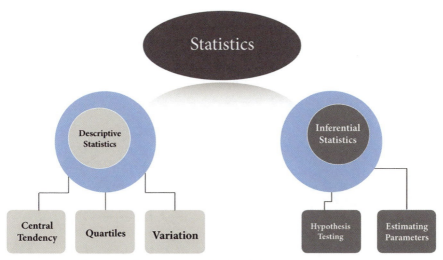

Figure 1.1.   Descriptive vs. inferential statistics

Each type of statistical approach provides a different way of looking at the data with regard to the population and the sample of the population that the researcher wishes to examine. For a useful summary for statistics formula, see appendix A.

1.4 Population Versus Sample

An important question that researchers often need to address is: What is being examined—the entire population or a sample of the population? The term *population* refers to all members of a group that the researcher has an interest in studying. But, what happens when the population is very large and the researcher has neither the access nor the resources to measure every single item in this huge collection? In these instances, the researcher usually takes a *sample*. The term *sample* stands for a section of the population. A famous example in which a population sample is used occurs every four years before the U.S. presidential election. At that time, various media organizations sample the opinions of the citizenry to try to determine which of the candidates the voters will elect. The measure of a characteristic of a population is called a *parameter*. In library science, researchers often use a sample in annotated bibliography and usability studies.

A sample consists of selecting subgroups from a population. For a sample to be useful it should reflect the similarities and differences found in the population. The main objective of drawing a sample is to make inferences about the entire population. A *statistic* is a summary measure computed from a sample to describe a characteristic of the population. To better illustrate this, figure 1.2 displays the difference between population and sample.

Another term that is often associated with both terms (*population* and *sample*) is *unit of analysis*. The unit of analysis refers to the person, collection,

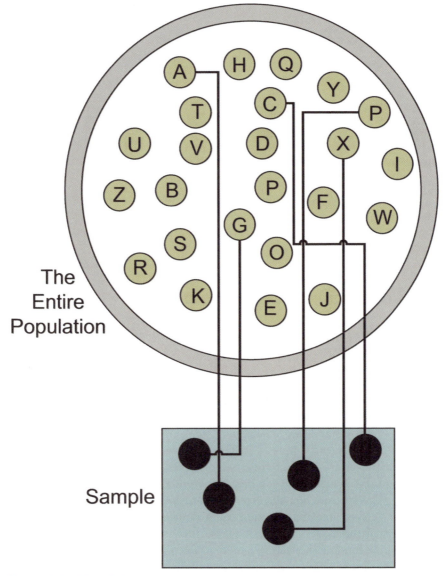

Figure 1.2. Population vs. sample

or object that is the target of the investigation. Units of analysis could include individuals, groups, organizations, countries, technologies, and artifacts. Many researchers often refer to the unit of analysis in their manuscript as a reference to their study population. Next, what are we measuring?

1.5 Data and Levels of Measurement

Throughout this book, we will discuss three important terms: *data, measurement,* and *variable.* The term *data,* in this book, is defined as the physical representation of a numerical collection of facts. We will be examining different types of data, for example, open source data, Dublin core data, and others. Data will be key as we set up our statistical analysis and visualization in order to communicate what we have analyzed.

   Measurement also plays a key role in determining the size, length, or amount of data. We will be able to establish what we have observed from data by measuring its content. Statistics often relies on empirical measurement derived from observation or experiments. Statisticians continue to develop different techniques that deal with the data in the context of variables that reflect the data types. A variable has two characteristics: (1) a variable is an attribute that describes a person, place, thing, or idea, and (2) the value of the variable can vary from one entity to another. In addition to the term *variable,* statisticians also use the term *level of measurement* as a critical factor in determining what kinds of tools may be used to describe the variable, and what types of analysis may be used for making inferences about the variable. In short, the level of measurement determines or constrains the types of descriptive and inferential statistics that may be applied to examine the variables defined in a researcher's study.

1.6 Introduction to Spreadsheets

Long before computers, ancient societies used to record their data on paper in order to facilitate their analysis and help them to make better decisions. One of many examples of this type of data recording was the creation in the United Kingdom of National Savings and Investments by the Palmerston government in 1861. This creation led to the Post Office Savings Bank, the world's first postal savings system. It would allow ordinary workers the ability "to save for themselves against adversity and ill-health" and provide the government with access to debt funding.

   To track people's deposits, a handwritten document that the bank official and the customer needed to sign was created. This document was designed in the

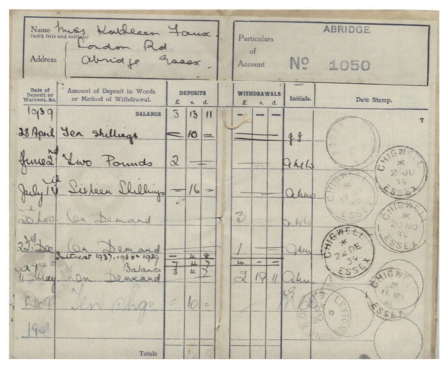

Figure 1.3.   Deposit slip made by Post Office Saving Bank 1869.

form of Z table. The Z table is short for the standard normal Z table (see appendix B). The standard normal distribution is used in hypothesis testing, including tests on proportions and on the difference between two means. The area under the whole of a normal curve is 1, or 100 percent. The Z table helps by telling us what percentage is under the curve at any particular point. In our example of the saving system's document, retrieved from London's Science Museum, the Z holds the records of all deposits made by a person as an account holder.

The use of spreadsheets is also known in the library, with the user often searching the card catalog for direction to material retrieval. Today, many libraries have destroyed their printed card catalog and replaced it with a VTS online system. We will learn how simple analytics will tell us more information about user behavior and how that can help the library improve its services to its community.

The change from paper tablet to computer spreadsheet came in 1978, when Daniel Bricklin, a Harvard Business School student, came up with the idea for an interactive visible calculator. Bricklin and Bob Frankston then co-created the software program VisiCalc. VisiCalc was the first personal computer application to be noticed for its effectiveness as a business tool; however, at that time not many people purchased this software. During the 1980s, Bill Gates, creator of

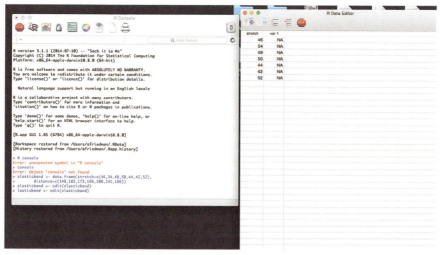

Figure 1.4. Open source R table.

Microsoft, developed Excel, which then became a popular application. Designed for both Mac and PC, Excel became the standard in spreadsheet applications. The computerized spreadsheet was designed such that each cell could contain either numeric or text data or the results of formulas that automatically calculate and display a value based on the contents of other cells. However, we are no longer limited to using Excel spreadsheets. This book will present another spreadsheet based on open source R. Figure 1.4 shows the R table interface.

1.7 Open Source Software

The term *open source* often refers to something that can be modified because its gate is publicly accessible. In the context of software, open source means that the software code can be modified or enhanced by anyone. The open source movement began in the late 1970s, when two separate organizations promoted the idea of software that is available for anyone to use or modify. The first organization that aimed to create a free operating system was General Public License (GPL). The leading person behind this movement was Richard Stallman. The second organization was Open Source Initiative (OSI), under the leadership of Bruce Perens and Eric S. Raymond.

R is a computer language that enables users to program algorithms and use tools that have been programmed by others. Open source R was invented by Professor John Chambers, who worked at Bell Labs during the 1970s. He developed the language called S, which debuted in 1976. During this time, he wanted to provide a more accessible way to calculate data using spreadsheets. However, private users and companies never adopted his creation. During the 1990s, two professors from the University of Auckland in New Zealand adopted the foundation of S and developed R, released in 1993 as an open source platform for statistical analysis. The name of the software, R, is based on their first names: Professor Robert Gentleman and Professor Ross Ihaka. R has become one of the most common open-source platforms used by academics and businesses alike, according to the *New York Times* (2009).

R is similar to other programming languages, such as C, Java, and Perl, in that it helps people perform a wide variety of computing tasks by giving them access to various commands. For statisticians, however, R is particularly useful because it contains a number of built-in mechanisms for organizing data, running calculations on the information, and creating graphical representations of datasets. Today, there are more than two thousand different packages devoted to R that enable users to manipulate the data in different formats and styles (http://www.r-project.org). We will review some of those packages to help us analyze and visualize today's library resources and audiences.

Students often ask, Why are we learning about R in the library environment? The answer is that R is open source and therefore free of charge, and it allows researchers to generate more insights from available data. Many researchers in the field of information science and library science have already started to use R as their platform for data analysis, such as Friedman (2014), Hensley et al. (2013), and many others.

1.8 How to Install R

The following information will introduce you to installing and running R. In addition to the resources provided in this book, other useful resources are http://www.r-project.org/ and R Wiki at http://rwiki.sciviews.org/doku.php.

This book provides examples for the use of R in statistical methodology. This will allow you to practice with the set of exercises in each chapter and be able to apply R to complete them.

Installing R:

1. Go to http://www.r-project.org/.
2. Click on the "Download R" link.
3. Select the location closest to you.
4. Click on your operating system (Linux, MacOS X, Windows) and follow the directions.

If you are a Mac user, download the latest .dmg file and follow the instructions. Once installed, R will appear as an icon in the Applications Folder. After you install R, you should go back to the same web page (where you obtained the latest .dmg file), click on "tools," which is located under "subdirectories," and install tcltk.dmg (universal build of Tcl/Tk for X11). This file includes additional tools that are necessary for building R on MacOS X.

If you are running Windows, click on the base, and then on the link that downloads R for Windows. (In the link, the current version number appears after "R.") When the dialog box opens, click Run and a "Setup Wizard" should appear. Keep clicking through Setup until the Wizard is finished. Now you should see an icon on your desktop, with a large capital R.

1.9 Summary

Statistics is the study of the science of regarding, collecting, measuring, controlling, and communicating data. In this book, we will focus on statistics in the library and information science settings using an open source spreadsheet, R, that is accessible to everyone, free of charge. We will cover basic terminology and models that will enhance your understanding of R. This will enable you to conduct a study, employ different statistical methodologies, and present the results in a visualization format.

1.10 Glossary

descriptive statistics—Collection of methods for organizing, displaying, and describing data, tables, and summary measures.

inferential statistics—Collection of methods based on sample results to make decisions for the population.

open source—A software program in which the source code is available to the general public for use and/or modification from its original design free of charge.

parameter—A summary measure that describes characteristics of an entire population.

population—An entire set of items or things under consideration.

R—An open source computer language that allows the user to program algorithms to produce statistical analysis and visualization.

sample—The portion of the population that is selected for analysis.

spreadsheet—A data listing on paper or computer that has rows and columns for recording data.

spreadsheet applications—Computer programs that let you create and manipulate tabular, organized data electronically.

statistic—A summary measure computed from sample data that is used to describe the entire population.

statistics—Group of methods used to collect, analyze, present, and interpret data to make decisions.

variable—A characteristic under study that assumes different values for different elements.

1.11 References

Friedman, A. 2014. "The Relationship between Research Methodology and Visual Display: A Study of Conference Proceedings in the Field Knowledge Organization." *Information Research: An International Electronic Journal* 19 (4). Available at www .informationr.net/ir/19-4/paper651.html.

Ruthenberg, J. 2013. "Data You Can Believe In, the Obama Campaign's Digital Masterminds Cash In." New York Times, June 23. Retrieved from http://www.nytimes .com/2013/06/23/magazine/the-obama-campaigns-digital-masterminds-cash-in.html.

Walker, S., J. Hensley , J. Eckert, R. M. Mason, and K. Nahon. 2013. *SoMe Tools for Social Media Research*. Fort Worth, TX: iConference.

Wattenberg, B. E., ed. 1966. *Statistical History of the United States: From Colonial Times to the Present*. New York: Basic Books.

CHAPTER 2

Research Design

2.1	Research Design
2.2	The Research Process and Design
2.3	Research Types
2.4	Types of Variables and Their Labels
2.5	Research Problem Statement
2.6	Hypothesis Testing and the Null Hypothesis
2.7	Scale Reliability and Validity
2.8	Summary
2.9	Glossary
2.10	References

The research design refers to the overall strategy that you choose to integrate the different components of the study in a coherent and logical way, thereby, ensuring you will effectively address the research problem; it constitutes the blueprint for the collection, measurement, and analysis of data. Note that your research problem determines the type of design you can use, not the other way around!

—William M. K. Trochim,
Research Methods Knowledge Base

2.1 Research Design

What is the most popular book among users between the ages of fourteen and twenty-one in the Tampa, Florida, public library? And what are the most common hashtags for the public library in Knoxville, Tennessee? These are examples of research questions a researcher addresses before starting to collect data. While these questions have different objectives, they also share a common ground—they are related to research that can be done in public libraries. Therefore, in this chapter we will begin to address these questions by looking at "What is a research process and design?" and "How do we raise a research question and hypothesis when we begin to assemble our research agenda?"

2.2 The Research Process and Design

In our first chapter, we defined the term *statistics* as a universal framework that refers to collecting, summarizing, and analyzing data. However, scientific research also demands a formal process, where the researcher needs to follow several steps in order to complete the research task toward discovering new knowledge. This process is documented and provides details to verify the researcher's process and conclusions. In this book, we will use the following established scientific process that includes a sequence of steps that lead from planning the research agenda, collecting the data, carrying out statistical procedures that will allow us to make informed conclusions based on our data analysis, and producing visual representations to provide more insight into the data analysis. The last step in this procedure is documenting the study findings. This strategy is organized into the following seven steps:

1. Understand the nature of the problem.
2. Decide what to measure and how to measure the research question.
3. Collect the data.
4. Analyze the data.
5. Conduct formal data analysis.
6. Visualize.
7. Create final written summary.

Step 1: Understand the Nature of the Problem
    The researcher needs to establish research questions and problems. It is important to have a clear direction before one starts to collect data, to ensure that the data that is collected addresses the research questions/problems. To illustrate the development of the problem, let's discuss "What can hashtags tell us about library users, habits, and engagements? Is their experience of using the library a good one? Why?" Our research question will consist of "What can we learn from user hashtags to understand user engagements with the library?" Our hypothesis will consist of "Older library users do use positive hashtags more than

younger users." The implementation will be the collection of all hashtags related to library use by both older and younger users.

Step 2: Decide What to Measure and How to Measure It

In this step, the researcher needs to make hard decisions on what data is needed to answer the question of interest. In our case, what is the most common hashtag used by users of the public library? In our study, we will examine users' hashtags with regard to their specific description of the library.

Step 3: Data Collection

The data collection step is a significant and fundamental one. The researcher must first decide whether an existing data source is adequate or whether new data must be collected. In cases where data already exist, it is important to understand how the data was collected and for what causes, so that any resulting limitations are fully understood and are taken into account when reporting the results of the study. If the researcher decides to collect new data, measuring tools need to be tested before the actual act of collecting in order to avoid unexpected problems. In our case, how do we measure library users' hashtags regarding library activity? One of many options is to log on to www.hashtag.org and type the name of the library and see the results.

Step 4: Data Analysis

After the data is collected, the next step is data analysis. This stage includes several steps where the initial analysis provides insight into general characteristics of the data and provides guidance in selecting appropriate methods for the next stage(s). In our case, a good starting point will be assessing the number of users who use hashtags for the library and what type of hashtags they used most often.

Step 5: Formal Data Analysis

The researcher must then select and apply a statistical model and methodology. Much of this book is devoted to this stage. In this case, we will employ content analysis that involves a methodology used to determine the presence of certain words or concepts within texts or sets of texts, according to Hodder (1994). We will then compare young adult users' postings to older users' postings by using correlation analysis (discussed later).

Step 6: Visualization

A researcher can employ different visualization strategies to find additional patterns in the data and then communicate the results. These will be discussed in the final sections of the book.

Step 7: Final Written Summary

The researcher summarizes the findings by writing and visualizing the results. Frequently at this stage, the researcher will need to address various questions that arise from the analysis; for example, "What can we learn from the data, what conclusion can be drawn from the analysis, and how can these results guide future research?" The researcher will need to report each stage of data analysis, with careful attention to make the data analysis comprehensible for readers.

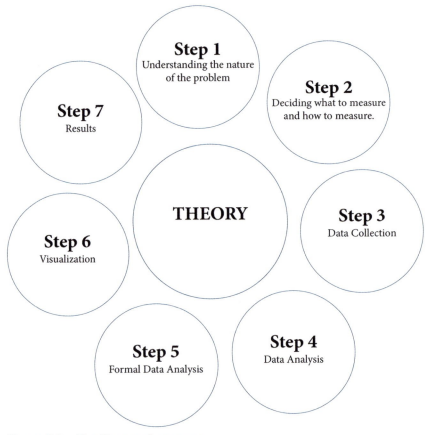

Figure 2.1. The Research process.

This research process also relies on theory. A theory is the explanation of the relationship that has been observed and attributes of the individuals or groups who are being observed. Information science researchers often use a theory to attempt to link what they observed and gain an understanding of any constraint phenomena that are related to that observation. In this book, we will not discuss in detail the various social theories often used by researchers in the field. Instead, we will focus on how to employ statistical theory to explore the more detailed analyses to be made from the data.

2.3 Research Types

As we saw, each step in the research process is different from the previous step; however, we need to understand the research types that a researcher needs to declare before starting the research project. We will focus on the four most common types of research, including observation, correlation, true experiments, and quasi-experiments. Each of these will be discussed further below.

Observation Research. The primary characteristic of *observation research* is that the subject of the study is being observed and recorded by the researcher. Often, these types of studies involve taking extensive notes based on observations of, and interviews with, the client. A detailed report with analysis would be a written record constituting the study of an individual case. In our study describing the use of hashtags, observation research would require our researcher to notice and record how the user used hashtags.

Correlation Research. The idea behind *correlational research* is to examine the relationship between two or more variables. In our study, we would evaluate the ages of library users as we follow the users' hashtags and the types of common words they use. These two variables, age and common concepts and words, could be found to convey data together. We want to see if that is the case.

Correlational research can be accomplished by a variety of techniques that include the collection of empirical data. However, in the past, researchers who conducted their studies based on only two variables often forgot that these variables can be affected by outside factors that are not noticed and documented. For example, the gender of library users and their use of the library catalog could be related to their current or future employment plans. The aim of correlation research is to examine the relationship between the two or more variables.

True Experiments. The *true experiment* is often thought of as taking place in a laboratory setting. However, this is not always the case. A true experiment is defined as a procedure conducted where an effort is made to impose control over all other variables, except the one under study. It is often easier to impose this sort of control in a laboratory setting. Thus, true experiments have often been erroneously identified as laboratory studies.

To fully understand the nature of the true experiment, we must first define a few terms: treatment group, control group, independent variable, dependent variable, random assignment, and double blind.

Experimental or *treatment group*—this is the group that receives the experimental treatment or manipulation, or is different from the control group on the variable under study;

Control group—this group is used to produce comparisons. The treatment of interest is deliberately withheld or manipulated to provide a baseline performance with which to compare the experimental or treatment group's performance;

Independent variable—this is the variable that the experimenter manipulates in a study. It can be any aspect of the environment that is empirically investigated for the purpose of examining its influence on the dependent variable;

Dependent variable—this is the variable that is measured in a study. The experimenter does not control this variable;

Random assignment—in a study, each subject has an equal probability of being selected to either the treatment or control group;

Double blind—neither the subject nor the experimenter knows whether the subject is in the treatment or the control condition.

Every experiment must have at least two groups: an experimental group and a control group. Each group will receive a level of the independent variable. The dependent variable will be measured to determine if the independent variable has an effect. As stated previously, the control group will provide us with a baseline for comparison. All subjects should be randomly assigned to groups and be tested as simultaneously as possible; the experiment should be conducted double blind. For example, we would have two groups: treatment group and control group. We would examine these two groups in a closed-environment setting with one group receiving some treatment and the other not receiving it. We would examine the two groups through testing.

Quasi-Experiments. Quasi-experiments are very similar to true experiments, but use naturally formed or preexisting groups. For example, if we wanted to compare younger and older library users on their library habits, it is impossible to randomly assign subjects to either the young or old group (naturally formed groups). Therefore, this cannot be a true experiment. When one has naturally formed groups, the variable under study is a subject variable (in this case—age) as opposed to an independent variable. As such, it also limits the conclusions we can draw from such a study. If we were to conduct the quasi-experiment, we would find that the older group might have more capacity for library usage when compared to the younger group, due to the fact that they have more free time than the younger generation. However, the researcher must be aware that there are many differences between the two groups that we cannot control and that these could account for differences in our dependent measures. Thus, we must be careful about making a statement of causality with quasi-experimental designs. For example, the library is conducting a special class over the weekend on techniques for searching in social media. We will divide the class based on alphabetical selection in order to examine their hashtags. Is this a naturally formed group?

2.4 Types of Variables and Their Labels

When thinking about research questions, it is also important consider the term *variable*. A variable is a characteristic under study that may assume different values for different elements. For example, income, age, and weight are common variables in human research subjects.

- A variable is an attribute that describes a person, place, thing, or idea;
- The value of the variable can "vary" from one entity to another.

In library science, many researchers examine the Dewey Decimal classification (DDC) codes as variables in their studies (Olson, 1998, Wang 2002, and others).

Variables can also be classified by type. We will begin our review with qualitative (categorical), or quantitative (numeric) types.

Qualitative variables may take on values that are names or labels. The color of a ball (e.g., red, green, blue) or the language type (e.g., English, Spanish, Korean) are examples of qualitative or categorical variables.

In comparison, *quantitative* variables are numeric. They represent a measurable quantity, for example, when we speak of a city's population in terms of numbers. For another example, quantitative variables might be numerical values (counts) of individuals comprising each of the percentages of the races in the total population: Hispanic/Latino, white, black or African American, Asian, Native American, and other. We can also select variables based on discrete or continuous information, as follows.

Discrete vs. Continuous Variables. Discrete variables are usually obtained by counting. There are a finite or countable number of possible choices available with discrete data. In our own example, discrete variables can be the new hashtags that were just generated today. It's not possible, however, to have 2.63 new hashtags. It is possible to have 2 or 3.

A *continuous variable* is one that can take on a value between any other two values, such as time spent waiting for the arrival of new book. Under this classification, the variable can take on any value between its minimum value and its maximum value. In our case study, the continuous variable would have a numeric value based on how many hashtags could be found in the last six months.

Before moving forward, we need to address the last variable classification: *univariate* versus *bivariate* data. These are not values, but a classification of variables in a study.

Statistical data and analysis is often classified according to the number of variables being studied: one variable versus two or more variables. When we conduct a study that looks at only one variable, we say that we are working with *univariate* data. Suppose, for example, that we are conducting a survey to estimate the average time a user borrows a book from the public library. Since we are working with only one variable—in this case, time—we would be working with univariate data.

When conducting a study that examines the relationship between two variables, we are working with *bivariate* data. In this case, we are conducting a study to see if there is a relationship between the race and income of users of public libraries. Since we are working with two variables, income and race, we would be working with bivariate data.

2.5 Research Problem Statement

As we outlined previously, research is a process. We usually establish our research agenda by writing a research problem statement and hypothesis. A research problem statement consists of three parts: 1) the ideal, 2) the reality, and 3) the consequences for the reader of the feasibility report. Well-constructed problem statements will convince your audience that the problem is real and worthy of your investigation. Your strategy is one of contrast: by situating the ideal scenario next to the situation as it exists, you can not only persuade the reader that a problem exists, but also emphasize the consequences of ignoring or addressing the problem.

The purpose behind the research problem statement is to compel the researcher to:

- Carefully determine the research problem and its objectives;
- Select the most appropriate and feasible research procedures, and
- Follow a specific and carefully developed plan of action.

Your problem statement is the backbone of your research proposal. Careful consideration of how you construct your problem statement will help you to focus on choosing the statistical methodologies and visualization patterns that will work best for your study.

Example:

Ranganathan's colon automatic classification is a well-known classification scheme that has been discussed in the field for a long time. However, this classification scheme has never been examined with regard to social media content. So, here is example of a research question: Can Ranganathan's colon automatic classification help classify the content of Twitter messages?

The research question must address the following steps.

- Choose an interesting general topic. Even directed academic research should focus on a topic in which the writer is at least somewhat personally invested. Writers should choose a broad topic about which they genuinely would like to know more.
- Do some preliminary research on your general topic. Do a few quick searches in current periodicals and journals on your topic to see what's already been done and to help you narrow your focus. What questions does this early research raise?
- Consider your audience. For most college papers, your audience will be academic, but always keep your audience in mind when narrowing your topic and developing your question. Would that particular audience be interested in this question?
- Start asking questions. Taking into consideration all of the above, start asking yourself open-ended "how" and "why" questions about your general topic. For example, "How did the slave trade evolve in the 1850s in the American South?" or "Why were slave narratives effective tools in working toward the abolishment of slavery?"
- Evaluate your question. Is your research question clear? With so much research available on any given topic, research questions must be as clear as possible in order to be effective in helping the writer direct his or her research.

2.6. Hypothesis Testing and the Null Hypothesis

A hypothesis is a specific, testable prediction about what you expect to happen in your study. To formulate the research question in a more standardized form, we employ a hypothesis testing statement to declare our research objectives. By now, you have already determined the variables that you wish to use and are looking to add a relationship between these variables. Do you expect that one variable caused another? Or do you expect that the two variables correlate in some way?

Hypothesis testing refers to the formal procedures used by statisticians to accept or reject statistical hypotheses. Hypothesis testing often captures a statement about the value of a population parameter and/or a statement about the kind of probability distribution that a certain variable can be observed as having.

In our example, do age and gender have direct effects on the content of hashtags that users employ when describing the library? In order to test whether your hypothesis is true or not, you have to determine a research statement to see if you can back it up. In order to address this issue, the researcher needs to state the null hypothesis and the alternative hypothesis.

- *Null hypothesis*—The null hypothesis, denoted by H_0, is usually the hypothesis that sample observations result purely from chance.
- *Alternative hypothesis*—The alternative hypothesis, denoted by H_1 or H_a, is the hypothesis that sample observations are influenced by some non-random cause.

For example, suppose we wanted to determine whether a particular flip of a coin is fair and balanced. A null hypothesis might be that half the flips would result in heads and the other half in tails. The alternative hypothesis might be that the number of heads and the number of tails would be very different. Symbolically, these hypotheses would be expressed as

$$H_0: P = 0.5 \quad H_a: P \neq 0.5$$

Suppose we flipped the coin fifty times, resulting in forty heads and ten tails. Given this result, we would be inclined to reject the null hypothesis. We would conclude, based on the evidence, that the coin was probably not fair and balanced.

Can we accept the null hypothesis? Some researchers say that a hypothesis test can have one of two outcomes: either you accept the null hypothesis, or you reject the null hypothesis. Many statisticians, however, take issue with the notion of "accepting the null hypothesis." Instead, they say that you "reject the null hypothesis" or you "fail to reject the null hypothesis."

Why the distinction between "acceptance" and "fail to reject"? Acceptance implies that the null hypothesis is true. Failure to reject implies that the data are not sufficiently persuasive for us to prefer the alternative hypothesis over the null hypothesis.

But what happens when we reject the null hypothesis when is it true? We call that a *decision error*.

Decision Errors. Two types of errors can result from a hypothesis testing—Type I or Type II errors. A *Type I* error occurs when the researcher rejects a null hypothesis and the hypothesis is actually true. The probability of committing a Type I error is called the *significance level*. This probability is also called *alpha*, and is often denoted by α.

A *Type II* error occurs when the researcher fails to reject a null hypothesis that is false. The probability of committing a Type II error is called *beta*, and is often denoted by β. The probability of *not* committing a Type II error is called the *power of the test*.

Hypothesis Format. There are two types of hypotheses—inductive and deductive. An *inductive hypothesis* is formed through inductively reasoning from many specific observations to tentative explanations. The researcher outlines a specific problem where he/she attempts to generate a general result. A *deductive hypothesis* is formed through deductively reasoning the implications of theory. In this case, the researcher outlines a general statement where he/she aims to find specifics.

2.7 Scale Reliability and Validity

A key concept relevant to a discussion of research methodology is the reliability and validity of the study. When an individual asks, "Is this study reliable and valid?" they are considering the consistency and legitimacy of some aspect of the study. There are four types of validity with respect to research and statistics. There are also five commonly used tests to establish reliability.

Each of the four types of validity will be briefly defined and described below. Be aware that this represents a cursory discussion of the concept of validity. Each type of validity has related threats that could pose a problem to a research study.

Statistical Conclusion Validity. Unfortunately, without a background in basic statistics, this type of validity is difficult to understand. Essentially, the question being asked is: "Are the variables under study related?" or "Is variable A correlated with variable B?" If a study has good statistical conclusion validity, we should be relatively certain that the answer to these questions is "Yes." Examples of issues or problems that would threaten statistical conclusion validity are the random heterogeneity of research subjects (the subjects represent a diverse group—this increases statistical error) or small sample size (it is more difficult to find meaningful relationships with a small number of subjects).

Internal Validity. Once it has been determined that the two variables (A & B) are related, the next issue to be determined is one of causality. Does A cause B? If a study is lacking internal validity, one cannot make cause-and-effect statements based on the research; the study would be descriptive, but not causal. There are many potential threats to internal validity. For example, if a study has a pretest, an experimental treatment, and a follow-up posttest, its own history is a threat to internal validity. If a difference is found between the pretest and posttest, it might be due to the experimental treatment, but it might also be due to any other event that subjects experienced between the two times of testing (for example, a historical event, a change in weather, etc.).

Construct Validity. One is examining the issue of construct validity when asking the questions: "Am I really measuring the construct that I want to study?" or "Is my study confounded (Am I confusing constructs)?" For example, if a researcher want to know whether a particular drug (variable A) will be effective for treating depression (variable B), he or she will need at least one measure of depression. If that measure does not truly reflect depression levels, but rather anxiety levels (confounding variable X), then the study will be lacking construct validity. Thus, good construct validity means that we can be relatively sure that construct A is related to construct B and that this might be a causal relationship. Examples of other threats to construct validity include subjects' apprehension about being evaluated, hypothesis guessing on the part of subjects, and bias introduced in a study because of the researcher's expectations.

External Validity. External validity addresses the issue of being able to generalize the results of a study to other times, places, and persons. For example, if a researcher conducts a study looking at art books in the library, can these results be generalized to food books? The researcher must ask the following questions to determine if a threat to the external validity exists: "Would I find these same results with a different sample?" "Would I get these same results if I conducted my study in a different setting?" and "Would I get these same results if I had conducted this study in the past or if I redo this study in the future?" If the answer is "No" to any of these questions, then the study's external validity is threatened.

Reliability is often defined as the consistency of the measurement of the instrument used by the researcher. The *instrument,* for the purposes of this book, is a formula that has already been proven and used by many in statistical analysis. Did the researcher measure the same way each time under the same conditions with the same subjects? We often encounter types of tests that measure the reliability of the instrument. Some of these are test-retest, split half, and inter-rater reliability.

Test-retest is a process done over a period of time in order to access the reliability and consistency of the instrument. The researcher records the scores on an instrument on different occasions to determine if the scores reflect results consistently.

Split half test indicates the correlation of scores from one half of an instrument with scores from the second half of the instrument. The researcher examines the results to see if the two sets of scores provide consistency with regard to the measurement of the testing instrument.

Inter-rater reliability is defined as the degree to which two or more outside observers rate the same variables in exactly the same way. The objective of this measure is to provide independent judges with the ability to judge the event independently, yet correlate the scores of the two in a consistent way.

2.8 Summary

We defined the term *statistics* as a process of applying statistical and logical techniques to describe, evaluate, and visualize data. We looked at the term *research process* where we introduced seven steps for conducting research:

1. Understand the nature of the problem.
2. Decide what to measure and how to measure it.
3. Collect data.
4. Begin the statistical analysis.
5. Conduct more advanced statistical analysis.
6. Create visualizations based on statistical analysis.
7. Summarize the findings.

We then discussed variables and their role in the research process. We reviewed different types of variables, including categorical versus numeric, discrete versus continuous, and univariate versus bivariate. We also discussed research problem statements and hypotheses testing. We stated that the research statement is the outline of your research goals. A hypothesis statement is concerned with the relationship between the variables you have selected to examine. In order to back up your hypothesis results, you test them against the opposite situation, also known as the null hypothesis. This asserts that things you tested are not related and that your results are not a product of random chance events. Then, in the last section, we examined validity and considered four types of validities: statistical conclusion validity, internal validity, construct validity, and external validity.

2.9 Glossary

alternative testing—Evaluates the hypothesis, denoted by H_1 or H_a, that sample observations are influenced by some non-random cause.

bivariate data—Occurs when the research study focuses on the relationship between two variables.

continuous variable—Numerical responses that arise from a measuring process.

correlation research—Research that tests for statistical relationships between two or more variables.

discrete variable—Produces a numerical response that arises from a counting process.

hypothesis testing—A process by which an analyst tests a statistical finding, with the goal of either accepting or rejecting the null hypothesis. The methodology employed by the analyst depends on the nature of the data used and the goals of the analysis.

instrument—For the purposes of this book, a formula, a survey, questionnaire, scale, or tool that has already been proven and used by many in statistical analysis.

inter-rater test—This process asks independent judges to examine your variables and analysis. You then compare their results for consistency.

null hypothesis—A statistical hypothesis to be tested.

observation research—Type of research in which researcher observes ongoing behavior.

qualitative variable—A variable that takes on values and names or labels; also known as a categorical variable.

quantitative variable—A variable that is measured based on numeric values.

quasi-experiment—A research design that lacks the full control of a true experiment design. The treatment variable often occurs naturally, but sometimes the researcher may be able to manipulate it.

reliability—The consistency of the measurement instrument.

research problem—A statement about an area of concern, a condition to be improved, a difficulty to be eliminated, or a troubling question that exists in scholarly literature, in theory, or in practice that points to the need for meaningful understanding and deliberate investigation. In some social science disciplines the research problem is typically posed in the form of a question.

research process—Seven steps in the research procedures that include understanding the nature of the problem, deciding what to measure, data collection, data analysis, formal data analysis, visualization, and results.

split-half test—The test of consistency of the instrument at two different times.

test-retest—The test of the consistency of the instrument over time.

true experiments—Research that focuses on one variable under a closed environment and setting.

Type I error—Occurs when the researcher rejects a null hypothesis when it is true.

Type II error—The failure to reject a false null hypothesis.

univariate data—Occurs when the research study focuses on just one variable.

validity—Accuracy of measurement, or legitimacy of the measurement.

2.10. References

Olson, H. A. 1998. "Mapping beyond Dewey's Boundaries: Constructing Classificatory Space for Marginalized Knowledge Domains." In Geoffrey C. Bowker and Susan Leigh Star, eds., *How Classifications Work: Problems and Challenges in an Electronic Age*, a special issue of *Library Trends* 47 (2): 233–54.

Wang, J. 2009. "An Extensive Study on Automated Dewey Decimal Classification." *Journal of the American Society for Information Science and Technology* (JASIS) 60 (11).

CHAPTER 3

Data (Types and Collection Methods)

3.1   Data Collection
3.2   Data Distributed by an Organization or Individual
3.3   Data Design Experiment
3.4   Data Survey Design
    3.4.1   Interview
    3.4.2   Questionnaire
    3.4.3   Focus Group
    3.4.4   Cross-sectional
    3.4.5   Long Cross-sectional or Longitudinal
    3.4.6   Time Series
    3.4.7   Panel Studies
    3.4.8   Examples in the Field of Information Science
3.5   Observation
3.6   Correlation
3.7   Sampling
    3.7.1   Sampling Methodologies
    3.7.2   Simple Random Sample
    3.7.3   Sampling with Replacement
    3.7.4   Sampling without Replacement
    3.7.5   Systematic Sample
    3.7.6   Stratified Sample
    3.7.7   Cluster Sample
3.8   Non-probability Methodologies
    3.8.1   Snowball Sampling
    3.8.2   Quota Sampling
3.9   Sampling Summary
3.10   Glossary
3.11   References

> Not everything that can be counted counts and not everything that counts can be counted.
>
> —Albert Einstein

3.1 Data Collection

Data collection procedures are an important step. It is important to keep in mind both what our research question is about and how we will analyze the data we collect. However, before gathering information we need to identify the source of data and, based on that knowledge, decide the methodology we will employ to collect the data. This chapter will discuss some of the different methodologies behind data collection.

The first questions you as a researcher need to address are: What is the source of your data? How will you collect your data?

Researchers have historically used four types of data collection sources: (1) data distributed by an organization or individual, (2) an experiment that they designed, (3) surveys, and (4) observation. However, with the growth of the Internet, we often encounter another resource, where the researcher collects data from multiple sources and tries to make sense out of them by analyzing the correlations between them. This type of source is called (5) a *data correlation*.

3.2 Data Distributed by an Organization or Individual

The most frequently used source is data that is created by organizations or individuals. This type of data is collected by those organizations or individuals who then publish it so that others might use it as a resource. For example, the United States federal government coordinates and distributes the data it has collected and then shares it with the public. The biggest source of government data is the Bureau of Labor Statistics, which offers two different websites full of information available for anyone to download to their collection. These websites are www.bls.gov and www.data.gov. In the private sector, an example of a source of available information is the sports channel ESPN, which allows sport fans, for a fee, to download data it has collected from various sporting events and scores.

In library science, many researchers use the library itself as their main data collection resource. For example, Lynch and Smith (2000) examined the changing role of the library as a workplace by collecting data from local and national library branches. They examined the common job titles found in different library branches and in the employment listings posted in the *College & Research Libraries Journal*.

3.3 Data Design Experiment

Experimental design occurs in a closed laboratory where the researcher conducts his/her own experiment under a controlled environment. The setting allows the researcher to impose a treatment, or condition, on a group of study objects or subjects in the interest of observing the response. The validity of an experiment is directly affected by both its construction and execution. Conducting this type of experiment requires the researcher to pay close attention to the setting of the experiment in order to avoid external influences on the subject(s) of the study. True experimental design is most often used in the field of pharmaceuticals, where companies manufacturing potentially medicinal agents attempt to test their new discoveries and evaluate their efficacy. In the field of library science, we usually do not encounter true experimental studies that take place in a closed laboratory. The most commonly registered complaint about experimental research is the high cost of maintaining a lab to support the rigorous requirements of research.

3.4. Data Survey Design

Survey design draws upon a variety of techniques for the collection of data. A survey may focus on opinions or factual information depending on its purpose, and many surveys involve administering a series of questions to individuals. Surveys can be implemented via interview (in person or via telephone) or self-report questionnaire (in person, mail, e-mail, or web). Additional methodologies include focus groups, cross-sectional, longitudinal, and others. We will start with the familiar interview.

3.4.1 INTERVIEW

The *interview* procedure involves an interviewer asking questions, perhaps face-to-face or over the phone, with the interviewee. Personal interviews can take place in the home, at a shopping mall, on the street, outside a library hall, and so forth. The interview procedures may vary according to the objectives of the researcher and the research question. Listed below are some of the advantages and disadvantages of this method.

The advantages of an interview include:

1. The ability to let the interviewee see, feel, and/or taste a product.
2. The ability to find the target population more easily. For example, you can find people who have frequented a public library much more easily directly outside a library hall, rather than, by comparison, calling phone numbers at random.
3. Longer conversations are sometimes tolerated. Particularly with in-home interviews that have been arranged in advance, subjects may be more willing to talk extensively when face-to-face, rather than when speaking to someone on the phone.

Disadvantages of interviews:

1. Personal interviews usually cost more per interview than other research methods. This is particularly true of in-home interviews, where travel time is a major factor.
2. Each interview has its own characteristics. It often draws its clientele from a specific geographic area, and that profile may also influence the type of client selected. These characteristics may differ from the desired target population and result in a nonrepresentative sample.

3.4.2 QUESTIONNAIRE

The *questionnaire* methodology consists of a series of questions and other prompts for the purpose of gathering information from respondents. The questionnaire may be delivered through various techniques such as by mail, website, or phone call.

The advantages of questionnaires:

1. They are economical to produce.
2. They are relatively easy to administer.
3. They can be conducted remotely, which may reduce or prevent geographical dependence.

The disadvantages of questionnaires:

1. Respondents may not feel encouraged to provide accurate and honest answers.
2. Respondents may not feel comfortable disclosing answers that reveal themselves in an unfavorable manner.

3. Survey questions could lead to inconclusive data because respondents may interpret certain options for answers differently than other participants. For example, the answer option "somewhat agree" may represent different levels of agreement to different subjects and thus have its own meaning for each individual respondent.

3.4.3 FOCUS GROUP

A *focus group* is a research interview process designed specifically to uncover insights from a small group of people in a face-to-face type of setting. The group interview is distinctive in that it uses a set of questions deliberately sequenced to proceed toward concepts of interest to the researcher. The focus group consists of a limited number of participants, discussing the topics the researcher raises before the group. Focus group interviews are used in a variety of ways and have gained popularity for helping researchers to gain insights on consumer behaviors and purchasing patterns.

The advantage of focus groups:

1. They yield insights into people's thoughts as a community.
2. The researcher is able to develop new research ideas.

The disadvantages:

1. The researcher's inability to control group influence.
2. The researcher's inability to measure the impact of external influences.

3.4.4 CROSS-SECTIONAL

A *cross-sectional* design is used for research that collects data on relevant variables one time only from a variety of people, subjects, or phenomena. This means that researchers record information about their subjects without manipulating the study environment. The defining feature of a cross-sectional study is that it can compare different population groups at a single point in time.

The advantages of a cross-sectional study:

1. Cheap and easy to conduct.
2. Data may be useful to future research.

The disadvantages of a cross-sectional study:

1. Cannot measure change across time.
2. No control of the independent variable.

3.4.5 LONG CROSS-SECTIONAL, OR LONGITUDINAL, STUDY

A longitudinal design collects data on the same setting, subjects, or both, over long periods of time. Measurements are taken on each variable over two or more distinct time periods. This allows the researcher to measure change in variables over time. There are two different types of longitudinal designs: time series and panel.

3.4.6 TIME SERIES

A *time series* design collects data on the same variable at regular intervals (weeks, months, years, etc.) in the form of aggregate measures of a population. For example, the Consumer Price Index (CPI), the FBI Uniform Crime Rate, unemployment rates, and poverty rates employ time series design.

The advantages of time series design are:

1. Establishing a baseline measure.
2. Describing changes over time.
3. Keeping track of trends.
4. Forecasting future (short-term) trends.

The disadvantages of time series design are:

1. Data collection methods may change over time.
2. Different structure is needed to show more than one variable at variable points in time.
3. Assumes present trends will continue unchanged.

3.4.7 PANEL STUDIES

Panel studies are a particular design of longitudinal study in which the unit of analysis is followed at specified intervals over a long period, often many years. The key feature of panel studies is that they collect repeated measures from the same sample at different points in time. The most often used technique in panel studies is a survey that follows the population of interest over an extended time period and is concerned with measuring change over time for the units of analysis within the population. The unit of analysis is typically an individual, but it could also be a firm or a dwelling or any other unit of analysis required by the research design. Panel studies typically collect data at relatively frequent intervals depending on the design requirements of a given study. Some run over many years, and others are short term, such as short panels conducted around elections.

An advantage of panel studies is:

1. The ability to examine the same sample at different points in times.

The disadvantages of panel studies are:

1. It takes a long time to conduct the study and report its report.
2. It is difficult to track the individuals around whom you have designed the study.

3.4.8 EXAMPLES IN THE FIELD OF INFORMATION SCIENCE

In the field of information science, many researchers employ different methodologies for their data collection. Here are few examples:

1. The Ithaka S+R US Library Survey 2013 report examines how the leaders of academic libraries are approaching systemic changes in their environment and the opportunities and constraints they face in leading their organizations. The study questionnaire was sent via e-mail to library deans and directors at four-year colleges and universities in the United States during the fall of 2013.
2. Baek (2013) conducted interviews with eight public librarians about STEM learning. This was the first time that STEM learning was examined by a researcher using interviews as the main tool to collect data.
3. Crowley et al. (2002) examined user perceptions of the library's web pages by using a focus group held at Texas A&M University.

3.5 Observation

Inherent within *observation* methodology is the idea that the researcher collects the data by carefully watching and documenting from the outside without adding any interventions. There are many types of studies that can be classified as observational research. These include case studies, ethnographic studies, and ethological studies. The primary characteristic of each of these types of studies is that phenomena are being observed and recorded.

In the field of information science, many researchers also employ this data collection methodology. Here are some examples:

1. Becker (2012) examined the patronage and usage of the children's section of a public library by observing patrons' behavior.
2. Hughes (2011) examined student utilization of physical spaces in the library by noting and recording the library usage habits and behaviors of individuals who were participants in the study.

3.6. Correlation

The *correlation* methodology allows the researcher to examine two or more different resources and make comparisons or correlation examinations between these variables. In statistics, this type of analysis is often labeled as *regression* and *correlation analysis*. Regression analysis involves identifying the relationship between the variables, where correlation analysis examines the degree to which the two variables are related. For more about regression and correlation analysis, see chapter 12.

Examples of correlation in our field include the following:

1. Tenopir (2012) examines the correlation between investment in university libraries and grant awards. The study examined eight institutions around the globe, where six demonstrated a greater than one-to-one (1:1) return in grant funding, with results ranging from 15.54:1 to 0.64:1. Equally significant is the result that two institutions showed a significant positive correlation between an increase in library investment over time and an increase in grant funding to the university.
2. Rao (2011) studied the correlation among library facilities in India, measuring different methods of optimal integration of services by the library providers.

Sampling methods play a crucial role in data collection for studies.

3.7 Sampling

In chapter 1, we introduced the idea behind the sample as part of a population being studied. In chapter 2, we discussed the most frequently used data collection methods including observation, true experiments, quasi-experiment, and correlation. However, we have not yet discussed how we can examine these data resources in regard to their population and the selection of our subjects. Rather than taking a complete census of the whole population, statistical sampling procedures focus on collecting a small representative group of the larger population. In the following sections we will discuss two types of sampling methods: probability samples and non-probability samples.

3.7.1 SAMPLING METHODOLOGIES

The sample begins with a frame. A *frame* is a list of all the items that compose the population. The frame is the source material or device from which a sample is drawn. The material can be population lists, directories, and even maps. The samples are drawn from these frames. However, in some cases, the source of the frame might not provide you with the information you need for your study. For example, a survey was created to establish the number of potential customers for a new service the New York City Public Library offers. The research team has drawn one thousand numbers at random from a telephone directory in the city, and, based on their list, they made two hundred calls each day from Monday to Friday from 8 a.m. to 5 p.m. and asked questions from a prepared list about the new service the library wants to offer.

In this example, *population* of interest is all inhabitants of the city; the *sampling frame* includes only those New York City dwellers who satisfy all the following conditions:

- Have a telephone;
- The telephone number is included in the directory;
- Are likely to be at home from 8 a.m. to 5 p.m. from Monday to Friday;
- Is not a person who refuses to answer any or all telephone surveys.

The *sampling frame* in this case is different from the *population*. It excludes members of the population, by its design, who may indeed be potential users of the proposed service. We need to understand what information a simple random sample can provide for a study and what it may, by its nature, exclude.

3.7.2 SIMPLE RANDOM SAMPLE

A *simple random sample* is one in which every individual or item from a frame has the same equal chance of selection as every other individual or item from that frame. Simple random sampling has often been considered the most popular technique.

With simple random sampling, n is used to represent the sample size and N to represent the frame size. Every item or person in the frame is numbered from 1 to N. The chance that any particular member of the frame is selected on the first draw $1/N$.

There are two basic methods by which samples are selected: with replacement and without replacement.

3.7.3 SAMPLING WITH REPLACEMENT

Sampling with replacement means that after a person or an item is selected, the subject is returned to the frame, where they have the same probability of being selected again if another drawing takes place.

An *advantage* with sampling with replacement is:

1. The sample will be free from bias—it is random.

   The *disadvantage* with sampling with replacement is:

1. As a result of the randomness of this technique, the results sometimes may not be representative of the population. In order to overcome this problem, researchers often use a larger sample size.

3.7.4 SAMPLING WITHOUT REPLACEMENT

In the sampling without replacement, the unit of the population in the sample has only one chance to be selected in the sample.

An advantage with sampling without replacement

1. Easy to follow

   The disadvantage with sampling without replacement

1. Hard to ensure unbiased section from the population.

3.7.5 SYSTEMATIC SAMPLE

In a *systematic sample*, the N individuals or items in the frame are partitioned into K groups by dividing the size of the frame N by the desired sample size n.

$$K = \frac{N}{n}$$

With this method, items are chosen from the population according to a fixed rule: for example, every tenth book in the basement floor in the library. This method should yield a more representative sample than the random sample (especially if the sample size is small). However, a systematic method can also introduce bias, for example, the period chosen might affect the result of the sample.

An advantage of the systematic sample is:

1. It can eliminate other sources of bias.

A disadvantage of the systematic sample is:

1. It can introduce bias where the pattern used for the samples coincides with a pattern in the population.

3.7.6 STRATIFIED SAMPLE

A *stratified sample* occurs where the population is broken down into categories, then a random sample is taken from each category. The proportions of the sample sizes are the same as the proportion of each category to the whole.

An advantage of a stratified sample is:

1. Yields more accurate results than simple random sampling.

A disadvantage of a stratified sample is:

1. Requires more administration effort than a simple random sample.

Random samples are also gathered from clusters in some studies.

3.7.7 CLUSTER SAMPLE

The cluster sample is used when populations can be broken down into many different categories, or *clusters* (e.g., church parishes). Rather than taking a sample from each cluster, first a random selection of clusters is chosen to represent the whole. Then, within each cluster, a random sample is taken. We will discuss this type of sample in more detail in chapter 9.

An advantage of the cluster sample is:

1. Cluster samples are less expensive and time-consuming than a full random sample.

Disadvantages of the cluster sample are:

1. It is not a genuine sample.
2. If only a few clusters are sampled, we might end up with a biased result.

Some sample methodologies, such as non-probability samples, cannot be used as studies of the general population.

3.8 Non-probability Methodologies

With *non-probability sampling*, we cannot specify the probability that each element will be included in the sample. As a result, non-probability sampling techniques *cannot* be used to infer from the sample to the general population. It may be used to investigate whether an issue or topic of concern exists to a sufficient extent that further investigation is possible. The most popular techniques of non-probability sampling include snowball sampling and quota sampling, but there are many others.

3.8.1 SNOWBALL SAMPLING

Snowball sampling may be defined as a technique for gathering research subjects through the identification of an initial subject who then is used to provide the names of other subjects. These subjects may themselves open possibilities for additional subjects for an expanding web of contact and inquiry. Snowball sampling can be placed within a wider set of methodologies that takes advantage of the social networks of identified respondents, which can be used to provide a researcher with an escalating set of potential contacts.

An advantage of snowball sampling is:

1. Easy to accomplish.

Disadvantages of snowball sampling are:

1. It is difficult to replicate the same method and result.
2. It does not reflect the entire population.

3.8.2 QUOTA SAMPLING

Quota sampling involves the selection of a portion of the population being studied. The idea of quota sampling is to set a target number of completed interviews with specified subgroups of the population of interest. The sampling procedure then proceeds, using a nonrandom selection mechanism, until the desired number of completed interviews is obtained.

An advantage of quota sampling is:

1. It is quick and easy to conduct.

A disadvantage of quota sampling is:

1. Not as representative of the population as a whole as other sampling methods.

3.9 Sampling Summary

In summary, data collection and sampling are key issues in any social research. The advantages of sampling are evident: feasibility of the research, lower costs, economy of time, and better organization of the work. We discussed two types of sampling: probability sampling, with and without replacement, and non-probability sampling. Each type of sampling addresses specific needs and has certain advantages and disadvantages.

As discussed in chapter 1, data can be collected from two sources, the entire population or a sample. A set in statistics is referred to as a population. Though this term is commonly used to refer to the number of people in a given place, in statistics, a population refers to any entire set from which you collect data.

As we have seen in the definition of statistics, data collection is a fundamental aspect and as a consequence, there are different methods of collecting data which when used on one particular set will result in different kinds of data. Let's move on to look at these individual methods of collection in order to better understand the types of data that will result.

3.10 Glossary

cluster sampling—Dividing a population into subgroups (clusters) and forming a sample by randomly selecting clusters and including all individuals or objects in the selected clusters in the sample.

correlation—The linear relationship between two variables.

cross-sectional study—A slice of the full data represented, cross-sectional designs collect data on relevant variables one time only from a variety of people, subjects, or phenomena.

design experiment—Refers to whether the experimental group changes significantly, over time on the outcome variable in comparison with the control group that is not exposed to the experimental treatment. The classic experimental design focuses on two variables: the treatment variable (also called the intervention or the independent variable) and the outcome variable (also called the dependent variable).

focus group—This technique involves having about a dozen people engage in an intensive discussion focused on a particular topic frame—a list of all the items that compose the population interview—a conversational practice where knowledge is produced through the interaction between a questioner (interviewer) and an interviewee or a group of interviewees (the subjects). Unlike everyday conversations, the research interview is most often carried out to serve the researcher's ends, which are external to the conversation itself (e.g., to obtain knowledge about a given topic or some area of human experience).

frame—A list of all the items that compose the population interview.

interview—A conversational practice in which knowledge is produced through the interaction between a questioner (interviewer) and an interviewee or a group of interviewees (the subjects). Unlike everyday conversations, the research interview is most often carried out to serve the researcher's ends, which are external to the conversation itself (e.g., to obtain knowledge about a given topic or some area of human experience).

long cross-sectional (longitudinal) study—A method in which the researcher collects data in the same setting, with the same subjects, or both, over long periods of time.

non-probability sampling—A method that does not permit the researcher to specify the probability that each element in the sample will be included in the population.

observation—The researcher collects the data by carefully watching and documenting from the outside without any intervention.

observational study—A study that involves watching the characteristics of an existing population.

probability sampling—The selection of a portion of the population to be used in estimating the likelihood of a distinct attribute's presence in the whole population.

questionnaire—a list consisting of a series of written inquiries and other prompts for the purpose of gathering information from respondents.

quota sampling—A method that sets a target number of completed interviews with specified subgroups of the population of interest; each element in the population has a known nonzero chance of being selected through the use of a random selection procedure.

simple random sample—A selection technique in which every individual or item from a frame has as equal a chance of selection as every other individual or item from that frame.

snowball sampling—A networking technique for gathering research subjects through the identification of an initial subject who then provides the names of other subjects, each of whom also may suggest others.

stratified sample—A collection design in which the population is broken down into categories, then a random sample is taken, in proportion to the makeup of the total population, from each category.

survey design—A data-collection method in which individuals answer specific questions about their behavior, attitudes, beliefs, or emotions. Surveys can be applied in different platforms including interview (in person or via telephone) or self-report questionnaire (in person, mail, e-mail, web).

systematic sample—A method that relies upon dividing the population into groups, then numbering the group members (K) and choosing those of the same specific number. In this case, the fifth group member of each of the smaller groups, from within the larger total population, collectively comprise the sample.

time series—A data collection instrument designed to collect data on the same variable at regular intervals (weeks, months, years, etc.) in the form of aggregate measures of a population.

3.11 References

Baek, J. Y. 2013. *The Accidental STEM Librarian: An Exploratory Interview Study with Eight Librarians.* StarNetScience-technology activities and resources for libraries.

Becker, K. 2012. "24 Hours in the Children's Section: An Observational Study at the Public Library." *Early Childhood Education* 40:107–14.

Crowley, Gwyneth H., et al. 2002. "User Perceptions of the Library's Web Pages: A Focus Group Study at Texas A&M University." *The Journal of Academic Librarianship* 28 (4): 205–10.

Hughes, A. M. 2011. "The Library as a Preferred Place for Studying: Observation of Students' Use of Physical Spaces." *Evidence Based Library and Information Practice* (EBLIP) 6 (2).

Long, M. P., and R. C. Schonfeld. 2013. *Ithaka S+R US Library Survey 2013.* http://www.sr.ithaka.org/sites/default/files/reports/SR_LibraryReport_20140310_0.pdf.

Lynch, B. P., and K. R. Smith. 2001. "The Changing Nature of Work in Academic Libraries." *College & Research Libraries* 62 (5): 407–20.

Rao, Y. S. 2011. "Correlation among Library Facilities: An Analytical Study." *Library Philosophy and Practice* 12 (1).

Tenopir, C. 2012. "Lib-Value: Measuring Value and Return on Investment of Academic Libraries." *Research Library Issues: A Bimonthly Report* from ARL, CNI, and SPARC, 271.

CHAPTER 4

How to Run R

4.1   Introduction to R Command Line Interface
4.2   The Story behind the R Programming Language
       4.2.1   The Logical Operator Syntax Table
       4.2.2   The Arithmetic Operator Table
       4.2.3   Installation of Package Command Line
4.3   Introduction to Basic Functionality in R
       4.3.1   Introduction to Vectors
       4.3.2   Writing Functions
       4.3.3   Introduction to Arguments
       4.3.4   The Return Value
       4.3.5   The Vector Index
4.4   Introduction to Variables in R
       4.4.1   Numeric Variable
       4.4.2   Integer Variable
       4.4.3   String Variable
       4.4.4   Character Variable
       4.4.5   Factor Variable
       4.4.6   Fraction Variable
       4.4.7   Logical Variable
       4.4.8   Summary
4.5   Importing Data to R
       4.5.1   Importing Data from Microsoft Excel
       4.5.2   Importing Data from Google Spreadsheet
       4.5.3   Importing Data from the Web
4.6   Summary
4.7   Glossary
4.8   Reference

4.1 Introduction to R Command Line Interface

Computer programs are collections of instructions that tell a computer how to interact with the user, interact with the computer hardware, and process data. These instructions are what stand behind the programming language, where the programmers write explicit instructions in order to directly manipulate the hardware/software/data. Most of the computer programs are based on a command line interface. The command line interface is what makes R so powerful. The command line is the user interface to a computer's operating system or an application, in which the user responds to a visual prompt by typing in a command on a specified line, receives a response back from the system and then enters another command, and so forth. After installing R, you will find the R icon on your desktop. Click on the icon and you will encounter the first R window greeting that will promote a window display called R's *console*.

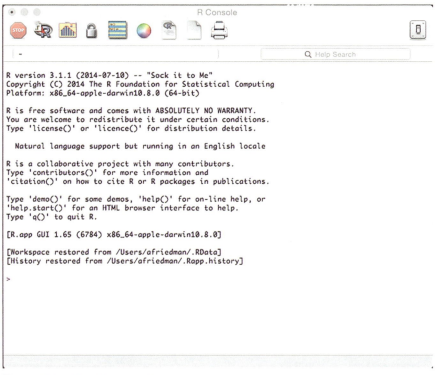

Figure 4.1.   The Rs console

Inside the R console window you will find the following text:

```
R version 3.1.1 (2013-05-16) -- "Good Sport"
Copyright (C) 2013 The R Foundation for Statistical Computing
Platform: x86_64-apple-darwin10.8.0 (64-bit)
R is free software and comes with ABSOLUTELY NO WARRANTY.
You are welcome to redistribute it under certain conditions.
Type 'license()' or 'licence()' for distribution details.
Natural language support but running in an English locale
R is a collaborative project with many contributors.
Type 'contributors()' for more information and
'citation()' on how to cite R or R packages in publications.
Type 'demo()' for some demos, 'help()' for on-line help, or
'help.start()' for an HTML browser interface to help.
Type 'q()' to quit R.
[R.app GUI 1.61 (6492) x86_64-apple-darwin10.8.0]
>
```

In the last line of the console you will find the prompt, the greater sign >, which is where you type the code to make R go to work. The convention in this book is that you will need to type your commands. After you have typed your commands, you will need to press the Return key to see the answer.

For example, for visualization demos, type:

>demo(graphics) and hit Return key

For basic calculation, type:

> 1 + 1 and hit the Return key

The result of 1 + 1 will present as a line [1]. In this case, [1] is equal to 2.

```
[1] 2
> 3 * 2 and hit the Return key.
[1] 6
> 5 + 6 + 3 + 4 + 1 and hit the Return key
[1] 18
> 4 * (4 + 4) and hit the Return key
[1] 32
```

Note: if you followed the directions, you have applied white space between each operator such as * and /. Another example of this would be typing 1 + 1, rather than 1+1. This is not necessary, but is encouraged as good coding practice. So, what stands behind the R programming?

4.2 The Story behind the R Programming Language

The "machine language" is divided into two types of languages: high level and low levels. The aim of the high level was to write programs that were less dependent upon a particular computer environment. Such machine languages are considered high level, because they are closer to human languages and further way from machine languages. In contrast, assembly languages are considered low level, because they are very close to machine languages.

The R programming language is *high level* and, as you will see, has shortcuts that make it easier to operate. The R programming language also comes with large sets of common function libraries. In a programming language, a library is a collection of pre-compiled routines that a program can use. These routines, sometimes called *modules*, are stored in object format. Those libraries are particularly useful for storing frequently used routines, because you do not need to explicitly link them to every program that uses them. We will learn to employ these libraries and these routines when we install different packages for R in order to produce different statistical equations and different visualization displays.

So, let's take a closer look at the syntax of the R language:

```
1. > a <- c(1,2,3,4)
> a
3. [1] 1 2 3 4
> a + 5
[1] 6 7 8 9
> a - 10
7. [1] -9 -8 -7 -6
> a*4
[1] 4 8 12 16
> a/5
[1] 0.2 0.4 0.6 0.8
```

In our example, the first line "a" is a *data container* that includes the numbers: 1, 2, 3, 4. By declaring "a" as a container we have the ability to add more functions and data manipulations.

In the third line, we ask R to add the number 5 to each of the numbers in the container: 1, 2, 3, 4. So, the answer R provides us is 1 + 5 = 6, 2 + 5 = 7, 3 + 5 = 8, and 4 + 5 = 9.

In the seventh line, we ask R to subtract 10 from each of the numbers the container holds, 1, 2, 3, 4. So, the answer R provides us is –9, –8, –7, –6. Note that R did not remember the calculation we conducted in the third line.

4.2.1 THE LOGICAL OPERATOR SYNTAX TABLE

Like any programming language, R has its own syntax, also known as operators. The operator syntax can be divided into two groups: arithmetic and logical operators. Table 4.1 shows the basic operators of logical syntax.

Table 4.1.

Operator	Description
<	Less than
<=	Less than or equal to
>	Greater than
>=	Greater than or equal to
==	Exactly equal to
! =	Not equal to
! X	Not x
X	y	X OR y
X & y	x AND y
isTRUE(x)	test if X is TRUE

R logical operators consist of <=, <, ==, >, >=, and != for less than or equal, less than, equal, greater than, greater than or equal, and not equal. These are the most often used operators. They can be used to create logical expressions that take the values of TRUE and FALSE (or T and F for short). Logical expressions may be combined with the logical operators for *OR* and & for AND.

4.2.2 THE ARITHMETIC OPERATOR TABLE

The arithmetic table is used to define a multiplication operation for an algebraic system.

Table 4.2.

Key Operator	Description	Example
+	Addition	2 + 1 = 6
−	Subtraction	3 – 1 = 2
*	Multiplication	2*1 = 2
/	Division	
^ or **	Exponentiation	10/2 = 5
x ^ y (or x ** y)	x raised to the power of y	2 ^ 5 = 32
x %% y	Modulus (x mod y) 5%%2 is 1	7%%3 = 1
x %/% y	Integer division 5%/%2 is 2	7%/%3 = 2

This table provides the basic mathematical functions we will practice in composing basic statistics formulas.

4.2.3 INSTALLATION OF PACKAGE COMMAND LINE

The R packaging system has been one of the key factors of the overall success of the R project. Packages allow for easy, transparent, and cross-platform extension of the R base system. An R package can be thought of as the software equivalent of a scientific article according to Leisch (2009). The articles are the de facto standard to communicate scientific results, and readers expect them to be in a certain format. We know that the aim of any academic article is to communicate a novel scientific idea to the peer group. In some cases, they may also serve as a tutorial on a certain topic, a survey, or a review. The overall format is always the same: text, formulas, and figures on pages in a journal or book, and nowadays we can find them in a PDF file on a web server. Some articles are intended for a worldwide audience, some only internally for a working group or institution, and some only for private use of a single individual.

R packages function the same way. The aim of the package is to maintain collections of R functions to datasets. The package is usually created by individuals who see the need to promote a new discovery of knowledge based on the dataset we have. As a written article distributes scientific ideas to others, a package distributes *statistical methodology* that has never been done before to others. The package system allows many more people to contribute to R while still enforcing some standards. But packages are also a convenient way to maintain private functions and share them with your colleagues. There are more than two thousand packages available on the Comprehensive R Archive Network's website, also known as Cran's website (http://www.r-project.org). We will not try all of them, but we will use a specific package with specific aims in mind, and we hope you will take the time to explore other packages.

How do we install the packages?

You type (the name of the package) after the > `install.packages`.
You can find the list of packages that are available on Cran's website at: http://cran.r-project.org/web/packages/.

For example, the `plyr` package was considered, according to Cran's log files, to be the top-ranking package in January 2013. The aim of the package is splitting and combining data. We will examine basic functionality in R as it relates to descriptive statistics.

4.3 Introduction to Basic Functionality in R

R is mainly used as an interactive program—you give R a command and it responds to that command. The result of your command may influence the next command that you give R.

Between the times you start R and it gives you the first prompt, any number of things might happen (depending on your installation). When working on different packages or different statistical models, you will work in a global environment. A global environment or workplace consists of a collection of named objects and a pointer to an enclosing environment. Every time you start a new session, you are creating a new environment. To find what the sense behind this environment is, you type:

```
> search ()
```

This will provide a list of all packages that are working in the background. The most common package is called `globalEnv` but there could be others.

To quit R, you type:

```
> q()
```

R will ask you if you want to save or delete the global environment when you quit. (At that point it is all or nothing—see Saving Objects for how to save just some of the objects.) If you do save the global environment, then you can start another R session with those objects in the global environment at the start of the new session. You are saving all the objects in the global environment.

The help function in R: The basic function command of help is > `help.start()`. R has a built-in help facility similar to the main facility of UNIX.

To get more information on any specific named function, for example "solve," the command is:

```
> help(solve)
```

An alternative is:

```
>?solve
```

For a feature specified by special characters, the argument must be enclosed in single or double quotes, making it a *character string*. This is also necessary for a few words with syntactic meaning including "if," "for," and "function."

4.3.1 INTRODUCTION TO VECTORS

A *vector* is the simplest type of data structure in R. Inside the vector are the functions that are self-contained modules of code that accomplish a specific task. A function usually takes in data, processes it, and returns a result. Once a function is written, it can be used over and over and over again. Functions can be called from inside other functions. The importance of a function in any another programming language, and in particular in R, is to pass an argument to other functions. They can also be nested, so that you can define a function inside of another function. In R, the functions are *first class objects*, which means that they can be treated much like any other R objects. The function is invoked by its name, then followed by the parenthesis and zero or more arguments.

The following examples illustrate the function "c" as a function that contains different numeric values:

```
> c(1, 2, 3)
[1] 1 2 3
```

In this example, the vector function "c" is a container to the values 1, 2, 3.

A more advanced example using the vector "x":

```
> x <- c("aa", "bb", "cc", "dd", "ee")
[1] "aa" "bb" "cc" "dd" "ee"
```

In this latter case the vector called "x," holds the values aa, bb, cc, dd, and ee. Vectors can also combine two or more other vectors.

For example, the vectors "n" and "t" are combined together:

```
>n <- c(1,2,3)
>t <- c("Bob", "Colleen", "Richard")
>c(n, t)
[1] "1" "2" "3" "Bob" "Colleen" "Richard"
```

In this case, we combine two different values: Bob, Colleen, and Richard with numeric values: 1, 2, and 3.

4.3.2 WRITING FUNCTIONS

When you write an R function there are two things you should keep in mind: the arguments and the return value. For example:

```
> p <- c("p1", "p2", "p3", "p4")
>p
>[1] p1, p2, p3, p4
```

We will encounter functions throughout the book. For example, there's a function named "+" that does simple addition. However, there are perhaps two thousand or so functions built in to R, many of which never get called by the user directly but serve to help out other functions.

4.3.3 INTRODUCTION TO ARGUMENTS

The arguments (or parameters) are the pieces of information you pass to the function. They can be of different sorts (lists, numeric vectors, data.frames, and so on).

Two things to remember about arguments:

1. The function above holds *local variables* (p1, p2, p3, p4). They live only inside the function and they *hide* any outside the function.
2. Arguments are passed *by value*. That means that no matter what you do to them, the original function values items are unaffected.

4.3.4 THE RETURN VALUE

In R, the return value is a function that has exactly one return value. If you need to return more than one thing, you'll need to make a list (or possibly a matrix, data.frame, or table display). We will discuss matrix, data.frame, and table display in chapter 17.

4.3.5 THE VECTOR INDEX

The vector index functionality allows us to declare an index inside square brackets [_]
Here is an example:

```
> t <- c("Bob", "Colleen", "Richard", "Ruth", "Alex")
>t[3]
[1] "Richard"
```

Vectors are not limited to being just a set of numbers. They may be or contain TRUE/FALSE values or have character strings attached:

```
> c(TRUE, TRUE, TRUE, FALSE)
[1] TRUE TRUE TRUE FALSE
```

However, only one type of entry may be used for vectors (for example, if a vector contains both numbers and character strings, then the numbers will be treated as if they are character strings).

4.4 Introduction to Variables in R

In chapter 3, we looked at different types of variables and the values they carried. In programming, the terminology of variables is a little different. Variables are given names, so that we can assign values to them and refer to them later. Variables typically store values of a given *type*. In any programming language, we often encounter seven types of data:

1. Numeric—decimal values, also known as numeric values
2. Integers—to store integer or "whole" numbers
3. Strings—a collection of characters

4. Characters—a single character such as a letter of the alphabet or punctuation
5. Factor—a variable in R which takes on a limited number of different values; such variables are often referred to as categorical variables
6. Fraction—represents a part of a whole or any number with equal parts
7. Logical—under logical variables the values are either *true* or *false*. In FORTRAN, they must be written as .TRUE. and .FALSE. Note that the two periods surrounding TRUE and FALSE must be there; otherwise, they become identifiers.

We will review each of the seven types of data and its variable values in R.

4.4.1 NUMERIC VARIABLE

Decimal values are called numeric in R. It is the default computational data type. If we assign a decimal value to a variable x as follows, x will be of numeric type. Here is an example of a single variable with a single numeric value:

```
> x <- 1
> x
[1] 1
> class(x) # The class command will display the data x
holds
[1] "numeric"
```

In R's environment, the variable offers a great deal of flexibility regarding the assignment.

So, how do I assign a variable? There are a number of ways to assign a value to a variable. The most common operator assignment is <- and ==, the first assignment being the preferred way. The assignment operation can be used successively to assign a value to multiple variables as the same time. For example:

```
> a < - b <-7
```

In this case, we assigned the value 7 to a and b. For example:

```
> a
[7]
> b
[7]
```

Another important aspect of a numeric variable is assigning a function. The `assign` function provides us the ability to assign a name to a value. For example:

```
> assign ("j", "4")
```

In this case, we assign two variables: j and 4:

```
> j
[1] 4
>4
```

Variable names can contain any combination of characteristics along with periods (.) and underscores (_).

For example:

```
> bob2 <- 38_a
> bob2
[1] 38_a
```

To remove a variable in R, we use the command rm:

```
> bob2 <- (12)
[12]
> rm (bob2) # remove bob2
> # now the variable bob 2 is removed and the R will
not recognize the variable called bob2.
```

4.4.2 INTEGER VARIABLE

The value of integers can carry negative numbers such as –3, –2, –1, plus 0 and positive numbers, such as 1, 2, 3. To declare an integer variable in R, we use a function called `as.integer`. We can be confident that y is an integer by applying the `is.integer` function. For example:

```
> x = as.integer(-3)
> x # print the value of x
```

```
[1] 3
> class(x) # print the class name of y
[1] "integer"
> is.integer(x) # is x an integer?
[1] TRUE
```

4.4.3 STRING VARIABLE

A *string* is a data type integer that presents in the form of text rather than numbers. It comprises a set of characters that can also contain spaces and numbers. For example, the single word "hamburger" and the phrase "I ate 3 hamburgers" are both strings.

```
> a <- "hello"
> a
[1] "hello"
> b <- c(,"there") # calling b a container that will
hold "there" strings
> b
[1] "there"
> paste(a, b) # paste function display the two
variables together
[1] "hello there"
> paste(a,b.. set="# ) With no space
>hellothere
```

4.4.4 CHARACTER VARIABLE

A character is used to represent a single element such as a letter of the alphabet or punctuation. In order to convert objects into character values in R, we need to declare this value as character with the as.character() function:

```
> x = as.character(0.14)
> x # print the character string
[1] "0.14"
> class(x) # print the class name of x
[1] "character"
```

4.4.5 FACTOR VARIABLE

As you recall from chapter 3, *categorical variables* represent types of data that may be divided into groups. For example, the color of the hair—black, white, or blond. In R, *a categorical variable is not designated as a factor.* R will treat it as such in statistical operations and create dummy variables for each level. If you import a variable with no numeric coding, R will automatically treat the variable as a factor. For example, the variable of hair color in the dataset is automatically treated as a factor. Once R thinks a variable is a factor, it has a series of special commands that can be used:

```
> a <- c("blond", "black", "white", "grey", "blond",
"white", "white", "black"))
> a <- factor (c("blond", "black", "white", "grey",
"blond", "white", "white", "black", "black"))
> a
[1] blond black white grey blond white black # You can
tell it's not a character vector because there are no
quotes.
Levels: blond black grey # Also the levels print out
> levels(a) # You can get the set of levels separately
[1] "blond" "black" "grey" "white"
```

4.4.6 FRACTION VARIABLE

In order to use fractions in R, we need to install a special package that will provide the calculation of fractions for us. A fraction in math is a way of representing division of a "whole" into parts. It has the form $\frac{Numerator}{Denominator}$. The numerator stands for the number of parts chosen, while the denominator is the total number of parts. For example, the pie consists of 5 slices, and if someone eats 2 slices, ⅗ of the pie remains. The package provides the ability to calculate the fraction variable. In this example, we illustrate the conversion of the value 0.14:

```
> install.packages(MASS)
> library(MASS) # call for the library
> fractions(.14) # write the fractions as function as
the value we want the R to
calculate for us.
[1] 7/50 # Results
```

4.4.7 LOGICAL VARIABLE

The logical value makes a comparison between variables and provides additional functionality by adding/subtracting/etc. For example:

```
> x = 1; y = 2 # sample value
> i> x + y
> i
[1] 3
```

It also provides us with two values for each element: TRUE or FALSE. Most often, R users use this value based on a questionnaire they want to record in R.

4.4.8 SUMMARY

We discussed seven different types of variables: numeric, integer, string, factors, fractions, character, and logical that will help us to hold different types of data. Establishing the variables will be an important part of our calculations when we introduce more advanced statistics.

4.5 Importing Data to R

Data is often kept in spreadsheets, and the most frequently used program is Microsoft Excel. In the following section, we describe how to import Excel spreadsheets to R. We will also review how to import data from the Google spreadsheet or directly from different websites.

4.5.1 IMPORTING FROM MICROSOFT EXCEL

There are several options for importing data from a Microsoft Excel spreadsheet into R. The following four steps are an easy way to import Excel to R:

Step 1—Open the data in Excel and prepare to export it as cvs. format.
Step 2—Close the Excel application and create a folder where you will keep this file.
Step 3—Open R and type the setwd command that designates it to be your working directory for R, where you will keep all your files with R.

Step 4—Type the following code: > `read.table` function in R to import the data.

We will illustrate each of these steps.

Step 1—We download a file from the state of Texas, which is a report on the status of its public libraries. We download the file to our computer and we call the file TXlibrary.xls. We then save the file as .cvs, TXlibrary.cvs. Figure 4.2 shows the screen capture.

Step 2—We create a specific folder called "R-library" where we will keep all our files.

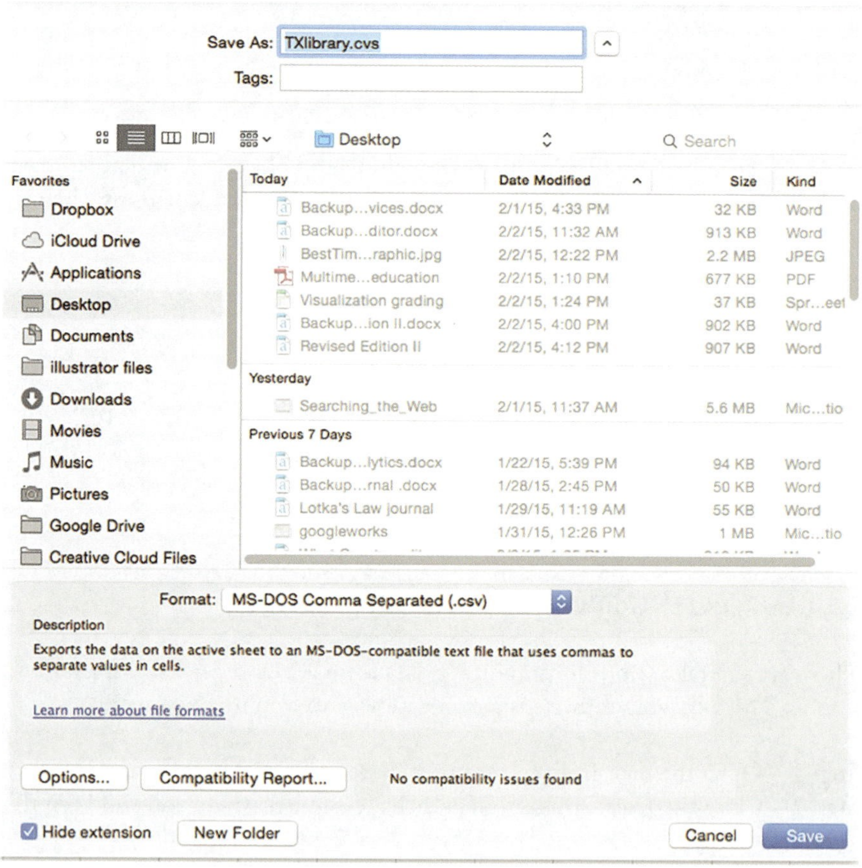
Save As: TXlibrary.cvs
Tags:
Desktop
Search
Favorites
Dropbox
iCloud Drive
Applications
Desktop
Documents
illustrator files
Downloads
Movies
Music
Pictures
Google Drive
Creative Cloud Files
Today
Date Modified
Size
Kind
Backup...vices.docx 2/1/15, 4:33 PM 32 KB Word
Backup...ditor.docx 2/2/15, 11:32 AM 913 KB Word
BestTim...raphic.jpg 2/2/15, 12:22 PM 2.2 MB JPEG
Multime...education 2/2/15, 1:10 PM 677 KB PDF
Visualization grading 2/2/15, 1:24 PM 37 KB Spr...eet
Backup...ion II.docx 2/2/15, 4:00 PM 902 KB Word
Revised Edition II 2/2/15, 4:12 PM 907 KB Word
Yesterday
Searching_the_Web 2/1/15, 11:37 AM 5.6 MB Mic...tio
Previous 7 Days
Backup...lytics.docx 1/22/15, 5:39 PM 94 KB Word
Backup...rnal .docx 1/28/15, 2:45 PM 50 KB Word
Lotka's Law journal 1/29/15, 11:19 AM 55 KB Word
googleworks 1/31/15, 12:26 PM 1 MB Mic...tio
Format: MS-DOS Comma Separated (.csv)
Description
Exports the data on the active sheet to an MS-DOS-compatible text file that uses commas to separate values in cells.
Learn more about file formats
Options...
Compatibility Report...
No compatibility issues found
Hide extension
New Folder
Cancel
Save

Figure 4.2. Excel Save window.

Step 3—We open R and type the `setwd` command that designates it to be our working directory for R, where we will keep all our files.

```
> setwd("<R-library>") # set working directory
```

Note that the forward slash should be used as the path separator even on Windows or Mac platforms. We called the new path R-library.

Our next command lets R know where our file is located:

```
setwd(file="/Users/AFriedman/Documents/R-library/
TXlibrary.cvs").
```

This code consists of the `read.table` command to read the file.

Step 4—We type the following command where R will open our library called R-library:

```
> txlibrary <- read.table(file.choose())
```

This code consists of a Read.table command to read the file. R will display the data in the following sequence (figure 4.3).

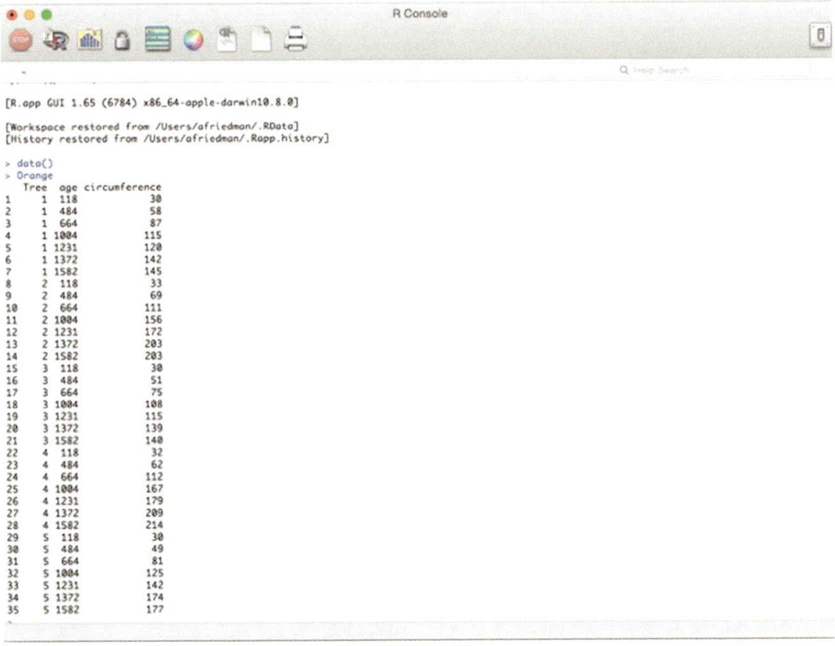

Figure 4.3.   R display of the data.

4.5.2 IMPORTING FROM GOOGLE SPREADSHEET

Google Drive offers an alternative to the Microsoft Excel spreadsheet. It allows us to create a special spreadsheet that holds URLs under the .csv file source. The process of converting it to R is a bit complex, but it only needs to be done once, and then you can share your data with anyone you like. That might be the biggest problem with this platform. If you have an account in Google Drive and you have already created a spreadsheet, click on "Share" in the toolbar of the spreadsheet. It will open a new window that will ask for Sharing Setting. Change the export type from Web Page to CSV (comma-separated values). Then change "all sheets" to "single sheet." Click "Publish Now."

The Publish box should look something like this:

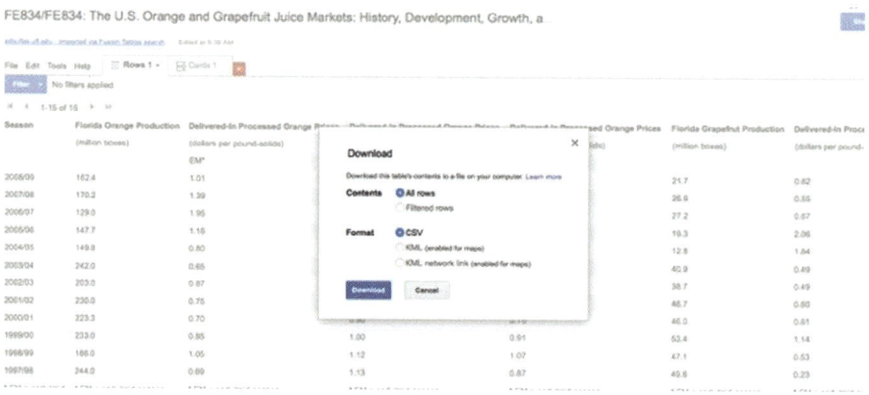

Figure 4.4.   Google Publish window.

Now, open R and type the name of the container you created in Google's spreadsheet inside the "read.table command."

Example:

```
> Tampa's catalog <- read.table(file= "https://docs.
google.com/spreadsheets/d/1RVuxJqOqKPvi7NVS2mDegv8tDOWYL
KAJZg3w4xdoKOY/edit?usp=sharing")
```

4.5.3 IMPORTING DATA FROM THE WEB

As we witnessed in the previous example, reading and importing data into R from the web is very easy; you simply specify where the file is located with the URL in the function. There are three common functions for reading, or importing, data into R, regardless of where the data is stored. These functions are read.table (for most text files—which have the extension .txt), read.csv (for comma separated values files—which have the extension .csv), and read.spss (for SPSS data files—which have the file extension .sav).

Here is an example of reading a text (.txt) file into R and naming the data example.3:

```
>example.3 <- read.table("http://statisticsforlib
.org/",)
```

Next, outline the summary of the file by typing the summary command:

```
>summary(example.3)
```

4.6 Summary

One of the great strengths of R is that it promotes reproducible research as an open-source system. The true witness of this is the ability to use different packages to produce analysis and visualizations for your own data. The command line in R is what makes R so powerful. In this chapter we reviewed basic syntax and data structures, and we explored different variables and the ability of the R to display them. We started our discussion on the vector as the main workhorse of R. We looked inside the vector's self-container that can hold not only different numeric values, but also text and TRUE or FALSE values. We also looked at different ways to import data to R through looking at the conversion of MS Excel and Google spreadsheets. In the next chapter, we will look closely at the heart of statistics by learning about descriptive statistics.

For other useful R commands, see appendix C.

4.7 Glossary

arguments—The pieces of information you pass to the function.

character—A single element such as a letter of the alphabet or numeric value.

distribution—A statement of the frequency with which units of analysis, or cases, are assigned to various classes or categories that make up a variable.

factors—Categorical variables that have a fixed number of levels.

first class functions—A building block of data that can be treated like any other R object.

fraction—A part of a whole or any numbers with equal parts.

functions—The fundamental building blocks of data in R.

Google—A top search engine.

integer—A whole number, whether negative or positive, or the number zero.

library—A collection of pre-compiled routines that a program can use, also called *modules.*

logical—Under logical variables the values are either *true* or *false.*

Microsoft Excel—The most frequently used platform and spreadsheet.

modules—Also called libraries.

numeric—The default computational data type, also known as decimal values.

spreadsheet—A program or display that displays numerical data in cells with a system of columns and rows similar to an accounting worksheet. Formulas may be included on the sheet to provide automatic calculations on or adjustments to the cell contents.

string—A data type integer that presents in the form of text, rather than numbers.

variable—Any of seven forms of data (numerics, integers, characters, strings, fractions, factors, and logical) that are given names so that we can assign values to them and refer to them later.

vector—May be, or contain, TRUE/FALSE values, numbers, or character strings.

vector index—This functionality allows us to declare an index inside a single square bracket [_].

Additional resources:

Administrative	Function	Description
	help()	Help for topic or package
	?	Help for a topic
	q()	Quit
	ls()	List of active objectives
	rm()	Remove active objective
	install.packages()	Install new packages
	library()	Load an installed package
	print()	Explicit print
	save()	Save objects
	load()	Load file
	gtwd()	Find out which directory by R is currently running
	setwd()	Set out your own directory
	#	Comments: When writing code in a file, sometimes it is nice to make comments to clarify what the code is doing. This can be done using the comment character, #.
	ca	

4.8 Reference

Leisch, F. (2008) "Creating R Package." Technical report #36. Department of Statistics, University of Munich. https://epub.ub.uni-muenchen.de/6175/2/tr036.pdf.

PART II

MAKING SENSE
OF STATISTICS

CHAPTER 5

Descriptive Statistics

5.1   Introduction to Descriptive Statistics
5.2   Summarizing the Dataset
5.3   Measures of Central Tendency
5.4   The Mean
5.5   The Median
5.6   The Mode
5.7   The Quartiles
5.8   Measures of Variability
5.9   Range
5.10   The Variance
5.11   The Standard Deviation
5.12   Measure of Position
5.13   Summary
5.14   Glossary

5.1 Introduction to Descriptive Statistics

In chapter 1, we outlined the idea behind descriptive statistics as the way to examine the population by summarizing the results. In this chapter, we will focus on the formulas and the methodologies that stand behind descriptive statistics. We will do so by using R.

5.2 Summarizing the Dataset

The American Library Association website often publishes the latest figures about the field. The following table came from the IMLS public library survey on the number of staff employed in libraries in 2011. Based on this report, we will explore the numerical data and their measurements and properties. The measures that we discuss in this chapter include measures of (1) central tendency, (2) position, and (3) spread.

Table 5.1.

	Librarians	Other Paid Staff	Total Paid Staff
Academic Libraries	26,606	59,145	85,751
Public Libraries	46,630	90,473	137,103
Public School Libraries	78,570	47,440	126,010
Private School Libraries	4,090	3,770	7,860
Bureau of Indian Education School Libraries	90	80	170
Total	155,986	200,908	356,894

5.3 Measures of Central Tendency

A measure of central tendency is a single value that attempts to describe a set of data by identifying the central position within that set of data. As such, measures of central tendency are sometimes called measures of central location. They are also classed as summary statistics. This section discusses different measures of central tendency that include the *mean*, the *median*, and the *mode*. We will look at the IMLS public library survey on the number of staff employed in libraries and use that information for our datasets.

Table 5.2.

Libraries	Academic Libraries	Public Libraries	Public School Libraries	Private Libraries	Bureau of Indian Education School Libraries
Units	85,751	137,103	126,010	7,860	170

5.4 The Mean

The arithmetic mean is the most common measure of central tendency. The formula of the mean is:

$$\bar{X} = \frac{\sum_{i=1}^{n} X_i}{n} = \frac{X_1 + X_2 + \cdots + X_n}{n},$$

where n stands for the sample size and x_n stands for the observed values. This formula is usually written in a slightly different manner using the Greek capital letter, Σ pronounced "sigma," which means "sum of":

$$\bar{X} = \frac{\sum x}{n}$$

You may have noticed that the above formula refers to the *sample mean*. So, why have we called it a sample mean? This is because in statistics, samples and populations have very different meanings, and these differences are very important even if, in the case of the mean, they are calculated in the same way. To acknowledge that we are calculating the population mean and not the sample mean, we use the Greek lowercase letter "mu," denoted as μ. In other words:

$$\text{Mean} = \frac{sum\ of\ all\ entries}{number\ of\ entries}$$

So, let's look at our data and calculate the mean of the total paid staff:

In this case, $\frac{85{,}751 + 137{,}103 + 126{,}010 + 7{,}860 + 170}{5}$ = 356,894/5 = 71,378

so the mean in this case is equal to 71,378.

An important property of the mean is that it includes every value in your dataset as part of the calculation. In addition, the mean is the only measure of central tendency where the sum of the deviations of each value from the mean is always zero.

When not to use the mean: The mean has one main disadvantage—it is particularly susceptible to the influence of extreme values.

To calculate the mean in open source R:

```
> librarynumbers <- c(85751, 137103, 126010, 7860, 170)
>mean (librarynumbers)
>[1] 71378
```

5.5 The Median

The median is the middle score for a set of data that has been arranged in order of magnitude, in other words, 50% of the observations are smaller and 50% of the observations are larger. The median is less affected by outliers and skewed data. The most common formula to calculate the median is:

$\{(n + 1) \div 2\}$th value

This formula corresponds to these two rules:

Rule 1: If there is an odd number of observations in the dataset, the median is represented by the numerical value corresponding to the positioning point $\frac{n-1}{2}$ of the ordered observations.

Rule 2: If there is an even number of observations in the dataset, then the positioning point lies between the two observations in the middle of the dataset. The median is then the average of the numerical values corresponding to these middle observations.

Example:

We will sort the data from the smallest to the largest numbers:

170, 7860, 85751, 126010, 137103
There are five numbers, so $((5 + 1) \div 2) = 3$
We will count three, so the median is the third number.
In our case: 85751

In R:

```
> librarynumbers <- c(137103, 126010, 85751, 7860, 170)
>median (librarynumbers)
> [1] 85751
```

5.6 The Mode

The mode is the value that occurs most often in the dataset. Unlike the mean, the mode is not affected by the occurrence of any extreme values.

In our example of numbers of libraries in the United States, we do not have a mode, as each number occurs with the same frequency: once.

In R:

```
>mode(librarynumbers)
>[1] "numeric"
```

This means that R did not find any mode in this dataset.

Here is another example, where a librarian is tracking unreturned books. The following data represent the number of books/manuscripts that were not returned to the library:

1, 3, 0, 3, 26, 2, 7, 3, 6, 3, 4, 12

So, in order to sort the data, we first ordered the array of these data from the smallest to the largest number:

0, 1, 2, 3, 3, 3, 4, 7, 12, 26

In this case, the most frequent value is 3. The value of 3 occurred three times.

The disadvantage of the mode is that there may be cases where we might find one mode and there might be cases where we will have more than one mode.

The relationship among the mean, median, and mode may be seen by looking at the shape of the curve and the values of the mean, median, and mode.

If a frequency distribution has symmetrical frequencies, the visualization of the curve will show that the mode, the median, and the mean are equal, as shown in figure 5.1:

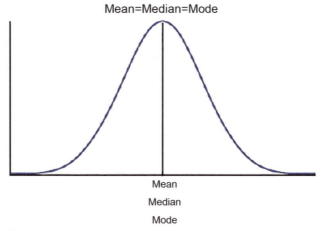

Figure 5.1. Symmetrical distribution.

The distribution is negative skewed when the mean is less than the median and less than the mode, as illustrated here:

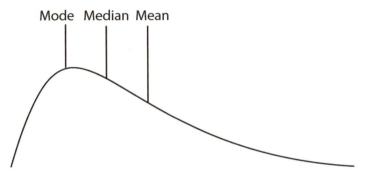

Figure 5.2.   Negative skewed distribution.

In the opposite direction, when the mean is bigger than median and mode, the distribution is called positive skewed:

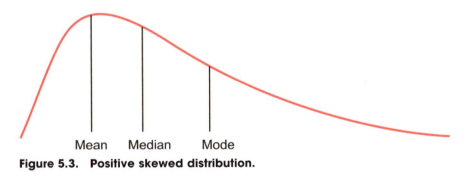

Figure 5.3.   Positive skewed distribution.

As a rule of thumb, median always lies between the mean and mode in a moderately skewed distribution, therefore it is considered the most realistic measure of central tendency.

5.7 The Quartiles

The quartiles are most often used to describe the properties of large sets of numerical data. The quartiles split a set of data into four equal parts (25%, 25%, 25% and 25%). The first quartile, Q1, divides the smallest 25% of the values from the other 75% that is larger. The second quartile, Q2, is the median—50% of the values are smaller than the median and 50% are larger. The third quartile, Q3, divides the smallest 75% of the values from the largest 25%.

First Quartile, Q1:

$$Q1 = \frac{n+1}{4} \text{ ranked value}$$

Third Quartile, Q3:
   75% of the values are smaller than or equal to the third quartile

$$Q3 = \frac{3(n+1)}{4}$$

In our case, we will use the library numbers: 98460, 8956, 7616, 3793, 1006, 265.

$$Q1 = \sigma/1 = 1702.75$$
$$Q3 = \frac{3(3+1)}{1} = 8621$$

In R:
```
> quartile(librarynumbers)
0% 25% 50% 75% 100%
265 1702.75 5704.50 8621 98460
```

5.8 Measures of Variability

Measures of variability indicate the degree to which the scores in a distribution are spread out. Larger numbers indicate greater variability of scores. Sometimes the word *dispersion* is substituted for variability, and you will find that term used in some statistics texts. We will divide our discussion of measures of variability into four categories: *range*, interquartile range, the *variance*, and the *standard deviation*.

5.9 Range

The range is equal to the largest value minus the smallest value:

$$\text{Range} = X_{largest} - X_{smallest}$$

In our example, the largest value is 98460, and smallest value 265:

$$98460 - 265 = 98195$$

The interquartile is the difference between the third and first quartiles in a set of data:

Interquartile range = Q3 – Q1

We calculated Q1 and Q3, where we found:

Q1 = 1702.75
Q3 = 8621
Q3 – Q1 = 6918.25

In R, IQR stands for the notation of the interquartile range:

```
>IQR(librarynumbers)
[1] 6918.25
```

While the range and quartiles measure the variation, they do not provide any value regarding how the values distribute or cluster between the extremes found in the dataset. Two commonly used methodologies to measure these variations are the variance and standard deviation. These two methodologies measure the *average scatter* around the mean—how larger values vary above it and how smaller values distribute below it.

5.10 The Variance

A simple measure of variation around the mean might take the difference between each value and the mean and the sum of these differences. However, if you did that, you would find that because the mean is the balance point in a set of data, for every set of data these differences would sum to zero. One measure of variation that differs from each dataset squares the difference between each value and the mean and then sums these squared differences. In statistics, this quantity is called a *sum of squares*. This sum is then divided by the number of values minus 1 (for sample data) to get the sample variance (S^2). The square root of the sample variance is the *standard deviation*.

Because the sum of squares is a sum of squared differences that by the rules of arithmetic will always be non-negative, neither the variance nor the standard deviation can ever be negative. For virtually all sets of data, the variance or the standard deviation will be a positive value, although both of these statistics will be zero if there is no variance at all in a set of data and each value in the sample is the same.

For a sample containing n values X_1, X_2, X_3, X_n, the sample variance (given by the symbol S^2) is:

$$S^2 = \frac{\sum_{i=1}^{n}(X_i - \overline{X})^2}{n-1}$$

$\bar{X}$= Mean
n = sample size
X_1 = i^{th} value of variable x

Variance is the sum of the squared differences around the mean, divided by the sample size minus one.

In our case, using the library numbers set (265, 1006, 3793, 7616, 8956, 98460)

S^2 = (98160-20026) / (6 – 1) = 1488842513

In our examples using R, var stands for variance in the R code:

```
>var (librarynumbers)
[1] 1488842513
```

5.11 The Standard Deviation

The most practical and most commonly used measure of variation is the standard deviation, which is represented by the symbol S. It shows how much variation, or dispersion, there is from the average (mean, or expected/budgeted value). A low standard deviation indicates that the data points tend to be very close to the mean, whereas high standard deviation indicates that the data is spread out over a large range of values.

Sample standard deviation:

$$S = \sqrt{\frac{\sum_{i=1}^{n}(X_i - \overline{X})^2}{n-1}}$$

In our case,

S = (98160 – 20026) / (6 – 1) = 38585.52

In R, sd is the code for the standard deviation, so for our example:

```
>sd(librarynumbers)
>[1] 38585.52
```

Another advantage to R is the ability to visualize basic statistics calculations. Chapter 14 will provide more in-depth review of the visualization procedure using R. For now, let's illustrate the power of R in producing histograms for the case study we examined regarding the library set. The command for R to create a simple histogram is hist(x) and we can add more attributes to this visualization.

```
> librarynumbers <- c((265, 1006, 3793, 7616, 8956,
98460)
> hist(librarynumbers, col="lightblue" main="My first
Histogram") # col= stands for the color scheme of the
histogram. Main stands for the title of the histogram.
```

The result:

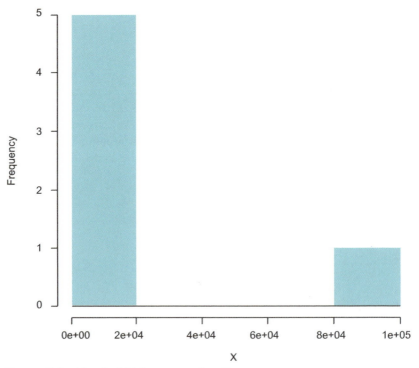

Figure 5.4. The first histogram using R.

5.12 Measure of Position

Standard deviation and variance are statistical measures of dispersion used to assess how far away individual data points are from the mean, or average, within a set of data. Knowing how far each data point lies from the average allows you to make more accurate conclusions about a dataset, population, or sample, because you can pick out outliers and extreme values and recognize how they affect your results. A large standard deviation indicates that the data values are far from the mean, and a small standard deviation indicates that they are clustered closely around the mean.

5.13 Summary

This chapter discussed descriptive statistics by looking at mean, median, mode, shape, quartile, range, interquartile, variance, and standard deviation. The mean is the most commonly used measure of central tendency. We calculated the mean by summing the observed numerical values of a variable in a set of data and then dividing it by the number of observations involved. Because its computation is based on every observation, the mean is greatly affected by any extreme value or values. The median is the value for which 50% of the observations are smaller and 50% of the observations are larger. The mode is the value in a set of data that appears most frequently. Unlike the mean, the mode is not affected by extreme values. The quartiles are not widely used in measuring non-central location, but they are used to describe properties of large sets of data. The quartiles split the data into four equal quarters. The next measure we covered is the range, which we calculated by taking the largest value minus the smallest value. The most commonly used measures of the spread, or dispersion, of the data are variance and standard deviation. We defined the variance as the sum of square differences around the mean, divided by the sample size minus one. The standard deviation is the square root of the sum of the squared differences around the mean, divided by the sample size minus one. We employ R to calculate those figures and, in many of the methodologies, the R code remains the same as the title of the methodology: mean was coded as `mean`, but variance and standard deviation have slight differences, as the code for the variance is `var` and for the standard deviation `sd`.

5.14 Glossary

central tendency—A single value that attempts to describe a set of data by identifying the central position within that set of data.

deviation—A measure of variation or dispersion from the mean.

interquartile range (IQR)—The difference between the third and first quartiles in a set of data.

mean—[or sample mean] The sum of the observed numerical values of a variable in a set of data divided by the number of observations involved.

median—The value for which 50% of the observations are smaller and 50% of the observations are larger.

mode—The value in a set of data that appears most frequently.

negative skewed—The term for a distribution where the mean is less than the median and the mode.

outlier [or extreme value]—A point or points that are distinctly outside of the pattern of dispersion for all other points in a dataset.

position—A measure of how far away individual data points are from the mean, or average, within a set of data.

positive skewed—The term for a distribution where the mean is bigger than both the median and the mode.

quartiles—A measure that splits a set of data into four equal parts (25%, 25%, 25%, and 25%).

range—The largest value minus the smallest value.

standard deviation—The square root of the sum of the squared differences around the mean, divided by the sample size minus one.

sum of squares—A measure of variation that differs from each dataset, squares the difference between each value and the mean, and then sums these squared differences.

variance [spread or dispersion]—The sum of square differences around the mean, divided by the sample size minus one.

CHAPTER 6

Bivariate Statistics

6.1 Introduction to Bivariate Statistics
6.2 The Foundation of Correlation Analysis
6.3 Introduction to Correlation Coefficient
6.4 Pearson's Sample Correlation Coefficient
6.5 The Spearman's Rank Coefficient
6.7 Summary
6.8 Glossary

6.1 Introduction to Bivariate Statistics

When we conduct research and find while collecting data that the research holds only two central variables, these variables become the theme of our research methodology. In order to analyze the correlation between two variables, we consult bivariate statistics to search out the embedded information. In this chapter, we review the bivariate data, which consists of two quantitative variables. Our first step in bivariate statistics is summarizing such data in a way that is analogous to summarizing single variables, as we did in chapter 5. We will start our review by looking at the differences between association, relationship, causation, and correlation. Then we will explore the idea of the correlation coefficient (from co- and relation), a numerical assessment of the strength of relationship between the x and y values in a bivariate dataset consisting of (x, y). We will look at the Pearson sample correlation coefficient and the properties of r. Finally, we will examine linear regression, fitting a line to bivariate data.

6.2 The Foundation of Correlation Analysis

The term *correlation* is often associated with the terms *association*, *relationship*, and *causation*. According to Beaumont (1992), the term *correlation* refers to: "The degree to which the points cluster about the line of best fit" (Howell, 2006, pp. 223). We will start with the term *correlation coefficient* as our basis for our discussion on correlation analysis.

6.3 Introduction to Correlation Coefficient

The correlation coefficient comes in many forms and has become the workhorse of bivariate statistics. Examination of the correlation coefficient determines the relationships among points or values in terms of whether they change together or separately. Generally, the correlation coefficient of a sample is denoted by small r, and the correlation coefficient of the population is denoted by ρ or R. In other words, a sample refers to a set of observations, or items, drawn from the population. This is in contrast to the population, where you examine each item from the entire population.

The correlation coefficient result will demonstrate a value between -1 and 1, with 1 or -1 indicating perfect correlation (all points would lie on a straight line in this case). A positive correlation indicates a positive association between the variables (increasing values in one variable corresponding to increasing values in the other variable), while a negative correlation indicates a negative association between the variables (increasing values is one variable corresponding to decreasing values in the other variable). A correlation value close to 0 indicates no association between the variables. To illustrate these values, figure 6.1 illustrates positive, negative, and no correlation.

A common formula to examine correlation coefficient is Pearson's sample correlation coefficient.

6.4 Pearson's Sample Correlation Coefficient

Pearson's sample correlation coefficient measures the strength of any linear relationship between two numerical variables. A Pearson's correlation attempts to draw a line of best fit through the data points of two variables. The Pearson correlation coefficient, r, indicates how far away all these data points are to this line of best fit, that is, how well the data points fit this new model/line of best fit. Its value can range from -1 for a perfect negative linear relationship to $+1$ for

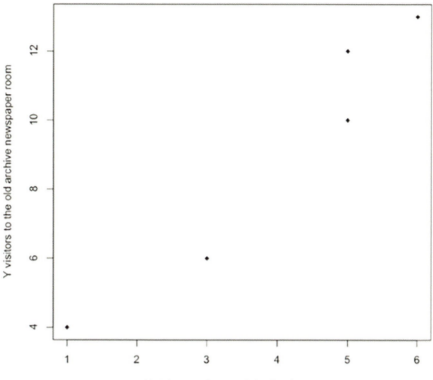

X visitors to the special collections room

Figure 6.1.   This figure illustrates a positive, a negative, and no correlation.

a perfect positive linear relationship. A value of 0 (zero) indicates no relationship between the two variables.

The Pearson's correlation coefficient formula:

$$r = \frac{\Sigma xy}{\sqrt{\Sigma x^2 - \Sigma y^2}}$$

Σ = Number of pairs of sources
Σxy = Sum of the products of paired scores
Σx = Sum of x scores
Σy = Sum of y scores
Σx^2 = Sum of squared x scores
Σy^2 = Sum of squared y scores

In order to practice the Pearson's correlation coefficient formula between two variables x and y, we will employ the data presented in table 6.1. In this table, the value of y refers to the number of visitors to the special collections room in the library, and y stands for the number of visitors to the old archive room. Our objective is to compute the similarity between these two variables, the data for the two rooms used in our library research.

Table 6.1.

	X Visitors to Special Collections Room	Y Visitors to Old Archive Room
	1	4
	3	6
	5	10
	5	12
	6	13
Total	20	45
Mean	4	9

Before proceeding with the calculations, let's consider why the sum of the xy columns reveals the relationship between x and y. If there were no relationship between x and y, then positive values of x would be paired with negative values of y, as with positive values. This would make negative values of xy as likely as positive values, and the sum would be small. On the other hand, consider table 6.1, in which high values of x are associated with high values of y and low values of x are associated with low values of y. You can see that positive values of x are associated with positive values of y and negative values of x are associated with negative values of y. In all cases, the product of x and y is positive, resulting in a high total for the xy column. Finally, if there were a negative relationship then positive values of x would be associated with negative values of y, and negative values of x would be associated with positive values of y. This would lead to negative values for xy.

Next, we need to calculate the mean of x and y in order to pursue the Pearson's coefficient analysis. This calculation is known as the *deviation score*, where the scores are expressed as difference deviations from mean. To convert data to deviation scores typically means to subtract the mean score from each score that x and y hold. Thus in our example, the first value of X is 1, so to calculate the deviation score we will take $1 - 4 = -3$, the second value is $3 - 4 = -1$, and so on.

Table 6.2.

	X	Y	x	y	xy	X^2	Y^2
	1	4	-3	-5	15	9	25
	3	6	-1	-3	3	1	9
	5	10	1	1	1	1	1
	5	12	1	3	3	1	9
	6	13	2	4	8	4	16
Total	20	45	0	0	30	16	60
Mean	4	9	0	0	6		

Pearson's *r* is designed to show the correlation between the number of visitors to the special collections room and number of visitors to both rooms. To achieve this value, Pearson's correlation is computed by dividing the sum of the xy column (Σxy) by the square root of the product of the sum of the x^2 column (Σx^2) and the sum of the y^2 column (Σy^2). Table 6.2 lays the ground for us to calculate the results from the numerator and denominator:

$$r = \frac{\Sigma xy}{\sqrt{\Sigma x^2 - \Sigma y^2}} = \frac{30}{\sqrt{(16)(60)}} = \frac{30}{\sqrt{960}} = \frac{30}{30.984} = 0.968.$$

An alternative way to examine this relationship is to visualize it.

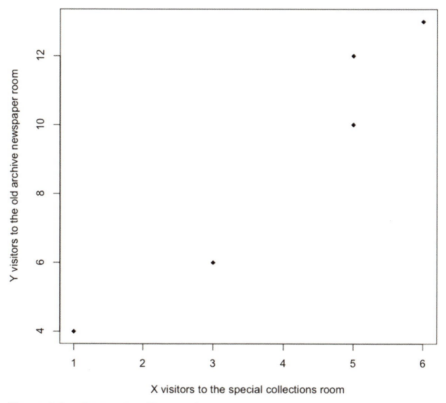

X visitors to the special collections room

Figure 6.2. Computing Pearson's.

The basic correlation function in R is achieved by typing `cor( )` function, to produce correlations and `cov( )` `function`, to produce covariances. A simplified format is `cor(x, use=, method= )`, where:

x	*Matrix or Data Frame*
use	Specifies the handling of missing data. Options are all.obs [assumes no missing data—missing data will produce an error], complete.obs [listwise deletion], and pairwise.complete.obs [pairwise deletion]
method	Specifies the type of correlation. R provides us with the options of Pearson, Spearman, or Kendall.

To code in R:

```
> x <- c(1,3,5,5,6)
> y <- c(4,6,10,12,13)
> cor.test(x, y) # The default in this case is
Pearson's r
> t = 6.7082, df = 3, p-value = 0.00676, alternative
hypothesis: true correlation is not equal to 0, 95
percent confidence interval: 0.5899134 0.9979838
sample estimates: cor 0.9682458
# In this case R calculated the following values for
us: t value, df, and p value.
plot (x,y, pch=18, xlab= "X-visitors to the special
collections room", ylab="Y of visitors to the old
archive newspaper room")
```

The difference between R and other statistical software such as SPSS, is that SPSS generates the correlation using Z scores when carrying out the calculation. The Z score is used for normal distribution. If we know the mean ("mu") and standard deviation ("sigma") and the set of scores are normally distributed, we can standardize each "raw" score by converting it into its Z scores by using the following formula on each individual score:

$$Z = \frac{x-\mu}{\sigma}$$

As a result, some of the Pearson's r formulas consist of Z scores as part of their calculation:

$$r = \frac{\Sigma Zx\, Zy}{n}$$

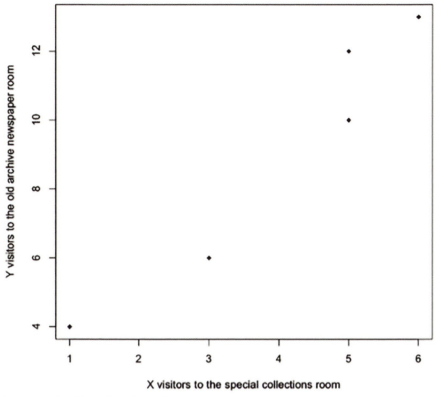

Figure 6.3.   The plot of our Pearson's.

6.5 The Spearman's Rank Coefficient

Another form of correlation is Spearman's rank correlation coefficient or Spearman's rho, named after Charles Spearman and often denoted by the Greek letter (rho) or as P^2, is a nonparametric measure of statistical dependence between two variables. It assesses how well the relationship between two variables can be described using a *monotonic function*. A monotonic function is a function that preserves the given order. The concept of order first rose in calculus and was later generalized to the more abstract setting of order theory. Nowadays, we encounter this sort of correlation in information retrieval environment settings. The monotonic relationship is a relationship that does one of the following: (1) as the value of one of the variables increases, so does the other variable; or (2) as the value of one variable increases, the other value decreases.

Under the Spearman's rank formula, if there are no repeated data values, a perfect Spearman correlation of +1 or –1 occurs when each of the variables is a perfect monotone function of the other. Examples of monotonic and non-monotonic relationships are presented in following diagrams.

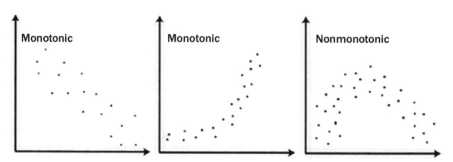

Figure 6.4.   The monotonic relationships in Spearman's correlation.

The attributes of the monotonic relationship are less restrictive than a linear relationship. The middle image in figure 6.4 illustrates this point well, where the nonlinear relationships exist, but the relationships are monotonic.

Spearman's rank correlation formula:

$$r_{rank} = 1 - \frac{6\Sigma d^2}{n(n^2-1)}$$

Where:

d = differences between ranks of corresponding X and Y

x = number of pairs of values (x, y) in the data

Example:

Library users participated in a competitive event that was organized by their town council. There were two contests. The first was a bicycle race, and the second was cooking a dish that was based on the local farmers' market. The following table depicts the ranks, which is in achievements of both the town competitions and in both tests. The library selected five users who often read about bicycles and cooking from their collection. The table also depicts the difference between the ranks and square of those differences.

Table 6.3.

The Library Users	Cooking Books	Cycling Books	Di	Di²
James	5	3	2	4
Greg	2	1	1	1
Ruth	4	5	1	1
Lisa	1	2	1	1
David	3	4	1	1

From the table, we can apply the Spearman's rank correlation formula:

$d^2 = 4 + 1 + 1 + 1 + 1 = 8$ (sum of the square of difference)
$n = 5$ (sample size)
$n^2 = 25$ (sample size squared)
$r_{rank} = 1 - \frac{6\Sigma d^2}{n(n^2-1)}$ Spearman's formula

Applying the formula and data above, the result is:

$$= 1 - \frac{6(8)}{5(25-1)}$$

$$= 1 - \frac{6(8)}{5(25-1)}$$

$$= 1 - \frac{48}{120}$$

$$= 1 - 0.4$$
$$= 0.6$$

In R:

```
> x <- c(5,2,4,1,3)
> y <- y (3,1,5,2,4)
>cor.test (x, y, method="spearman")
ata: x and y
S = 8, p-value = 0.35
rho: 0.6
```

6.7 Summary

Bivariate statistics involves the analysis of two variables, often denoted as X and Y, for the purpose of determining the type of relationship between them. In this chapter we review correlation analysis, and in particular Pearson's correlation coefficient, properties of Pearson's r, correlation, and causation. We examined these through the use of R. We employed R and provided examples of the code required to run R.

6.8 Glossary

association—Any relationship between two variable quantities that shows them to be dependent statistically.

bivariate statistics—The analysis of two variables, often denoted as X and Y, for the purpose of determining the type of relationship existing between them.

causation—A conclusion often viewed as implied by data, when the data point out an association or relationship only, and not the definitive result of what is driving it, often stated, "Correlation does not imply causation."

correlation—The degree to which the points cluster about the line of best fit.

correlation coefficient—A number between −1 and +1 that describes the type of relationship an independent variable has with a dependent variable; a 0 would mean there is no relationship, −1 means a perfectly aligned negative relationship, and +1 indicates a perfectly aligned positive relationship.

monotonic function—A mathematical relationship that maintains a given order.

multivariate analysis—Research and evaluation on many observations and variables to find applicable relationships.

Pearson's r—Also called the Pearson's product moment correlation coefficient, the covariance of two variables divided by the product of their standard deviations.

relationship—Variables, such as x and y, are considered to be related when the value of the second variable can be approximated based on what is known about the first one.

Spearman's rank coefficient—A correlation test of the association between a ranked variable and a measured variable.

univariate analysis—Measures and analysis of one observation.

## CHAPTER 7

Probability Theory

7.1	Introduction to Probability
7.2	Introduction to Random Events
7.3	Sample Space and Events
7.4	Some Probability Rules
	7.4.1	Mutually Exclusive
	7.4.2	Collectively Exhaustive
7.5	Multiplication Rule for Independent Events
7.6	Union of Events
7.7	Addition Rules
7.8	Bayes's Theorem
7.9	In R
7.10	Summary
7.11	Glossary

Probability is expectation founded upon partial knowledge. A perfect acquaintance with *all* the circumstances affecting the occurrence of an event would change expectation into certainty, and leave neither room nor demand for a theory of probabilities.

—George Boggle (1854)

7.1 Introduction to Probability

The term *probability* has most often been associated with the outcome of winning or losing in gambling. Probability is the likelihood or chance that some particular event will occur. From the gambler's perspective, the winning is the event he or she is looking for. Probability is not often used in the library environment, but by reviewing the fundamentals of probability we will have a more solid foundation for methodologies of taking a sample or calculating your hypothesis. In this chapter, we will focus on the randomization of probability.

7.2 Introduction to Random Events

Probability theory is concerned with the analysis of random events. The central objects of probability theory are random variables, stochastic procedure, and events we are trying to measure. The idea, under probability theory, is that a numerical measure indicates the likelihood of an event occurring. All probability values are between 0 and 1, inclusively. When the probability of an event is equal to 0, it means that this event is impossible. When the probability of an event is equal to 1, it means the event is certain to occur. Events with probabilities nearer to 1 are likely to occur.

If an individual rolls a coin or dice a single time, the outcome is considered to be a random event. If this event is repeated many times, the sequence of random events will exhibit certain patterns that can be studied and predicted. The following is the assignment of probability formula:

Probability of occurrence P(A) $= \frac{X}{T}$

X = number of ways in which the event occurs

T = total number of elementary outcomes

Events we measure can be named with capital letters A, B, C . . .

So, P(A) means the probability of A occurring, and it will read "P of A." In other words, we will try to find the value of P where 0 P(A) 1.

For example, suppose we consider tossing a fair die.

There are six possible numbers that could come up, *outcomes*, and since the die is fair, each one is equally likely to occur. So we say each of these outcomes has a probability of 1/6, which is equal to 0.166.

In this case, 1 is equal to the number of ways in which the event occurs, and 6.0 is the total number of outcomes.

Under probability theory, we have three assignments: intuition, experience, and judgment.

1. Under the intuition approach, the probability assignment is more subjective when it comes down to the chance of the occurrence assigned to an event by

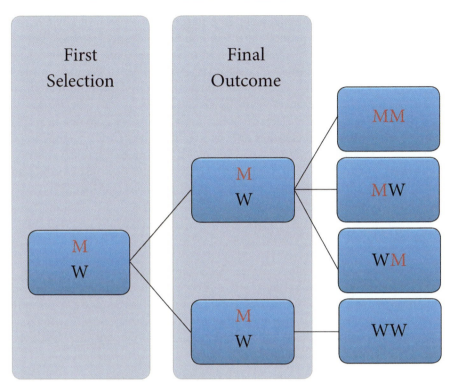

Figure 7.1. Illustration of probability.

a particular individual. As a result, this assignment will be different when we assigned it to another individual.

2. The next assignment is based on experience. It is also known as an *a priori probability assignment*. This assignment can be described as making a conclusion based upon deductive reasoning, rather than research or calculation. The largest drawback to this method of defining probabilities is that it can only be applied to a *finite set* of events.

3. The last step is judgment, also known as empirical assignment probability. This approach is based on observed data, not on prior knowledge or intuition.

7.3 Sample Space and Events

The basic elements of probability theory are the outcomes of the processes or variables under study. They entail an event, simple event, joint event, or sample space. However, in order to achieve these processes or variables, we need to comprehend what a statistical experiment is. A statistical experiment is any random activity that results in a defined outcome. For example, select tossing a coin *n* times and recording the score each time. In this example, the event is a collection of one or more outcomes in a statistical experiment. Under the statistical experiment, a simple event is an event that includes one and only one of the final outcomes for an experiment. It is usually denoted by E_i.

Suppose we randomly select two library users who visit the library on a daily basis. We then observe these users as: a man or a woman. Let us denote the selection of a man by M and that of a woman W. We can compare the selection of two outcomes, where each result in the outcome man or woman. As we can see from the Venn and tree diagram, there are four outcomes: MM, MW, WM, WW. In the Venn Diagram, M is red and W is black.

S = {MM, MW, WM, WW}

A joint event occurs when an event has more than two or more characteristics. The notation for joint event is p(A and B). What is the probability of event A and event B occurring? It is the probability of the intersection of two or more events. The probability of the intersection of A and B may be written p(A ∩ B). Table 7.1 summarizes a sample of library user loans by type paper books vs. eBooks. The formula for a joint event:

$$P \text{ (A and B)} = \frac{The\ number\ of\ outcomes\ satisfying\ A\ and\ B}{Total\ number\ of\ possible\ outcomes}$$

Example:

Table 7.1.

Borrow a Book or Electronic Device	Yes	No	Total
Physical book	20	5	**25**
eBook	10	6	**16**
Total	**30**	**11**	**41**

The sample space consists of 41 events. The two events are classified as physical book and eBook based on joint probability that refers to situations involving two or more events, such as the probability of physical book and eBook. Recall that a joint event A (physical book) and B (eBook) must occur simultaneously. In order for us to find if a randomly selected library user selected physical paper, we will examine the probability that users took a physical book by

$$P(\text{Physical book and eBook}) = \frac{number\ of\ physical\ books}{Total\ number\ of\ both\ types\ of\ books}$$

$$= \frac{20}{41} = 0.48$$

Sample space is defined as where the set of all simple events occur. In our example, 41 is the sample space.

We can use this reminder to determine the probability that an event will not occur. The complement of an event is the opposite, an event where A does not occur. A^c designates the complement of event A.

1. $P(A) + P(A^c) = 1$
2. $P(\text{event A does not occur}) = P(A^c) = 1 - P(A)$

For example, the probability that a college student takes a physical paper book loan from the library is 0.45. What is the probability that a college student will not take advantage of the library services during his/her academic year?

Solution:
    $P(\text{will borrow a book from the library}) = 0.45$
    $P(\text{will not borrow a book from the library}) = 1 - P(\text{will borrow a book from the library}) = 1 - 0.45 = 0.55.$

7.4 Some Probability Rules

Before we introduce the computation and multiplication rules, we will review some basic conditions that need to be fulfilled in order for us to calculate these probability rules correctly.

7.4.1 MUTUALLY EXCLUSIVE

Under this condition, two events are *mutually exclusive* if both events cannot occur at the same time. This condition is often called a *disjoint*. The formula is: $P(\text{A and B}) = 0$. For example, you can't flip a coin and get a head and a tail at the same time.

Probability (Heads or Tails) = Probability (Heads) + Probability (Tails)

7.4.2 COLLECTIVELY EXHAUSTIVE

Under this second condition, a set of mutually exclusive events is collectively exhaustive if one of the events must occur. A famous example is the toss of a coin. If we toss a coin that has {heads, tails}, in this example, the event will be collectively exhaustive: only one side of the coin will face out.

The formula for collectively exhaustive:

$$A \cup B = S$$

S stands for sample space.

Independent events. Two events are said to be independent if the occurrence of one does not affect the probability of the occurrence of the other. In other words, A and B are independent events if:

Either $P(\frac{A}{B}) = p(A)$ or $P(\frac{B}{A}) = P(A)$

If it can be shown that one of those two conditions is true, then the second will also be true. And if one is not true, then the second one will also be not true.

If the occurrence of one event affects the probability of the occurrence of the other event, then the two events are said to be *dependent events*.

Example:

In table 7.1, we refer to a joint probability of library users borrowing physical books and eBooks. Are both types of books independent?

In order to address this question, we will employ the formula of independent events and, in this case, the probability of books (A) and probability of eBooks (F), $P(A) = P(\frac{A}{F})$

$$P(A = \frac{0.48}{41} = 0.011) \neq \frac{0.48}{0.52} = 0.923$$

As a result, the physical book and eBook are not independent, but dependent, and as a result we must take into account the changes in the probability of one event caused by the occurrence of the other event. The notation P (A, given B) denotes the probability that event A will occur if event B has occurred. This is called a *conditional probability*. We note P (A, given B) as "probability of A given B." If A and B are dependent events, then P(A) P (A, given B) because the occurrence of event B has changed the probability that event A will occur.

Calculating the conditional probability. The formula for calculating the conditional:

$$P\left(\frac{B}{A}\right) = \frac{P\ (A\ and\ B)}{P(A)} \text{ and } P\left(\frac{A}{B}\right) = \frac{P\ (A\ and\ B)}{P(B)}$$

Given that p(A) ≠ 0 and P(B)) ≠ 0

Example:

Given that a randomly selected library user is age 50 or above is 0.20 and the joint probability that the user is a woman is 0.03, find the conditional probability that a student selected at random is a woman given that the user is a senior above the age of 50.

Solution:

Let's define the two events:

A = Library user selected, and he or she is above the age of 50
B = Library user selected, and she is a woman

From the given information

P(A) = 0.20
P(A and B) = 0.03

Time to employ our conditional formula:

$$P\left(\frac{B}{A}\right) = \frac{P\ (A\ and\ B)}{P(A)} = \frac{0.03}{0.20} = 0.15$$

As a result, the (conditional) probability is 0.15 that the woman is a public library user and she is above the age of 50.

7.5 Multiplication Rule for Independent Events

In the previous case, we examined two events that are dependent. Now, suppose that events A and B are independent. Then,

$$P(A) = P\left(\frac{A}{B}\right) \text{ and } P(B) = P\left(\frac{B}{A}\right)$$

By substituting P(B) for $P\left(\frac{A}{B}\right)$ into the formula for the joint probability A and B, we acquire:

$$P(A \text{ and } B) = P(A)\ P(B)$$

So, the role of the multiplication rule to calculate the probability of independent events or the intersection of two independent events A and B is:

P(A and B) = P(A) P(B)

Example:

The library building has two fire detectors. The probability is 0.02 that any fire detector of this type will fail to go off during a fire. Find the probability that both fire detectors will fail to go off in case of a fire.

Solution:

In this example, the two fire detectors are independent because whether or not one fire detector goes off during a fire has no effect or direct connection to the second detector. As a result, we define the following two events:

A = the first fire detector fails to go off during fire
B = the second fire detector fails to go off during fire.

The joint probability of A and B will count for:

P (A and B) = P(A) P(B) = (0.02)(0.02) = 0.004

7.6 Union of Events

This section discusses the union of events and the addition rule that is applied to compute the probability of the union of events.

The union of two events A and B includes all outcomes that are either in A or in B or in both A and B. The definition of union of events is:

Let A and B be two events defined in a sample space. The union of events A and B is the collection of all outcomes that belong to A or to B or both A and B and is denoted: A or B or A B.

Example:

A library group has been organized to listen to a special guest speaker's lecture on the subject of home gardening. The group accounts for 300 active members. Of them, 140 are women and among them they participate in at least one event in the library group's event calendar. The library posted a Facebook message where 95 responded to the posting and provided confirmation that they will attend the talk. Describe the union of the events *woman* and *will attend the guest speaker talk.*

Solution:

Let's first define the following events

F = library members who are female
M= library members who are male
A = A library group member
B = A library member who is not a group member

The union of the events *who will attend the guest speaker talk in the library group event* can be either woman or participate in library group events. The number of library group counts is

140 + 210 − 95 = 225.

Why did we subtract 95 from 140? The reason is that 95 of those who responded to the Facebook posting represent the intersection of events Male and Female. To avoid double counting, we subtracted 95 from the sum of the two members. We can observe this double counting in table 7.2 which displays this information. The sum of numbers in the three shaded cells gives the number of members of the library group who are either women or will responded to the Facebook message event or both. However, if we add the totals of the row labeled F and the column labeled A, we count 95 twice.

Table 7.2.

	A– Responded to the Facebook Message	B– Did Not Respond to the Facebook Message	Total
F	95	45	140
M	115	45	160
Total	210	90	300

7.7 Addition Rules

The method used to calculate the probability of the union of events is called the addition rule. The rule states: The probability of the union of two events A and B is:

P(A or B) = P(A) + P(B) − P(A and B)

In order to calculate the probability of the union of two events (A and B), we add their marginal probabilities and subtract their joint probability from this sum. We must subtract the joint probability A and B from the sum of their marginal probabilities to avoid double counting because of common outcomes in A and B. This is the case where A and B are not mutually exclusive events.

Example:
The chief librarian proposed that all the library visitors and staff will be introduced to a new online service the state's public library will offer this spring. Three hundred staff and visitors were asked about their opinions on this new service. Table 7.3 gives a two-way classification of the responses of stuff and visitors.

Table 7.3.

	Favor	Oppose	Did Not Respond	Total
Staff	45	15	10	70
Visitors	90	110	30	230
Total	135	125	40	300

Example:
Find the probability that one person selected at random among 300 is a staff member and he/she is in favor of this proposal.

Solution:
Let A and B define the following events

A = the person selected is a staff member of the library
B = the person selected is in favor of the proposal

From the information given in table 7.3 we have:

$$P(A) = \frac{70}{300} = 0.233$$

$$P(B) = \frac{135}{300} = 0.450$$

$$P(A \text{ or } B) = P(A) + P(B) - P(A \text{ and } B) = 0.233 + 0.450 - 0.155 = 0.533$$

Based on your calculations, the probability of a randomly selected person from these 300 people being a staff member and in favor of this proposal is 0.5333.

This probability can be calculated without using the addition rule. In this case:

$$45 + 15 + 10 + 90 = 160$$

Then, $P(A \text{ or } B) = \dfrac{160}{300} = 0.533$

We know from an earlier discussion that the joint probability of two mutually exclusive events is zero. When A and B events are mutually exclusive events, the term P(A and B) in the addition rule becomes zero and is dropped from the formula. So, what happens with the probability of the union of two mutually exclusive events? We turn to the addition rule to find the probability of the union of mutually exclusive events.

Addition Rule for Mutually Exclusive Events:
   $P(A \text{ or } B) = P(A) + P(B)$

Example:
   Back to our example of the proposal offered by the chief librarian. This time, the offer that all staff and visitors to the library will need to apply the new service as a requirement to answer the questionnaire will be put forward. Three hundred staff and visitors were asked their opinion on this subject. The following results are captured in table 7.4.

Table 7.4.

	Favor	Oppose	Did Not Respond	Total
Staff	45	15	10	70
Visitors	90	110	30	230
Total	135	125	40	300

What is the probability that a randomly selected person from these 300 staff and visitors is in favor of the proposal or did not respond?

Solution:
   F = the person selected is in favor of the proposal of mandatory use of the new services
   N = the person selected did not respond

Stage I:

$P(F) = \dfrac{70}{300} = 0.233$

$P(N) = \dfrac{135}{300} = 0.4500$

$P(A \text{ and } B) = P(A) \, P(\frac{B}{A}) = 0.233 + 0.4500 - 0.1500 = 0.533$

The addition rule formula can be easily extended to apply to more than two events:

$$P(A \text{ or } B \text{ or } C) = P(A) + P(B) + P(C)$$

Example:

In 2010, Huang et al. (2010) conducted a survey on the Internet about book reviews and borrowing intention. We did not receive the full dataset from them, and as a result, we will assume that among those responding to their survey, based on 8,002 people who responded, 3,201 were female and 3,201 were male.

Table 7.5.

Favorite Book	Female Vote	Male Vote
The Great Gatsby by Fitzgerald	1518	531
The Catcher in the Rye by Salinger	218	127
The Grapes of Wrath by Steinbeck	685	686
To Kill a Mockingbird by Lee	312	463
The Color Purple by Walker	431	219
Ulysses by Joyce	458	649
Beloved by Morrison	387	103
The Lord of the Flies by Golding	792	523

Suppose that one person is selected at random from these 8,002 respondents. Find the following probabilities:

a. Probability of the union of events female and favorite book by *The Color Purple* by Walker.
b. Probability of the union of events male and *Beloved* by Morrison

Solution:

F = the person selected is a woman
N = the person selected is a man

Stage I:

$$P(F) = \frac{4801}{8002} = 0.599$$

$$P(M) = \frac{3201}{8002} = 0.40$$

$$P(A \text{ and } B) = P(A) \, P\left(\frac{B}{A}\right) = (0.599)(0.667) = 0.399$$

Stage II:

P(F or M) = P(F) + P(M) − P(F and M) = 0.599 + 0.4 − 0.399 = 0.6

An addition rule formula can be easily extended to apply to more than two events:

P(A or B or C) = P(A) + P (B) + P(C).

7.8 Bayes's Theorem

Bayes's theorem is a theorem of probability theory originally stated by the Reverend Thomas Bayes (1702–1761). It can be seen as a way of understanding how the probability that a theory is true is affected by a new piece of evidence. It has been used in a wide variety of contexts, ranging from marine biology to the development of Bayesian spam blockers for e-mail systems. In the philosophy of science, it has been used to try to clarify the relationship between theory and evidence. We did not find any study in library science, of yet, that uses Bayes's theorem as its methodology.

Bayes's theorem examines the relation between two conditional probabilities that are the reverse of each other. This theorem is also referred to as Bayes's law or Bayes's rule (Bayes and Price, 1763). Bayes's theorem expresses the conditional probability, or "posterior probability," of an event A after B is observed in terms of the "prior probability" of A, prior probability of B, and the conditional probability of B given A. Bayes's theorem is valid in all common interpretations of probability. This function provides one of several forms of calculations that are possible with Bayes's theorem.

The basic formula for Bayes's theorem entails conditional probability, joint probability, and mutually exclusive and collectively exhaustive events. In many cases, under this theorem, many researchers measure the probability of the future success of events. Bayes's theorem allows us to measure the impact factor of a new event:

$$P(B_i \mid A) = \frac{P(A \mid B_i)P(B_i)}{P(A \mid B_1)P(B_1) + P(A \mid B_2)P(B_2) + \cdots + P(A \mid B_k)P(B_k)}$$

where:

B_i = i^{th} event of k mutually exclusive and collectively exhaustive events
A = new event that might impact $P(B_i)$

Example:

The popularity of cooking has been a major consideration to publishers. Recent reports showed that the probability of producing a successful cookbook received 0.6 from a library support group. Thus, the probability of an unsuccessful book is $1 - 0.6 = 0.4$ (see table 7.6). Under the Bayes's theorem we find the following:

Event S = successful report
Event F = favorable report
Event S' = unsuccessful report
Event F' = unfavorable report

Table 7.6.

	Prior Probability	Conditional Probability	Joint Probability	Revised Probability
S= success	0.4	0.8	0.32	0.64
S' = unsuccessful	0.6	0.3	0.18	0.36

$P\ (S) = 0.40$
$P\ (S') = 0.60$
$P(\frac{F}{S}) = 0.80$
$P(\frac{F}{S'}) = 0.30$
$$P\ (\frac{S}{F}) = \frac{(0.8)((0.4)}{(0.8)(0.4)+(0.3)(0.6)} = \frac{0.32}{0.32+0.18} = \frac{0.32}{0.50}$$

7.9 In R

Much of the work in software applications and probability focuses on the basic notion of the random sample. The basic notion then, is that a random sample will provide us a more accurate reading of the cards or the experiment we will conduct.

In R you can simulate these situations with the `sample` function. If you pick randomly a number from the set 1–20, then you can type:

```
>sample (1:20, 5)
```

The R will come back with five randomized numbers, in this case:

```
[1] 18 14 8 1 4
```

Notice that the default behavior of the sample function is sampling without replacement. That is, the samples will not contain the same number twice, and size obviously cannot be bigger than the length of the vector to be sampled. If you want the result of sample with replacement, you will need to add the argument = TRUE:

```
>sample (1:20, replcement=T)
{1] 13 1 19 17 8 16 8 1 11 3 5 1 18 20 18 12 15 20 9 3
```

In fair coin tossing, the probability of heads should equal the probability of tails, but the idea of a random event is not restricted to symmetric cases. It should be equally applied to other cases as the successful outcome of any procedure.

A sample space in R is usually represented by a *data.frame*, that is, a rectangualr collection of variables. Another function of a data.frame is for storing data tables. It is a list of vectors of equal length. For example, the following variable df is a data.frame containing three vectors n, s, b:

```
> n = c(2, 3, 5)
> s = c("aa", "bb", "cc")
> b = c(TRUE, FALSE, TRUE)
> df = data.frame(n, s, b)
```

How to build a data.frame:

```
> book <- c(20, 5)
> ebook <- c(10, 6)
> df <- data.frame(book, ebook)
> table(book, ebook), row.vars=1:2) # this will allow
us to present the table.
book ebook
5    6     1
     10    0
20   6     0
     10    1
```

7.10 Summary

This chapter developed concepts concerning basic probability, calculating probability, conditional probability, and Bayes's theorem. We then reviewed R and the package called *prob*. We reviewed the basic terminology in probability that entail: sample spaces and events, contingency tables, simple probability, and joint probability. We also reviewed the general addition rule, the additional rule for mutually exclusive events, and the rule for collectively exhaustive events. We also looked at statistical independence, marginal probability, and Bayes's theorem.

7.11 Glossary

Bayesian—Methods in probability and statistics, especially in statistical inference, named after Thomas Bayes.

classical probability rule—The method of assigning probabilities to outcomes or events of an experiment with equally likely outcomes.

conditional probability—The probability of an event subject to the condition that another event has already occurred.

dependent events—Two events for which the occurrence of one changes the probability of the other.

event—A collection of one or more outcomes of an experiment.

experiment—A process with well-defined outcomes that, when performed, results in one and only one of the outcomes per repetition.

independent event—Two events are independent if the occurrence of one does not change the probability of the other occurring.

joint probability—The probability that two or more events occur together.

marginal probability—The probability of one event or characteristics without consideration of any other event.

mutually exclusive events—Two or more events that do not contain any common outcome and as a result, cannot occur together.

probability—A numerical measure of the likelihood that a specific event will occur.

sample space—The collection of all simple points or outcomes of an experiment.

## CHAPTER 8

Random Variables and Probability Distributions

8.1   Random Variable
8.2   Discrete Distributions
    8.2.1   Mean of Discrete Distributions
    8.2.2   Standard Deviation of Discrete Distributions
8.3   Binomial Distribution
    8.3.1   The Characteristics of Binomial Distribution
8.4   Continuous Distributions
8.5   Normal Distribution
    8.5.1   Normal Disribution under Binomial Distribution
8.6   Summary
8.7   Glossary

8.1 Random Variable

In statistics, a random variable has two basic circumstances regarding the possibility of the outcome of the variable. The random variable is subject to variations due to chance or a result of it taking on a set of different possible values. The random variable is often associated with two conditions: fixed and conditional. Under the fixed condition, the variable does not change its attributes. The most famous example in the business world is rent. The rent as a variable does not fluctuate with changes of the weather, nor due to the day of the week. Again, this is true given a general assumption that the owner of the property does not change his or her mind every single day. Under the second condition, the characteristics of the variable change due to its probability. The most famous example

105

is flipping a coin. The coin always holds two sides, a head and a tail. When we flip the coin, the result will always consist of two random conditions, head or tail, unless we have the power to manipulate these probability conditions. Under this condition, we encounter two types of probability: discrete random variable and continuous random variable. We will discuss these distributions later in this chapter, but we will start with random variables.

A random variable in R. In R, you can generate a random number under two commands: `sample` and `runif`. Using the `sample` command, you will need to select the sample size and number of random numbers you want to retrieve from the sample size you selected.

The `sample` *function.* When you want to pick up four numbers at random from a set of 1–40, under `sample` function, you will type:

```
>sample (1:40, 4)
> [1] 36 28 15 2
```

The first argument (x) is a vector of values to be sampled, and the second part of the argument is the sample of 4. So, in this case, the actual sample size is 40 and we asked for 4 random numbers to be selected from this sample.

The `runif` *function.* To generate a decimal number where any value (including fractional values) between the stated minimum and maximum is equally likely, use the `runif` function. This function generates values from the uniform distribution. Here's how to generate one random number between 5.0 and 7.5:

```
> x1 <- runif(1, 5.0, 7.5)
> x1[1] 6.715697 # Be sure to type this x1, then Enter,
to retrieve your values.
```

In this case, the first argument is declaring that x1 is the variable that will hold our arguments. The second argument is included inside parentheses. The first is the number of values I want R to generate, in this case 1, and the two values that describe the range of the possibilities, 5.0 to 8.5.

You can also generate multiple random values by specifying the number of values you want as the first argument to `runif`. Here's how to generate 10 values between 5.0 and 7.5:

```
> x2 <- runif(10, 5.0, 7.5)
```

```
> x2 [1] 6.339188 5.311788 7.099009 5.746380 6.720383
7.433535 7.159988 [8] 5.047628 7.011670 7.030854
```

However, random selection has additional conditions: with replacement and without replacement.

With replacement means that once a person/thing is selected to be in the sample, that item is placed back in the population sample and thus has equal opportunity to be sampled again. *Without replacement* means that once an individual/thing is sampled, that item is not placed back in the population for resampling.

In R, we often use the replacement function. We indicate that the function to `replace` is true:

```
> x4 <- sample (1:40, 5, replace=T) #
```

We used the same values as in our first example:

```
>x4 [1] 34 25 35 12 11
```

8.2 Discrete Distributions

A discrete random variable is defined as a countable variable versus a continous random variable, where the variable can take infinitely many values. (for example, the number of copies of Dostoyevsky's *Humiliated and Insulted* found in the library at the current time). This number will not change. In contrast, the time it takes to travel between the local high school and the local public library is a continuous variable. The reason is that the traffic, the weather, and other conditions can affect the outcome of the drive.

Two characteristics of probability distribution are:

1. $0 \leq p(x) \leq 1$ for each value of x
2. $\Sigma \, P(x) = 1$

These two characteristics are also known as the two conditions that a probability distribution must satisfy.

In order to illustrate discrete distributions, we will use one of the simplest discrete distributions, the Bernoulli distribution. The creator of this distribution was the Swiss scientist Jacob Bernoulli (1655–1705). He was known for his work on probability statistics and was one of the founders of the calculus of variations. Under this distribution—that is, discrete probability—there are only two possible values of the random variable, x = 0 or x = 1. When drawing numbers from this distribution, if selecting x = 0, the probability is P(x) = 0.3, while the probability of selecting x = 1 is 0.7.

In our case, we want to count the number of copies of Dostoyevsky's *Humiliated and Insulted* at the local library. x will stand for the total number of copies and P(x) its probability:

Table 8.1.

X	P(x)
0	0.3
1	0.7
	Sum = 1

Because this distribution is based on discrete random variables, it will not show us normal distribution, as we discussed before. We will employ R to visualize this distribution:

```
> x = c(0,1)
> y = c(0.3, 0.7)
>plot (X, Y. type="h", xlim=c(-2, 2), ylim=c(0,1),
lwd=2, col="blue", ylab="p")
```

It will yield the graph in figure 8.1:

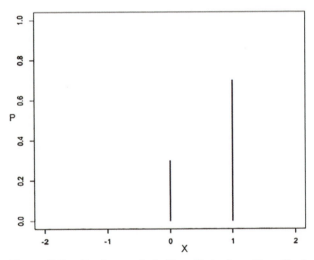

Figure 8.1.   Dostoyevsky's *Humiliated and Insulted*.

The plot consists of x and y, and `xlim = c(-2, 2)` represent the x axis from –2 to 2 and `ylim = c(0,1)` represent by the Y axis.

In order to make our point more transparent, we will add points so you will see the nature of this distribution.

```
>points(x, y, pch=16, cex=2, col="dark red")
```

Figure 8.2 is the result of the four lines and produces a better illustrations of the distribution of the book found in the library:

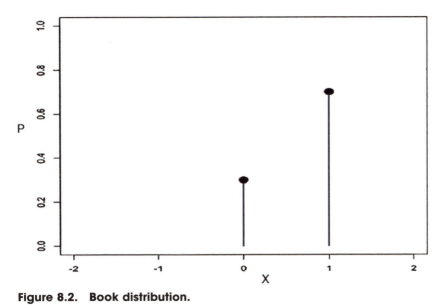

Figure 8.2.   Book distribution.

8.2.1 MEAN OF DISCRETE DISTRIBUTIONS

The mean of a discrete variable is denoted by μ. It is the actual mean of its probability. It is also called the *expected value* and is denoted by E(x). The mean or expected value of a discrete variable is the value that we expect to observe per repetition of the experiment we conduct over a large number of times. To calculate the mean of a discrete random variable x, we multiply each value of x by the corresponding probability and sum (hence the symbol, Σ), the resulting products. This sum gives us the mean (or expected value) of the discrete random variable x.

The formula of the expected discrete random variable:

$$\mu = \Sigma x P(x)$$

To illustrate this formula, table 8.2 shows the extended measurement of copies of Dostoyevsky's *Humiliated* at the campus library.

In order to calculate the xP(x), we need to multiple it by x:

Table 8.2.

X	P(x)	xPx
0	0.015	$0 \times 0.015 = 0$
1	0.235	$1 \times 0.235 = 0.235$
2	0.425	$2 \times 0.425 = 0.85$
3	0.245	$3 \times 0.245 = 0.735$
		$\Sigma xP(x) = 1.82$

8.2.2 STANDARD DEVIATION OF DISCRETE DISTRIBUTIONS

The standard deviation of a discrete random variable is denoted by σ and measures the spread of the probability distribution. A higher level for the standard deviation of a discrete random variable indicates that x can assume values over a larger range from the mean. In contrast, a smaller value for the standard deviation indicates that most of the values that x can assume are clustered closely to the mean. The basic formula to compute the standard deviation of a discrete random variable is:

$$\sigma = E[X - \mu)2 \times Px]$$

Example:

The library loan program often ships books from one library to another within the same state. Despite the fact that two quality control officers were assigned to check that a book will arrive at its final destination, library users continue to complain about the poor condition of the books received. Let x denote the number of books that arrive from the library service in bad condition out of four hundred books that were shipped. The following distribution provides us with the following table of the probability distribution of x:

Table 8.3.

X	0	1	2	3	4	5
P(x)	0.02	0.2	0.3	0.3	0.1	0.08

In order to address this question, we create a new table, where we have four new columns for P(x), xP(x), x^2, and $x^2P(x)$:

Table 8.4.

X	P(x)	xP(x)	X²	X²P(x)
0	0.02	0	0	0
1	0.2	0.2	1	0.2
2	0.3	0.6	4	1.2
3	0.3	0.9	9	2.7
4	0.1	0.4	16	1.6
5	0.08	0.4	25	2
		$\Sigma xP(x) = 2.50$	$\Sigma x^2P(x) = 7.70$	

Our analysis steps:

Step 1: We compute the mean of the discrete random variable.

Square each value of x and record it in the fourth column of the table. Then we multiply these values of x^2 by the corresponding values $P(x)$. The resulting values of $x^2P(x)$ are recorded in the fifth column. The sum of this column is $\Sigma x^2P(x) = 7.70$.

Step 2: Compute the value of $\Sigma x^2P(x)$.

Substitute the value of μ and $\Sigma x^2(x)$ in the formula for the standard deviation of x and simplify.

By performing this step, we obtain:

$$= \Sigma x2\ Px - \mu2 = 7.70 - (2.5)2 = 1.45 = 1.204$$

Thus, a given shipment of 400 books is expected to contain an average of 2.5 defective books with a standard deviation of 1.204.

8.3 Binomial Distribution

Another form of discrete probability distribution is binomial distribution. When a mathematical expression is available, the exact probability of occurence of any particular outcome of the random variable can be computed. In such cases, the entire probability distribution can be obtained and listed. Many mathematical models have been developed to represent various discrete variables that can occur in the business and academic worlds. The library environment is not an exception. One of those models is binomial distribution. The power of this model is the ability to match it to many everyday applications. Binomial distribution has four major characteristics:

1. The sample consists of a fixed number of observations, *n*.
2. Each observation is classified into one of two mutually exclusive and collectively exhaustive categories, usually referred to as success and failure and nothing in between.
3. The probability of an observation being classified as success, p, is constant from observation to observation. Thus, the probability of an observation being classified as failure, 1 − p, is constant over all observations.
4. The outcome (success or failure) of any observation is independent of the outcome of any other observation. To ensure independence, the observation can be obtained by using two different sampling methods. Each observation is randomly selected either from an infinite population without replacement or from a finite population with replacement.

Binomial distribution is used when the discrete random variable of interest is the number of successes obtained in a sample of *n* observations. If, for example, a sample of four invoices is considered, three could be none, one, two, three, or four tagged order forms. Can the binomial random variable, the number of tagged order forms, take on any other value? This is impossible because the number of tagged order forms cannot be more than the sample size *n* and cannot be less than zero. Thus, the range of a binomial random variable is from 0 to *n*.

Suppose that the following result is observed in a sample of four orders:

Table 8.5.

First Order	Second Order	Third Order	Fourth Order
Tagged	Tagged	Not Tagged	Tagged

What is the probability of obtaining three successes (tagged order forms) in a sample of four orders in this particular sequence? Because the assumption can be made that selecting an order is a stable process with a historical probability of 0.1 of problems occurring, the probability that each order occurs as noted is as follows:

Table 8.6.

First Order	Second Order	Third Order	Fourth Order
0.1	0.1	1 − P = 0.90	0.1

Each outcome is independent of the others, because the order forms are being selected from an extremely large or practically infinite population without replacement. Therefore, the probability of obtaining this particular sequence is:

$$Ppp(1 - p) = p^3 (1 - p) = (0.10)^3 (0.90)1 = 0.0009$$

However, this indicates only the probability of obtaining three tagged orders out of a sample of four forms in a specific sequence.

Before moving toward binomial distribution, we will address the notion of factorials that presents itself in binomial distribution. Factorials are recognized by their notation, which includes the symbol ! This exclamation point is used to denote factorials and is read as (the number) factorial, for example, 6! is read as "six factorial." The value of the factorial of a number is obtained by multiplying all of the integers from that number to 1. 6! is evaluated by multiplying all the integers from 6 to 1. By definition, 0! is equal to 1.

The formula for factorials is :

$$n! = [n(n-1)(n-2)(n-3)...]$$

Let's look at an example.

If the likelihood of a tagged order form is 0.1, what is the probability that three tagged order forms are found in the sample of four forms?

Let's apply the binomial formula:

$$P(x = 3) = \frac{4!}{3!(4-3)} (0.1)^3 (1-0.1)^{4-3}$$

$$= \frac{4!}{3!(4-3)} (0.1)^3 (0.9)^1$$

$$= 4(0.1)(0.1)(0.1)(0.9) = 0.0036$$

The formula for binomial distribution:

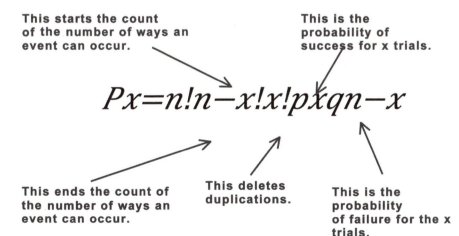

This starts the count of the number of ways an event can occur.

This is the probability of success for x trials.

$$Px = n!n - x!x!p\overset{x}{q}n - x$$

This ends the count of the number of ways an event can occur.

This deletes duplications.

This is the probability of failure for the x trials.

Figure 8.3.   Binomial distribution.

P(x) = Probability of x success given the parameters n and p
n = sample size
p = probability of success
$1 - p$ = probability of failure
x = number of successes in the sample (x = 0,1,2,3,4......n)

The binomial distribution in R is noted as `dbinom`; therefore, for the previous example:

```
> dbinom(3, 4, 0.1) where
(x = 3, size = 4, prob = 0.1)
[1] 0.0036
```

In R, the arguments that can add to this equation are as follows:

x, q = are vectors of quartiles
P = vector of probabilities
n = number of observations. If length (n) > 1, the length is taken to be the number required.
Size = number of trials
Prob = number of successes on each trial

8.3.1 THE CHARACTERISTICS OF BINOMIAL DISTRIBUTION

Each time a set of parameters (n and p) is specified, a particular binomial probability distribution is generated. Next, the mean and standard deviation of binomial distribution is explained.

Mean of binomial distribution. The mean of binomial distribution is obtained as the product of two characters (n and p). The formula of the mean of binomial distribution is equal to the sample size n multiplied by the probability of success p.

$$\mu = E(x) = np$$

The standard deviation of the binomial distribution:

$$\sigma = npq$$

Example:
According to the Institute of Museum and Library Services, 56% of public libraries in the United States are small and rural libraries. Assume that this result

is true for the current population of the United States. A sample of 60 libraries is selected. Let x be the number of small and rural libraries. Find the mean and standard deviation of the probability distribution of x.

Solution:
This is a binomial experiment with a total of 60 random variables. Each variable that is selected has two outcomes: (1) the selected library is a small and rural library, or (2) the selected library is not small and not a rural library. The probabilities p and q for these two outcomes are 0.56 and 0.44 respectively:

$n = 60$
$p = 0.56$
$q = 0.44$

Using the formula for the mean and standard deviation of the binomial distribution, we obtain:

$\mu = np = 60(0.56) = 33.60$
$\sigma = npq = (60)(0.56)(0.44) = 14.784 = 3.845$

The mean of the probability distribution of x is 33.60 and the standard deviation is 3.845. The value of the mean is what we expect to obtain, on average, per repetition of the experiment.

8.4 Continuous Distribution

A continuous random variable is a random variable whose values are not countable. A continuous random variable can assume any value. A good example of a continuous variable is the life of a battery or the price of print book. These are both good examples of a continuous random variable.

Example:
Suppose 5,000 females volunteer to help the library, and x is the continuous random variable that represents the number of books those volunteers read. Table 8.7 lists the frequency and relative frequency distribution of x. Frequency stands for number n_i of times the event occurred in an study. Relative frequency refers to the absolute frequency normalized by the total number of events.

Table 8.7.

Number of Books Read By the Volunteers (x)	Frequency	Relative Frequency
1 to 2	90	0.018
3 to 4	170	0.034
5 to 6	460	0.092
7 to 8	750	0.15
9 to 10	970	0.194
11 to 12	760	0.152
13 to 14	640	0.128
15 to 16	440	0.088
17 to 18	320	0.064
19 to 20	220	0.064
21 and above	180	0.036
	N= 5000	Sum 1.0

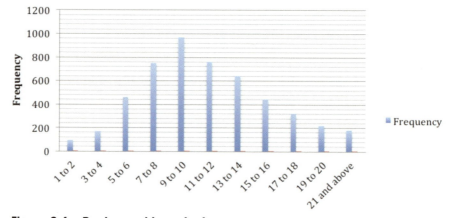

Figure 8.4. Books read by volunteers.

As you can see, relative frequency is calculated based on the frequency divided by the total. As illustrated in graph 1, this is called normal distribution.

8.5 Normal Distribution

As discussed in chapter 5, normal distribution describes a distribution in the form of a bell shape where the mean is equal to 0 and standard deviation is equal to 1. To better illustrate, figure 8.5 shows the core values of this distribution.

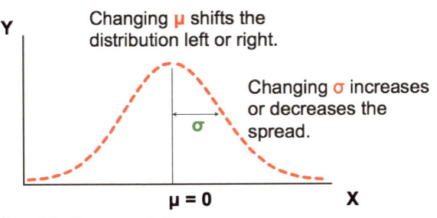

Figure 8.5. The common bell curve.

Normal distributions vary in two ways: the mean μ may be located anywhere on the x axis, and the bell shape may be more or less spread according to the size of the standard deviation σ. Furthermore, normal distribution also plays an important part when we deal with a random variable that processes the standard normal distribution and is denoted by Z. In other words, the units for the standard normal distribution curve are denoted by Z and are called the *Z value* or *Z scores*. The Z value is equal to the difference between x and the population mean, μ divided by the standard deviation σ:

$$Z = \frac{(x - \mu)}{\sigma}$$

Where
    x represents the data value
    μ represents the mean
    σ represents the standard deviation.

Example:
    Suppose you are studying the reading behavior of your library's regular visitors. One of your regular visitors, Dan, reads 10 books a month. In addition, the American Library Association recently published some figures of reading behavior across the country. They found that the mean population of the public library reads 8 books per month, with a standard deviation of 12. Another private company conducted the same research and found that the number of library books the average reader reads per month is 4. Their standard deviation was 10.

Based on our formula:

$$\text{First case } Z = Z = \frac{(x-\mu)}{\sigma} = \frac{10-8}{12} = \frac{2}{12} = 0.333$$

$$\text{Second case } Z = \frac{(x-\mu)}{\sigma} = \frac{10-4}{10} = \frac{6}{10} = 0.66$$

So Dan, your regular visitor to your library, reads above the number reported by the American Library Association, and his reading counts are considerably higher than the findings of the private company. We will come back to Z score in chapter 9, when we compare two independent sample tests for the difference between two means.

What percentage are the two scores we calculated for the Z case? R provides us with the answer. The code to calculate the Z score is pnorm (x), so in this case:

```
>pnorm(0.33)
>0.6304329
```

For the second score:

```
>pnorm(0.66)
>0.7453731
```

As a general rule, all Z scores have a mean of zero and standard deviation of 1, and range (roughly) between –3.00 and +3.00. A Z score of "0" is average; a positive Z score is above average; a negative Z score is below average. Based on figure 8.6, a normal curve shows that about 68% of a sample falls between –1 and +1 standard deviations, and about 98% falls between –2 and +2 standard deviations.

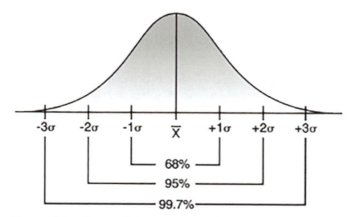

Figure 8.6.   The distribution percentages of a bell curve.

In our case, Dan's reading habits are under 68% and are within the first standard deviation.

8.5.1 NORMAL DISTRIBUTION UNDER BINOMIAL DISTRIBUTION

As you recall, earlier in this chapter we discussed binomial distribution under discrete distribution. However, binomial distribution can also appear under normal distribution, where the probability is that we will obtain is an approximation to the exact probability. The approximation is obtained by using the normal distribution and is very close to the exact probability when n is large and p is very close to 0.50. However, this does not mean that we should not use the normal approximation when p is not close to 0.50. The reason the approximation is closer to the exact probability when p is close to 0.50 is the binomial distribution is symmetric when $p = 0.50$.

The formula of normal distribution as an approximation to binomial distribution is:

$np > 5$ and $nq > 5$

Usually, the normal distribution is used as an approximation to the binomial distribution when np and nq are both greater than 5.

Example:
According to an estimate, 50% of the people of the United States have visited the library at least one time. If a random sample of 30 persons is selected, what is the probability that 19 of them have visited the library?

Solution:
Let n be noted as the total number in the sample.
x will stand for the number of persons in the sample who visited the local library at least one time.
P is the probability that 19 of the persons selected have visited the library one time.

Then, this is a binomial problem because:

First count

$n = 30$
$p = 0.50$
$q = 1 - p = 0.50$

Second count

x = 19
n − x = 30 − 19 = 11

From the binomial formula, the exact probability that 19 persons in a sample of 30 have visited the library at least one time is:

np = 30(0.50) = 15 (visited) and nq = 30 (0.50) = 15 (did not visit)

Because in both cases, np and nq are greater than 5, we can use the normal distribution as an approximation to solve this binomial problem.

We then do the following three steps:

Step 1:

Compute μ and σ for the binomial distribution
The formula for finding the mean is μ = np
In our case, 30 (0.50) = 25
The formula for finding the standard deviation σ = *npq*
In our case, *npq* = 30(0.50)(0.50) = 2.7361

Step 2:

Convert the correlation for continuity. As we showed previously, the binomial distribution applies to discrete random variables, so how can we convert it to continuous distribution? We employ a correction for continuity.

The definition of continuity correlation factors is: the addition of 0.5 and/or the subtraction of 0.5 from the values of x when the normal distribution(s) is/are used as an approximation to the binomial distribution. Where x stands for the number of successes in *n* trials, this is called the *continutity correction factor.*

In our case, the probability was 19 successes in 30 trials. To make the correction for continuity, we use the interval 18.5 to 19.5 for 15 persons. This interval is P (18.5 ≤ × ≤ 19.5).

Step 3:

Compute the required probability using the normal distribution.

We will calculate the Z score by using the formula $Z = \frac{(x-\mu)}{\sigma}$ and using the Z score table.

Then, we will calculate each probability 18.5 and 19.5 and compare the difference.

For x = 18.5 Z = $\frac{18.5-15}{2.7386}$ = 1.28

For x = 19.5 , Z = $\frac{19.5-15}{2.7386}$ 1.64

Then, the last calculation:

P(18.5 ≤ × ≤ 19.5) = P(1.28 ≤ × ≤ 1.64) = 0.9495 – 0.8997 = 0.0498

Based on the normal approximation, the probability that 19 persons in a sample of 30 will have the library at least visited one time is 0.0498.

8.6 Summary

We started by defining the random variable where we reported that any variable holds two conditions: fixed and conditional. Under the fixed variable, the variable did not change its attributes or values. However, the conditional variable was subject to variations due to chance or a result anywhere within a possible range of different values. In addition, we looked at two types of distributions to be random variables: discrete versus continuous distributions. We defined discrete as countable distributions of countable items, such as the number of books the library holds on the subject of statistics. We also looked at continuous random distribution, defining it as ongoing variables that continue to change. We considered how to calculate the mean, the standard deviation, and binomial under these two distributions.

8.7 Glossary

binomial distribution—This model consists of the probabilities of each of the potential numbers of successes x on N trials for independent events that each have a probability of π (the Greek letter pi) of occurring.

conditional variable—The attributes of the variable vary due to chance or a result anywhere within a possible range of different values, which influence its probability.

continuous distribution—If a random variable in the distribution is a continuous random variable, then the distribution is continuous distribution.

continuous random variable—A value, subject to chance, in which the data may take on any of an infinite number of values, especially ones that are not purely countable.

discrete distribution—A model that may take on a countable number of distinct values such as 0, 1, 2, 3, 4. Discrete random variables are usually, but not always, countable.

fixed variable—The attributes of the variable cannot be changed; they stay the same.

random variable—Subject to variations due to chance or a result of taking on a set of possible different values.

variable—One of the possible values from the outcome of a statistical experiment.

Z—The value equal to the difference between x and the population mean, divided by the standard deviation.

CHAPTER 9

Sampling

9.1   Introduction
9.2   What Is a Sample
9.3   Types of Sampling
9.4   Sampling Distribution
9.5   Sampling Distribution of Means and Proportions
         9.5.1   Sampling Distribution of Hat p
         9.5.2   Application of Sampling Distribution of [Equation]
9.6.   Summary
9.7   Glossary
9.8   References

9.1 Introduction

We often like to know something about the entire population; however, due to time, cost, and other restrictions, we can only take a sample of the target population. This chapter introduces the subject of sampling distributions. In the field of information science and librarianship, many scholars have utilized samples in their own studies. For example, Savolainen (2010) used this methodology to investigate dietary blogs and the types of information those blogs represent. The author reported that his entire population consisted of 644 blogs that were written in the Finnish language and contained the words *dieting* and *weight loss*. In order to study the blogs and the type of information they represented, he took samples of 50 blogs and examined their content more closely. In this chapter, we will cover the considerations in taking a sample and how we can employ R to help us calculate the sampling findings.

9.2 What Is a Sample?

The idea of a sample (as discussed in chapter 1) is an exploration from the part to the whole. The population is considered to be the entire universe, whereas the objective of a sample is to capture a small group of subjects that represent accurately the entire universe under investigation. As a result, the sample must be chosen carefully by following established procedures and distributions. Figure 9.1 represents a visual aspect of the idea of a sample of library users.

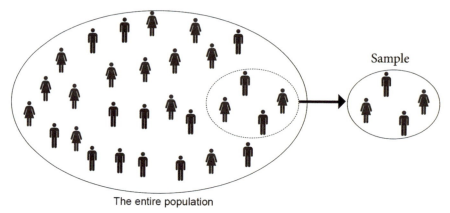

The entire population

Figure 9.1.   Population and sample.

As discussed in the previous chapters, distribution is a statement of the frequency with which units of analysis or cases are assigned to the various classes or categories that make up a variable. In this chapter, we draw a distinction between population distributions and sample distributions. A population distribution is made up of all the classes or values that we could observe or examine. The idea behind the population distribution is that it is derived from the information on all elements of the population being studied. In comparison, a sampling distribution consists of a random sample that represents the entire population. There are many types of sampling methodologies, but five are the most common.

9.3 Types of Sampling

There are five common types of sampling: random, systematic, convenience, cluster, and stratified.

- *Random sampling* is analogous to putting everyone's name into a hat and drawing out several names. Each element in the population has an equal chance of occurring. While this is the preferred way of sampling, it is often difficult to do. It requires that a complete list of every element in the population be obtained. R can generate random numbers by using a simple command line. (See below for more details.)
- *Systematic sampling* is a nonrandom sampling method in which every nth element is chosen from a list of numbered elements. Thus, every element does not have a chance of being drawn once the starting point is selected. The start is often chosen randomly and sometimes changed several times during the selection process to improve the chances of representativeness that occurs under ordered lists. In practice, every kth element is taken. This is similar to lining everyone up and numbering off "1, 2, 3, 4; 1, 2, 3, 4." When done numbering, all people numbered 4 would be used. R can generate systematic sampling in a simple command by using the kth element. Under R, several options exist to run systematic sampling.
- *Convenience sampling* is also a nonrandom sampling method in which the researcher uses some convenient group or objects as the sample. Under this methodology, R cannot produce sampling that is systematically justified.
- *Cluster sampling* is a random sampling procedure. The sampling method uses a group of population elements rather than a single element. Often the sampling is carried out in two stages. In the first stage, the clusters are sampled; in the following stages, the elements of the chosen clusters are sampled. R provides different methodologies to employ for the cluster sampling.
- *Stratified sampling* divides the population into groups called *strata*. In this probability sampling method, the elements are randomly selected from each designed subpopulation (stratum) of a population. The strata are determined according to differing types or amounts of a variable that the researcher decides may be associated with the major variable. The advantage of this methodology is that it incorporates all the advantages of random sampling plus it increases the precision of the analysis due to the homogeneous groupings.

In R:

Simple Random sampling command:

```
> x <- 1:10 # Your dataset from 1 to 10
> sample(x) # Your sample
[1] 3 2 1 10 7 9 4 8 6 5
sample(10) # asking the R to generate 10 number.
[1] 10 7 4 8 2 6 1 9 5 3
```

The systematic sampling command:

```
# population of size N
# the values of N and n must be provided

>sys.sample = function(N,n){
> k = ceiling(N/n)
# ceiling(x) rounds to the nearest integer that's
larger than x.
#This means ceiling (2.1) = 3
> r = sample(1:k, 1)
> sys.samp = seq(r, r + k*(n-1), k)
> cat("The selected systematic sample is: \"", sys.
samp, "\"\n")
# Note: the last command "\"\n" prints the result in a
new line
}
# To select a systematic sample, type the following
command
# providing the values of N and n
# sys.sample(50, 5)
```

Convenience sampling. R does not support convenience sampling even through researchers can use utilities R to summarize the data that were collected from convenience sampling.

Stratified sampling. R has an amazing variety of functions for cluster analysis. The most common approaches include hierarchical agglomerative, partitioning, and model based. The procedure for conducting stratified sampling will be posted on the book's website.

9.4 Sampling Distribution

The sampling distribution of a particular statistic is the distribution of all possible values of the statistic, computed from samples of the same size randomly drawn from the same population. In order to conduct a successful sampling distribution, we need to provide an equal chance of selection for all units found in the entire population. Sampling distributions are also important in statistics because they allow analytical considerations to be based on the sampling distribution, rather than on individual outcomes. The calculation of the sampling distribution needs to be an estimation of the entire population distribution versus the sample distribution. These values are often called *parameters* for the entire population and *statistics* for the samples. Table 9.1 represents the different measurements we will encounter in this chapter regarding sampling distribution and the entire population.

Table 9.1

Measure	Population Values Also Known as Parameters	Sample Values Also Known as Statistics
Mean	μ also known as mu	$\bar{x}$ also called x bar
Variance	σ^2	s^2
Standard deviation	σ	S
Proportion	p	P

Let's take an example of five common readers who often visit the library and borrow books. We counted the number of books they read and compiled it into a table.

We labeled the patrons as Person A, B, C, D, E. The frequency is the number of books that particular patron read in the last month, A = 3, B = 3, C = 2, D = 2, E = 1.

The next measurement is relative frequency, which is the actual number of specific events divided by the total number of events. In this case, these are a user and his/her selection of books read in the last month. Therefore, if a user borrowed 3 books out of the 11 books that all 5 users borrowed from the library, 3 divided by 11 equals 0.2727.

The relative frequency is based on the following formula:

$$\text{Relative frequency} = \frac{\text{frequency}}{\text{sum of all frequences}}$$

Table 9.2.

X	Frequency	Relative Frequency
A	3	3/11 = 0.2727
B	3	3/11 = 0.2727
C	2	2/11 = 0.1818
D	2	2/11 = 0.1818
E	1	
		1/1 = 0.090
	SUM 11 1	

The mean for the entire population in this case is: $\mu = (Xi) = 2.2$

Parameter variance $\sum \frac{(Xi-\mu)^2}{N} = 15.48$

Parameter standard deviation = 15.48 = 3.93

Now we will look at the sampling distribution for the sample mean, x.

Sampling Distribution of x⁻. The concept behind a sampling distribution is the probability distribution of a sample based on all possible random samples of the same size from the same population, given a finite population with mean (μ) and variance ($\sigma2$). When sampling from a normally distributed population, it can be shown that the distribution of the sample mean will have the following properties:

1. The distribution of **x⁻** will be normal.
2. The mean μx, of the distribution of the values of **x⁻**, will be the same as the mean of the population from which the samples were drawn; $\mu x = \mu$.
3. The variance, $\sigma x2$, of the distribution of **x⁻**, will be equal to the variance of the population divided by the sample size; $\sigma_x^2 = \frac{\sigma_x^2}{n}$

So, in our case, we took three separate random samples from the dataset to determine if we will receive the same result. The symbol of the sample will be marked as *x*, read as "x bar."

The result is as follows:

Sample I: [1] A B C
Sample II: [1] E C D
Sample III: [1] C D B

Sample I: $x = \dfrac{3+3+2}{5} = 8/5 = 1.6$

Sample II: $x = \dfrac{1+2+2}{5} = 5/5 = 1$

Sample III: $x = \dfrac{2+1+3}{5} = 6/5 = 1.2$

Mean and standard deviation of the sampling distribution x are denoted by μx and σx.

As a result, we can see that the mean of three samples (1.6, 1, 1.2) provides us different results than the mean from the entire population $\mu = 2.2$. The closest score was the mean of sample I that was equal to 1.6. In order to address the problem, we need some way to distinguish between these estimated values and the actual descriptive values of the population. We will look to the mean and standard deviation in sample distributions to yield information about those differences.

The mean in sampling distributions. The mean of the sampling distribution of the mean is the mean of the population from which the scores were sampled. Therefore, if a population has a mean μ, then the mean of the sampling distribution of the mean is also μ. The symbol μ_M is used to refer to the mean of the sampling distribution of the mean. Therefore, the formula for the mean of the sampling distribution of the mean can be written as $\mu M = \mu$.

The standard deviation in sampling distribution. The standard deviation of the sampling distribution of a statistic is referred to as the *standard error* of that quantity. For the case where the statistic is the sample mean, and samples are uncorrelated, the standard error stands for: $\sigma_{\bar{x}} = \dfrac{\sigma}{\sqrt{n}}$, where σ is the standard deviation of the population and n is the sample size. This formula is used when $\dfrac{n}{N} \leq 0.05$ where N is the population size.

In our case:

Sample I: $x = \dfrac{3+3+2}{5} = 8/5 = 1.6$

Sample II: $x = \dfrac{1+2+2}{5} = 5/5 = 1$

Sample III: $x = \dfrac{2+1+3}{5} = 6/5 = 1.2$

An important implication of this formula is that the sample size must be quadrupled (multiplied by 4) to achieve half (½) the measurement error. When designing statistical studies where cost is a factor, this may have a role in understanding cost-benefit tradeoffs.

In order to understand why we see different values for x, we must first explore the characteristics of sample distributions in the form of shape, mean value, and standard deviation. We will begin with general properties of the sampling distribution.

General properties of the sampling distribution of x. Let x denote the mean of the observation in a random sample of size n from a population having mean μ and standard deviation σ. The following denotes the mean value of the x distribution by μx and the standard deviation of the x distribution by μx. Then the following rules will hold:

Rule # 1: $\mu x = \mu$

Rule # 2: $\sigma_{\bar{x}} = \dfrac{\sigma}{\sqrt{n}}$

Rule # 3: When the population distribution is normal, the sampling distribution of x is also normal for any sample size n.

Rule # 4: Also known as *central limit theorem*. When n is sufficiently large, the sampling distribution of x is well approximated by a normal distribution curve, even when the population distribution is not itself normal.

Rule # 1 states that the sampling distribution of x is always centered around the mean of the population sampled.

Rule # 2 states that the spread of the distribution x decreases as n increases but it also establishes the relationship between the standard deviation of the x distribution and its standard deviation and sample size. Then $n = 16$ for example:

$$\sigma_{\bar{x}} = \frac{\sigma}{\sqrt{n}} = \frac{\sigma}{\sqrt{n}} = \frac{\sigma}{\sqrt{16}} = \frac{\sigma}{4}$$

So the sample distribution has a standard deviation only half as large as the population standard deviation. This rule is exact if the population is infinite and is approximately correct if the population is finite and *no more than 10% of the population* is included in the sample.

Rule # 3 states that when the population distribution is normal, the sampling distribution of x is also for any sample size.

Rule # 4, the central limit theorem, states that when n is sufficiently large; the sampling distribution of x is well approximated by a normal curve, even when the population distribution is not itself normal.

Then the following statements are true:

a. The *x* distribution is a normal distribution.
b. The mean of the *x* distribution is μ.
c. Then standard deviation of the *x* distribution is $\frac{\sigma}{\sqrt{n}}$.

We can conclude from the theorem that when x has a normal distribution, the *x* distribution will be normal for any sample size *n*. Furthermore, we can convert the *x* distribution to the standard z distribution using the following formulas:

$$\mu_x = \mu$$

$$\sigma_{\bar{x}} = \frac{\sigma}{\sqrt{n}}$$

$$Z = \frac{\bar{x} - \mu_{\bar{x}}}{\sigma_{\bar{x}}} = \frac{\bar{x} - \mu}{\frac{\varrho}{\sqrt{n}}}$$

Where *n* is the sample size,
  μ is the mean of the *x* distribution,
  σ is the standard deviation of the x distribution.

The theorem states that the *x* distribution will be normal provided the x distribution is normal. The sample size *n* could be 2, 3, 4, or any fixed sample size we wish. Under this case, the mean of the *x* distribution is μ (same as for the x distribution) but the standard deviation is $\frac{\sigma}{\sqrt{n}}$, which is smaller than σ.

Example:
  Suppose a team of researchers examine the type of books library users borrow for the long Christmas holiday. These researchers classify the type of books based on the Dewey Decimal classification scheme in order to employ this classification into the theorem deviation. The researchers have determined that the population of readers x has a normal distribution with μ = 10.2 and standard deviation σ = 1.4.

A. The team raises the question: What is the relationship where a random library user will borrow a book that can be classified between the language (5) and technology (7) classifications?

Table 9.3.

		Dewey Decimal Classification Classes
1	0	General works, Computer Science and Information
2	100	Philosophy and Psychology
3	200	Religion
4	300	Social Sciences
5	400	Language
6	500	Pure Science
7	600	Technology
8	700	Arts & Recreation
9	800	Literature
10	900	History & Geography

Solution:

As discussed in chapter 6, with $\mu = 10.2$ and $\sigma = 1.4$, the Z score will provide us with the following formula:

$$Z = \frac{(x - \mu)}{\sigma} = \frac{x - 10.2}{1.4}$$

As a result,

$$P(8 < 10) = P(\frac{8 - 10.2}{1.4} < Z < \frac{10 - 10.2}{1.4})$$
$$= P(-1.57 < Z < 0.14)$$

Next, convert those values to Z score table:

$$= P\ (0.582 - 0.557) =$$
$$= 0.25$$

Therefore, the probability that a single book taken from the library by a single random reader is related to language and technology is about 0.25.

B. What is the probability (of the mean length x) that five random patrons selected will choose books that are classified under arts and recreation (8) and history & geography (10)?

If $\sigma x = \mu = 10.2$. If σx represents the standard deviation of the x distribution, then by using the theorem equation:

$$\sigma_{\bar{x}} = \frac{\mu}{\sqrt{n}} = \frac{1.4}{\sqrt{5}} = \frac{1.4}{2.236} = 0.63$$

To create a standard Z variable from x, we subtract μx and divide by σx:

$$Z = \frac{\bar{x}-\mu_{\bar{x}}}{\sigma_x} = \frac{\bar{x}-\mu}{\frac{\sigma}{\sqrt{n}}} = \frac{\bar{x}-10.2}{0.63}$$

To standard the interval $5 < x < 8$, we use 5 and then 8 in place of x in the preceding formula for Z:

$$8 < x < 10$$
$$= \frac{8-10.2}{0.63} < Z < \frac{10-10.2}{0.63}$$
$$= -3.49 < Z < -0.31$$

The theorem, part (a) tells us that x has a normal distribution. Therefore,

$$P(5 < x < 8) = P(-11.19 < Z < -8.19).$$

Next, convert those values to Z scores:

$$= .9999 < Z < 0.003$$
$$= 0.999 - 0.003$$
$$= 0.996$$

The probability is about 0.996, the mean length based on a sample size of 5, and between 8 and 10 under the Dewey Decimal classification.

C. Looking at the results of parts A and B, we see that the probability size one to sample (0.25) size 4 (0.996) are quite different. Why is this the case?

According to the theorem, both x and x have a normal distribution and both have the same mean of 10.2. The difference is in the standard deviation for x and x. The standard deviation of the x distribution is $\sigma = 1.4$

The standard deviation of x is:

$$\sigma_{\bar{x}} = \frac{\mu}{\sqrt{n}} = \frac{1.4}{\sqrt{5}} = \frac{1.4}{2.236} = 0.63$$

The standard deviation of the x distribution is less than half the standard deviation of the x distribution, although the means are the same.

Log onto our website for more exercises on this subject.

Standard error. The standard error is the standard deviation of a sampling distribution. For the x sampling distribution:

$$\text{Standard error} = \sigma_{\bar{x}} = \frac{\sigma}{\sqrt{n}}$$

The expression standard error refers to the standard error of the mean.

In R, the standard error equals sd/$\sqrt{n}$:

```
> x <- c(1,2.3,2,3,4,8,12,43,-4,-1)
> se <- sd(x)/sqrt(length(x))
> se
[1] 4.236195
```

The distribution given x follows any distribution.

Under the theorem, part 1 gives us complete information about the x distribution, provided the original x distribution is known to be normal. What happens if we do not have the information about the shape of the original x distributions? The central limit theorem tells us what we can expect.

The central theorem for any probability distribution. If x processes any distribution with mean μ and standard deviation σ, then the sample mean x, based on a random sample of size *n*, will have a distribution that approaches the distribution of a normal random distribution that approaches the distributions of a normal random variable with mean μ and standard deviation σn as *n* increases without limit.

The central limit theorem says that x can have any distribution, but as the sample size gets larger, the distribution of *x* based on a random sample of size *n* will have a distribution that approaches the distribution of a normal variable with mean μ and standard deviation $\frac{\sigma}{\sqrt{n}}$ as *n* increases without limit.

The formula of the central limit theorem to convert the x distribution to the standard normal distribution is:

$$\mu x = \mu$$

$$\sigma_{\bar{x}} = \frac{\sigma}{\sqrt{n}}$$

$$Z = \frac{\bar{x} - \mu_{\bar{x}}}{\sigma_x} = \frac{\bar{x} - \mu}{\frac{\sigma}{\sqrt{n}}}$$

Sampling distributions for proportions.

Given:

N = number of binomial trials (fixed constant)
r = number of success
p = probability of success on each trial
q = 1 – p = probability of failure on each trial

If np >5 and nq > 5, then the random variable $\hat{p} = \frac{r}{n}$ can be approximated by normal variable (x) with mean and standard deviation:

$$\mu p = p$$
$$\sigma_{\hat{p}} = \sqrt{\frac{pq}{n}}$$

The values of the mean and standard deviation calculated for the probability distribution are calculated as follows:

$$\mu = \frac{70+78+80+80+95}{5} = 80.60$$

The definitions of mean and standard deviation of sampling are always defined as *X*.

The formula of the mean of the sampling distribution of *X* is always equal to the mean of the population:

$$\mu x = \mu$$

Example with R:

We will employ R to address the central limit theorem.

We will use the rnorm command to draw 500 numbers at random distribution while the mean for this distribution is 100 and standard deviation is 10.

Our command:

```
> x = rnorm(500, mean=100, sd=10)
> x # we will ask to see the result of some of the
results
```

Table 9.4.

[1] 111.55209	97.24050	92.68848	82.52463	109.31802	108.32459	83.00670	89.26875
[9] 75.70270	123.58992	102.09190	119.77364	88.12079	106.97782	98.59419	103.14760
[17] 94.61791	88.13449	99.29828	91.85665	104.26802	94.80050	108.50890	84.33962
[25] 101.09177	81.12858	91.36644	96.93328	99.12372	112.96364	107.81306	107.95731
[33] 96.43726	108.51994	109.68077	104.83131	99.32821	103.60105	104.19988	93.96107
[41] 102.33610	93.78330	124.02103	94.78894	105.64514	95.79113	104.30137	89.44551
[49] 113.75918	93.31709	117.63567	107.31241	128.34292	112.88165	107.20717	113.37049
[57] 100.59420	113.03992	115.58488	88.73811	72.85903	105.96066	107.92803	103.03057
[65] 104.83090	105.81510	87.53651	94.72101	111.60492	107.54120	91.60892	90.55675
[73] 93.22649	101.25328	107.63417	102.67403	81.29807	83.06487	93.36482	93.70351
[81] 108.06343	107.03462	95.92501	93.33976	109.85680	91.24292	105.56427	90.46225
[89] 96.69797	99.28140	99.63375	91.76809	94.70627	96.59201	95.13531	117.79783
[97] 92.33372	86.74711	88.56511	102.06469	119.70357	104.40460	102.09666	101.34539
[105] 103.59292	99.32866	101.01474	101.58607	93.74571	108.59612	100.67548	116.78889
[113] 96.80618	92.62621	107.17173	96.38856	100.68643	110.06115	112.36466	105.30423
[121] 92.38832	100.10897	97.82776	111.70773	88.82512	95.20199	114.80327	97.45863
[129] 107.50334	98.10763	102.99769	106.39846	99.29961	93.20238	93.00196	100.03094
[137] 113.50025	115.03300	106.32779	89.58524	85.14172	103.70424	100.34439	108.09727
[145] 79.72313	96.22978	109.05198	101.18664	126.50670	98.57598	92.38971	99.55717
[153] 103.14452	109.05158	100.54290	112.65490	106.79928	107.35994	90.53019	81.14386
[161] 98.61420	107.48035	103.12688	87.12294	99.08614	92.89029	105.88213	82.92831
[169] 96.59139	105.29636	87.87654	105.41993	89.64116	101.23920	103.23246	114.41911
[177] 90.83871	94.73443	122.92020	105.40389	113.58954	117.54110	97.64189	89.95689
[185] 93.08089	88.92455	87.16113	84.23658	95.56815	95.85473	87.22373	105.84172
[193] 92.83464	120.95720	83.94792	107.77612	103.19188	95.49539	108.04202	96.85295
[201] 84.46574	105.08998	83.23930	97.22247	102.00901	92.78544	86.53811	104.21367
[209] 97.33453	85.86610	108.69772	132.01008	97.67792	103.33140	106.23286	111.31900
[217] 102.36186	100.79340	108.32016	102.86359	88.64807	107.88597	82.06701	110.22867
[225] 100.56341	116.09703	101.08097	90.05288	105.50572	106.99322	87.18559	106.81418
[233] 86.26361	95.58739	81.64357	80.85432	95.59627	96.56567	106.28033	96.22533
[241] 122.20326	99.91373	100.35222	106.86913	89.19629	93.93497	101.01534	106.37162
[249] 87.15815	123.24625	104.89270	111.01097	90.56193	105.84058	79.86703	93.41226
[257] 93.70946	106.57830	92.83771	108.41502	102.25140	92.66213	102.31731	99.12675
[265] 119.67439	93.27267	83.21695	110.74516	99.94568	107.07684	84.85125	96.75518
[273] 112.35921	84.27979	90.43687	112.41555	103.83653	93.43820	112.05262	102.78605
[281] 103.96401	106.47644	86.41875	103.98403	112.21884	91.61851	103.52600	99.98722
[289] 105.73103	106.45804	73.32174	113.81926	86.30343	111.53781	94.86229	86.85868
[297] 110.95911	93.40308	99.60810	111.86818	93.71954	88.57434	98.63304	94.37386
[305] 100.48269	100.69264	86.07424	105.78913	83.79600	94.39545	95.09701	88.31949
[313] 102.05952	94.12686	91.06158	84.04382	95.39729	91.38391	96.83824	101.20211
[321] 89.17918	121.25700	122.52074	94.68952	97.63818	119.14110	92.14390	91.88988
[329] 113.75349	91.35794	74.76314	105.51984	111.06501	84.27096	86.24828	102.40973
[337] 104.25186	97.94886	109.30634	92.43647	99.71722	95.93561	85.92015	85.50492
[345] 107.81461	106.31641	104.20502	88.97319	100.24124	95.01394	104.78500	103.32714
[353] 104.20762	91.42431	99.56947	102.71849	95.55139	93.43830	92.29035	86.74374
[361] 102.31213	99.86325	80.84533	97.25405	108.02706	100.67164	104.06942	104.42769
[369] 95.64327	109.67884	92.69703	114.91947	82.97577	95.49521	124.46985	104.86343
[377] 96.00504	100.57825	104.14272	98.45316	114.32171	95.36987	82.69245	86.88861
[385] 101.88278	107.88787	110.60463	96.09254	106.85077	116.36704	103.05464	79.10533
[393] 106.07226	95.35260	95.05443	82.31125	91.84258	87.62534	106.14509	100.58569
[401] 85.90184	100.76999	102.43461	109.64790	96.92951	100.46193	90.81334	81.38203

```
[409] 106.13624 104.94034  93.40309  90.61116  97.41716 109.74482  85.08824 120.28829
[417]  94.94676 109.19260 112.24533  98.41927  97.95787 100.95752 102.60309 101.35629
[425] 109.01787  95.92091 110.40156 108.74196 102.84021 109.40487 101.92498 104.08255
[433]  98.13174 106.96881  89.61117  93.13745 114.03345 108.75272 107.21131  93.17538
[441] 103.96577  81.18744 120.59262 103.66089 112.42153 100.22605  97.28623 102.52154
[449]  80.32988  90.94998  83.25729  92.70170 105.04413 112.67451  91.90482  99.54297
[457]  95.13043 117.91574 102.77992  97.96377  91.23315 105.69915 102.54660  66.25475
[465]  84.98554 102.48492 110.85954  84.19404 108.13689 109.41963  91.33799 113.34345
[473]  86.90366  96.23221 111.91153  98.64547  83.28638 102.55118  97.14488 118.38495
[481]  95.12027  97.51625  94.63760 105.75733 103.73914 105.37714 112.00177 120.35917
[489] 104.20671  89.17663 100.23328  99.87450 116.70476  86.93272 110.40801 102.18216
[497] 100.51997  82.10726 105.22389 105.46758
```

When you examine the numbers stored in R generated for x, it is hard to see if the mean of this distribution is equal to 100 as we asked. In order to overcome this perception, we will employ the histogram to see the visual distribution of 500 random variables.

The code for the histogram in R is hist(x), where you can add more attributes to the visual display:

```
> hist(x, prob=TRUE, col="red")
```

The result:

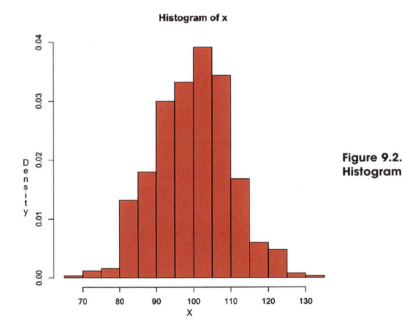

Figure 9.2. Histogram

The result of this histogram shows that this random number provides normal distribution. The mean of this histogram is located near 100, as we requested. In addition, it appears that almost all the values appear within 3 increments of 10 from the mean, suggesting that the random numbers were drawn from a distribution having a standard deviation of 10.

Histogram of x

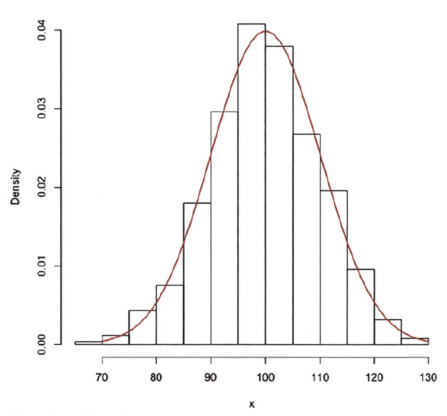

Figure 9.3.   Fitting the normal curve to the histogram.

9.5 Sampling Distribution of Means and Proportions

When a sample is drawn from a population, there are many different samples that could have been chosen. That means that the mean of the sample, *x*, will vary depending on which sample is picked. Thus *x* is a random variable, because the sample mean varies from sample to sample. Every sample has a mean and variance. Since x depends on the sample picked, theoretically all the possible sample means could be found, and then the true mean and variance of the sample means could be calculated.

The concept of proportion is the same as the concept of relative frequency, as discussed in chapter 8, and the concept of probability of success in a binomial experiment. The relative frequency of a category or class gives the proportion of the sample or population that belongs to that category or class. Similarly, the probability of success in a binomial experiment represents the proportion of the sample or population that possesses the given characteristics.

The population proportion, denoted by p, is obtained by taking the ratio of the number of elements in a population with a specific characteristic to the total number of elements in the population. The sample proportion denoted is p; hat p gives a similar ratio for a sample.

9.5.1 POPULATION AND SAMPLE PROPORTION FORMULAS

The population and sample proportions, denoted by p and p are calculated as:

$$P = \frac{X}{N} \text{ and } \hat{p} = \frac{x}{n}$$

Where
> N = total number of elements in the population
> n = total number of elements in the sample
> X = number of elements in the population that possess a specific characteristic
> x = number of elements in the sample that possess a specific characteristic

Example:
Suppose there are a total of 4,255 library members in the local library and 2,521 of them own homes. A sample of 200 library members is taken from this library, and 158 of them own homes. Find the proportion of library members who own homes in the population and in the sample.

Solution:
For the population of library members:

N = population size = 4255
X = membership in the population who own homes = 2521

The proportion of all library members in this local library who own homes is:

$$P = \frac{X}{N} = \frac{2521}{4255} = 0.59$$

Now, for a sample of 200 library members and 158 of them own homes:

n = sample size, 200
x = library members who own homes, 158

The sample proportion is:

$$\hat{p} = \frac{X}{n} = \frac{158}{200} = 0.79$$

As in the case of the mean, the difference between the sample proportion and the corresponding population proportion gives the sampling error, assuming that the sample is random and no non-sampling has been made:

Sampling Error = $p - p$

In this case,

$$p - p = 0.59 - 0.79 = -0.2$$

The sample error = −0.2

9.5.1 SAMPLING DISTRIBUTION OF P HAT p

Sampling distribution of the sample proportion, p, gives the various values that the researcher can assume and their probabilities.

Example:

The chief librarian at the local library in NYC asked her five employees to assess their knowledge in statistics. Table 9.5 gives the names of these five employees and their answers concerning their knowledge of statistics.

Table 9.5.

Name	Knows of Statistics
Ally	Yes
John	No
Susan	No
Margret	Yes
Jerry	Yes

If we define the population, p, as the proportion of employees who know statistics, then

$$P = \frac{3}{5} = 0.60$$

Now, suppose we draw all possible samples of the three employees and compute the proportion of employees, for each sample, who know statistics. The total number of samples of size three that can be drawn from the population of five employees is:

$$\text{Total number of samples} = {}_5C_3 = \frac{5!}{3!(5-3)!} = \frac{5*4*3*2*1}{3*2*1*2*1} = 10$$

Table 9.6 summarizes the proportion of employees who know statistics for each of those samples.

Table 9.6.

Sample	Proportion Who Know Statistics
Ally, John, Susan	1/3 = 0.33
Ally, John,	
Ally	
Ally	
Ally	
Ally	
John	
John	
Susan	

Table 9.5 will allow us to prepare the frequency distribution of p.

Table 9.7 captures the relative frequency of classes, which is obtained by dividing the frequencies of classes and the population size.

Table 9.7.

p̂	F	Relative Frequency
0.33	3	3/10 = 0.30
0.67	6	6/10 = 0.60
1	1	1/10 = 0.10
Σf = 10		Sum = 1.0

Mean and standard deviation of p. The mean of p, which is the same as the mean of the sampling distribution of p, is always equal to the population proportion, p, just as the mean of the sampling distribution of x is always equal the population mean, μ.

Mean of the sample proportion formula. The mean of the sample proportion p is denoted by μ and is equal to the population proportion, p.

As a result, $\mu p = P$

The standard deviation of p denoted by σp is given the following formula. This equation is true only when the sample is small compared to the population size.
    Standard deviation of the sample proportion is denoted by p and is referred to as σp and is given the formula

$$\sigma_{\hat{p}} = \sqrt{\frac{pq}{n}},$$

where p is the population proportion q = 1 − p, and n is the sample size. This formula is used only when $\frac{n}{N} \leq 0.05$, where N is the population size.

However, in cases where $\frac{n}{N}$ is greater than 0.05, then σp is calculated as follows:

$$\sigma_{\hat{p}} = \sqrt{\frac{pq}{n}} = \sqrt{\frac{N-n}{N-1}}$$

Shape of the sample distribution of p. The shape of the sampling distribution of p is often inferred from the central limit theorem. According to the central limit theorem for sample proportion, the sampling distribution of p is approximately normal for a sufficiently large sample size. In the case of proportion, the sample size is considered to be sufficiently large if np and nq are both greater than 5; that is, if:

np > 5 and nq > 5

Note, the sampling distribution of p will be approximately normal if np > 5 and nq > 5. This is the same condition that was required for the binomial probability.

Example:
According to a survey conducted by the Librarian Association during 2006, 56% of U.S. teens visit the library more than once a week. Assume that this result is true for the current population of U.S. teens. Let p be the proportion of U.S. teens in a random sample of 15,000 who visit the library. Find the mean and standard deviation of p and describe its sampling distribution.

Solution:
Let p be the population of all U.S. teens who visit their local library more than one time during the week.
Then,

P = 0.56
q = 0.44

The mean of the sampling distribution of p is:
μp = p = 0.56

The standard deviation of p is:

$$\mu_{\bar{p}} = \sqrt{\frac{pq}{n}} = \sqrt{\frac{(0.56)(0.44)}{1500}} = 0.0128$$

The values of np and nq are:

np= 1500(0.56) = 840
nq= 1500(0.44) = 660

Because np and nq are both greater than 5, we can apply the central limit theorem to make an inference about the shape of the sampling distribution of p. Therefore, the sampling distribution of p is approximately normal with a mean of 0.56 and a standard deviation of 0.0128, as illustrated in figure 9.8.

9.5.2 APPLICATION OF SAMPLING DISTRIBUTION OF P

So far in this chapter, we covered that when we conduct a study, we usually take only one sample and make all decisions or inferences on the basis of the results of that one sample. We use the concepts of mean, standard deviation, and shape of the sampling distribution of p to determine the probability that the value of p computed from one sample falls within a given interval. In this section, we will reintroduce the Z value in order to find more.

The Z value for the value of p:

$$Z = \frac{\hat{p} - p}{\sigma_p}$$

Example:
According to Conscious Consumer Report, 515 of the adults surveyed said that they are willing to pay more for electronic reading devices than buying print books (*USA Today*, June 12, 2012). Suppose this result is true for the current population of American adults. Let p be the proportion in a random sample of 1,050 adults who will hold the stated opinion. Find the probability that the value of p is between 0.53 and 0.55.

Solution:
$$n = 1050$$
$$p = 0.51$$
and q = 1 − p = 1 − 0.51 = 0.49 → q = 0.49,

where p is the population of all adults American who will hold the stated opinion.

The mean of the sample proportion p is:

$$\mu p = p = 0.51$$

The standard deviation of p is:

$$\sigma_{\hat{p}} = \sqrt{\frac{pq}{n}} = \sqrt{\frac{(0.51)(0.49)}{1050}} = 0.15437$$

The values of np and nq are:

$$np = 1050\ (0.51) = 535.5$$

and

nq = 1050 (0.49) = 514.5

Because np and nq are both greater than 5, we can infer from the central limit theorem that the sampling distribution of p is approximately normal. The probability that is between 0.53 and 0.55, given as the area under the normal curve for p between $p = 0.53$ and $p = 0.55$, is shown in figure 9.3.

The first step in finding the area under the normal curve between $p = 0.53$ and $p = 0.55$ is to convert these two values to their respective Z values. The Z values for p are computed using the following formula:

$$Z = \frac{\hat{p} - p}{\sigma_p}$$

The two values of p are converted to their respective Z values and then the area under the normal distribution between these two points is found using the normal distribution table.

For = 0.53, $Z = \frac{0.53 - 0.51}{0.01542} = 1.30$

For = 0.55, $Z = \frac{0.55 - 0.51}{0.01542} = 2.59$

Thus, the probability that p is between 0.53 and 0.55 is given by the area under the standard curve between $Z = 1.3$ and $Z = 2.59$. This area is shown in figure 9.4:

$$P(0.53 < .055) = P(1.30 < Z < 2.59) = P(Z < 2.59) - P(Z < 1.30) = 0.9952 - 0.9032 = 0.0920$$

Thus, the probability is 0.0920 that the proportion of U.S. adults in a random sample of 1050 who will be willing to pay for electronic books, rather than print, is between 0.53 and 0.55.

9.6 Summary

We started this chapter with a discussion of sample and population. We reviewed five different sampling methodologies: random, systematic, convenience, cluster, and stratified. We then moved to sampling distributions. We defined sampling distribution as a particular statistic that counts the frequency distribution of possible values of the statistic over all possible samples under the sampling design.

We looked at the general properties of the sampling distribution of x, where we reviewed five rules:

Rule # 1: $\mu x = \mu$

Rule # 2: $\sigma_{\bar{x}} = \dfrac{\sigma}{\sqrt{n}}$

Rule # 3: When the population distribution is normal, the sampling distribution of x is also normal for any sample size n.

Rule # 4: Also known as central limit theorem.

We examined how each rule plays an important part in the exploration of sampling distributions. We then looked at the p value and its application to sampling distributions.

9.7 Glossary

cluster sample—A sampling technique used when "natural" groupings are evident in a statistical population.

convenience sample—Sample that made up of people who are easy to reach.

P value—The probability of obtaining the observed sample results (or a more extreme result) when the null hypothesis is actually true.

random sample—Sampling technique where we select a group of subjects (a sample) for study from a larger group (a population). Each individual is chosen entirely by chance, and each member of the population has a known, but possibly non-equal, chance of being included in the sample.

sampling distribution—The probability distribution, under repeated sampling of the population, of a given statistic (a numerical quantity calculated from the data values in a sample).

sampling error—The error caused by observing a sample instead of the whole population.

stratified sample—Obtained by taking samples from each stratum or subgroup of a population.

systematic sample—An equal-probability method for each person out of the population.

9.8 Reference

Savolainen, R. 2010. "Dietary Blogs as Sites of Informational and Emotional Support." *Information Research* 15 (4). Retrieved from htttp://www.informationr.net/ir/15-4/ paper438.html.

## CHAPTER 10

Confidence Interval Estimation

10.1   Introduction
10.2   Confidence Intervals
10.3   General Estimation Framework
10.4   Interpreting Confidence Intervals
10.5   Standard Error of the Mean
10.6   Estimating a Population Proportion
10.7   Computing a Confidence Interval for the Population Proportion
10.8   Confidence Intervals When σ (Population Standard Deviation) Is Unknown
10.9   Estimating the Population Mean with σ Unknown
10.10   Determining Sample Size
10.11   Strategies for Determining Sample Size
10.12   Working in R
10.13   Summary
10.14   Glossary
10.15   References

10.1 Introduction

The aim of taking a sample is to obtain an accurate reading of the population. However, the sample will never be as accurate as the measure of the entire population. This is an important aspect of *randomization* control. In this chapter, we will explore the calculation behind the sample. This type of statistics is called *inference*. Statistical inference makes use of information from a sample to draw conclusions (inferences) about the population from which the sample was taken.

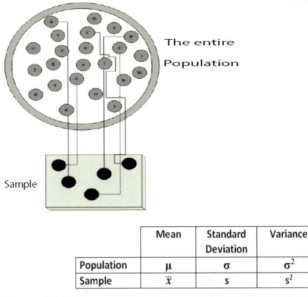

	Mean	Standard Deviation	Variance
Population	μ	σ	σ^2
Sample	$\bar{x}$	s	s^2

Figure 10.1. Populations may contain any number of samples which approximate, but may vary somewhat from, the values of the entire population.

The calculation of the entire population and sample is divided into two different types of processing: parameter and statistic.

Parameter: A number that describes the population. It is fixed, but we rarely know it. Examples include the true proportion of all American adults who visit the library to browse for a new book or the true mean of all residents of New York City who have a library card.

Statistic: A number that describes the sample. This value is known since it is produced by our sample data, but can vary from sample to sample (e.g., if we calculated the mean heights of a random sample of 1,000 library members of the New York City Public Library). Calculating this mean would most likely vary from the mean calculated from another random sample of 1,000 residents of New York City.

Example:
A survey is carried out at a university to estimate the proportion of undergraduate students who drive to campus to attend classes. One thousand students are randomly selected and asked whether they drive to campus to attend classes. The population is all of the undergraduates at that university campus. The

sample is the group of 1,000 undergraduate students surveyed. The parameter is the true proportion of all undergraduate students at that university campus who drive to campus to attend classes. The statistic is the proportion of the 1,000 sampled undergraduates who drive to campus to attend classes.

10.2 Confidence Intervals

Confidence intervals provide a range of values that is likely to contain the population parameter of interest. It gives an estimated range of values that is likely to include an unknown population parameter, the estimated range being calculated from a given set of sample data. We base the calculations of the confidence intervals on two parameters:

- A point estimate is a single number.
- A confidence interval provides additional information about the variability of the estimate.

Figure 10.2. Illustration of the point estimate's relationship to the confidence interval.

How much uncertainty is associated with a point estimate of a population parameter versus a confidence interval?

Example:
Suppose we want to know what percentage of the public library members in Tampa, Florida, browsed the latest novel from J. K. Rowling, the author of the Harry Potter series? To estimate this, we take a random sample of 100 library members and find out what percentage of those 100 members read J. K. Rowling's last novel. Then, we say that the sample percentage should come close to the actual percentage of *all* Tampa public library members who read J. K. Rowling.

In this example:

Population of Interest: All public members of the public library in Tampa
Sample Size: $n = 100$

Statistic from the sample: The percentage of library members sampled who read
J. K. Rowling's latest novel
Parameter in the Population: The percentage of all Tampa library members who
read J. K. Rowling's latest novel

How do we actually estimate the parameter, though?

10.3 General Estimation Framework

Suppose we want to estimate a parameter (e.g., population proportion, population average, etc.). The first thing to notice is that it would be impossible to exactly pinpoint the value with 100% accuracy *without sampling every single member* of the population, since there would always be some uncertainty. As a result, the best we can do is to make a guess at the true value, and then include a margin of error based on a certain level of confidence we have in our results. The estimate and the margin of error form something called a confidence interval. A confidence interval is made of two different parts:

1. The *point estimate* is the sample statistic (this is our best guess at the true parameter value given our sample).
2. The *margin of error* is added and subtracted from the point estimate to make the interval.

It can also be subdivided into two parts:

a. A critical value from a distribution (more to come on this later)
b. The standard error of the point estimate (more to come on this as well)

The confidence interval (CI) has this form:

CI = (Point Estimate) ± (Margin of Error)
= (Point Estimate) ± (Critical Value)*(Standard Error)

Of course there is no guarantee that the true population parameter will be in this interval, so we have to make some sort of statement about the chances that this will be true.

The *confidence level* is the probability that the interval actually covers the true population parameter. Often, the confidence level is denoted $(1 - \alpha)$, where α is the chance that it does *not* cover the true parameter. For example, if $\alpha = 0.05$, then the confidence level is 0.95, or 95%. Thus we would say that we are 95% confident that the interval covers the parameter.

An example of a 95% confidence interval is shown below:

$72.85 < \mu < 107.15$

There is good reason to believe that the population's mean lies between these two, 72.85 and 107.15, since 95% of the time confidence intervals contain the true mean. If repeated samples were taken and the 95% confidence interval was computed for each sample, 95% of the intervals would contain the population mean. Naturally, 5% of the intervals would not contain the population mean.

10.4 Interpreting Confidence Intervals

Let's consider the example from earlier, where we want to estimate the percentage of library members who read the latest novel from J. K. Rowling. Suppose that of our sample of size 100, 15 members already purchased the new book by J. K. Rowling. This gives a point estimate of 15%, or 0.15 for the population parameter.

Suppose also that we calculated a critical value of 1.645 and a standard error of 0.0357, with a confidence level of 95%. In this case, the confidence interval will be:

$$CI = (Point\ Estimate) \pm (Margin\ of\ Error)$$
$$= (Point\ Estimate) \pm (Critical\ Value)*(Standard\ Error)$$
$$= 0.15 \pm 1.645*0.0357$$
$$= 0.15 \pm 0.0587$$

This gives the interval (0.0913, 0.2087). To interpret this interval, any of the following statements are equivalent:

1. We are 95% confident that the true percentage of all public library members who own the latest book by J. K. Rowling is between 9.13% and 20.87%.
2. If we repeatedly took different samples consisting of 100 members and computed a CI for each of those samples, 95% of the computed intervals would cover the true percentage of all public library members who own the book.
3. There is a 95% chance that the interval (0.0913, 0.2087) covers the true percentage of all public library members who own J. K. Rowling's new novel.

A General Note: Depending on the parameter you want to estimate, formulas for the point estimate, critical value, and standard error will change. However, the format of a confidence interval is always the same.

10.5 Standard Error of the Mean

The standard deviation of a sampling distribution is called the standard error of the mean (basically they are measures of sampling variability or estimates of dispersion or spread). A standard error generally has a *level of confidence* associated with it. You use the standard error of the mean to determine how close to the true population mean you can expect your sample mean to be and how much confidence you can place in that expectation. To reduce the amount of sampling variability, you can make your sample larger and more homogeneous.

Example:

Two hundred randomly selected Tampa public library members were asked how much money they spent on new technology that related to their reading purchases over the past month. The sample mean for the 200 library members was $42.35.

a. Did the selected library members spend an average of $42.35 on technology purchases last month?
b. What can be inferred from the result that the sample mean is $42.35?
c. How could you be more confident in the sample mean?

Solution:

a. Answer: No. The 200 library members selected may just happen to be bigger spenders than those who were not chosen. In fact, the average for all the library members (the population mean) could be very different from the sample mean of $42.35. One can never know with absolute certainty even approximately what the population mean is. For instance, what if one library member not polled happened to spend $1,000 on new technology purchases last week? The effect of including that library member might be to raise the mean figure to over $1,000.
b. The information can be used to suggest the probability of library member spending trends, but not with absolute certainty (unless the sample includes the entire population).
c. By increasing the sample size, we can be *more* confident that the population mean lies *fairly close* to the sample mean we obtained. This idea of *confidence*, as opposed to *certainty*, is what is important to statisticians.

Next, we examine the result when the standard deviation of the population is unknown.

10.6 Estimating a Population Proportion

To estimate a population proportion, we will be using normal approximation. There are three conditions that must be satisfied for us to estimate the population proportion:

1. The sample must be a simple random sample.
2. The binomial conditions are satisfied:

   a. Fixed number of trials (this is the sample size n)
   b. Independent trials (this follows from the simple random sample requirement)
   c. There are two types of outcomes—success and failure
   d. The probability of success/failure is the same in each trial (this should be true if the population is large)

3. There are at least five successes and five failures.

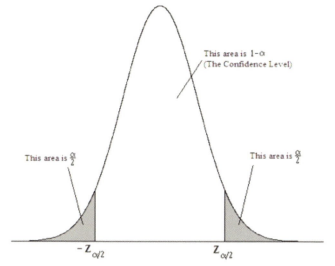

Figure 10.3. An Illustration of a Confidence Level.

Some Notation:

p = the population proportion (unknown quantity that we want to estimate)

$\hat{p} = \dfrac{x}{n}$ the sample proportion of x successes in a sample of size n

$\hat{q} = 1 - \hat{p}$ the sample proportion of failures in a sample of size n

$Z_{\alpha/2}$ = the Z score with an area *above* $\alpha/2$ (see figure 10.3 above)

Common Values of $Z_{\alpha/2}$:

Confidence Level	α	$Z_{\alpha/2}$
90%	0.1	1.645
95%	0.05	1.96
99%	0.01	2.575

10.7 Computing a Confidence Interval for the Population Proportion

For a sample size of n, confidence level $1 - \alpha$, and sample proportion $\hat{p}$, the parts of the confidence interval are:

Point Estimate: $\hat{p}$

Critical Value: $Z_{\alpha/2}$

Standard Error: $\sqrt{\dfrac{\hat{p}\hat{q}}{n}}$

So the confidence interval is:

CI = (Point Estimate) ± (Margin of Error)
= (Point Estimate) ± (Critical Value) × (Standard Error)

$$= \hat{p} \pm Z_{\alpha/2}\sqrt{\dfrac{\hat{p}\hat{q}}{n}}$$

Example:

Librarians at the University of Texas, Austin, are interested in estimating the percentage of defective manuscripts found in different locations. To do this, they take a simple random sample of 100 books and manuscripts and find that 8 of them are defective. Find a 95% confidence interval for the percentage of defective books and manuscripts found by librarians at University of Texas, Austin, and interpret it.

Solution:

First, we note a few things:

- The three conditions above are met.
- The sample proportion is $\hat{p} = \dfrac{X}{n} = Z_{0.05/2} = 0.08.$

- The confidence level is 95% = 0.95 = 1 − α, so α = 0.05.
- The critical value is $Z_{\alpha/2} = Z_{0.05/2} = Z_{0.0025} = 1.96$.
- The standard error is $\sqrt{\dfrac{\hat{p}\hat{q}}{n}} = \sqrt{\dfrac{(0.08)(0.92)}{100}} = \sqrt{\dfrac{0.0736}{100}} = 0.0271$.

Therefore, the confidence interval is:

$$\hat{p} \pm Z_{\alpha/2}\sqrt{\frac{\hat{p}\hat{q}}{n}} \;\rightarrow\; 0.08 \pm (1.96)(0.0271) \;\rightarrow\; 0.08 \pm 0.0532 \;\rightarrow\; (0.0268, 0.1332)$$

Therefore, we can say that we are 95% confident that the percentage of defective manuscripts in this facility is between 2.68% and 13.32%.

10.8 Confidence Intervals when σ (Population Standard Deviation) Is Unknown

Estimating a Population Mean—σ Unknown. In the previous section, we estimated the population mean by using the fact that $\bar{X}$ was normally distributed with a mean of $\mu_{\bar{X}} = \mu$ and a standard deviation of $\sigma_{\bar{X}} = \dfrac{\sigma}{\sqrt{n}}$.

For this reason, Z had a standard normal distribution, where:

$$Z = \frac{\bar{x} - \mu_{\bar{x}}}{\sigma_x} = \frac{\bar{x} - \mu}{\frac{\sigma}{\sqrt{n}}}.$$

Now, however, we no longer know σ.

How do we address it? Many statistical textbooks recommend instead estimating σ with the sample standard deviation s. The question, however, is if T has a standard normal distribution, where:

$$T = \frac{\bar{X} - \mu}{s/\sqrt{n}}$$

The distribution of T is called the Student-t distribution, or just the t distribution.

Unfortunately, T does *not* have a standard normal distribution because we have to account for the fact that s will not be exactly equal to the true population standard deviation σ. However, through statistical theory it turns out that the distribution of T can be specified.

Recall: The reason we divided by $n - 1$ instead of n in the sample standard deviation formula $s = \sqrt{\dfrac{1}{n-1}\sum_{i=1}^{n}(x_i - \bar{x})^2}$ was because of something called *degrees of freedom.* In this case, there were only $n - 1$ degrees of freedom because we already knew the sample mean $\bar{x}$.

It turns out that the t distribution changes shape depending on the degrees of freedom of s. For this reason, in finding critical values, you have to know the degrees of freedom, which are always $n - 1$.

A note about the t distribution. The t distribution is also symmetric, like the standard normal distribution, and has a similar shape. However, it is a bit narrower and tapers off less quickly to the right and left (see figure 10.4).

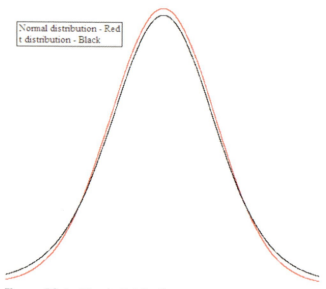

Normal distribution - Red
t distribution - Black

Figure 10.4. The t distribution compared to the standard distribution.

In computing the confidence interval, we will need to use the value $t_{\alpha/2}$. This is exactly like the value $Z_{\alpha/2}$ from before, except for the t distribution (see figure 10.5).

To find the value of $t_{\alpha/2}$, we use table A-3 (in appendix A). Choose the row with "Degrees of Freedom" = $n - 1$ and the column with "Area in One Tail" = $\alpha/2$ (or equivalently, "Area in Two Tails" = α). The critical value is listed at the intersection of that row and column.

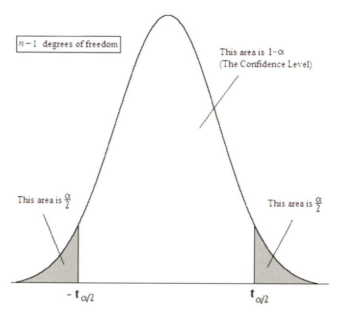

Figure 10.5. Confidence level and t distribution.

(*Note*: If the degrees of freedom do not appear in the first column, just choose the closest value in the table.)

10.9 Estimating the Population Mean with σ Unknown

To estimate a population mean in this new situation, two conditions must be met:

1. The sample is a simple random sample.
2. Either the population is normally distributed or $n > 30$ (so we can use the central limit theorem).

As before, the best point estimate of the population mean is the sample mean, $\bar{x}$.

We will start with the t distribution with $n - 1$ degrees of freedom.

Computing a Confidence Interval for the Population Mean (σ Known). For a sample size of n, confidence level $1 - \alpha$, and sample mean $\bar{x}$, the parts of the confidence interval are:

Point estimate: $\bar{x}$

Critical value: $t_{\alpha/2}$ (with $n - 1$ degrees of freedom)

Standard error: $\dfrac{s}{\sqrt{n}}$

So the confidence interval is:

$$CI = \text{(Point Estimate)} \pm \text{(Margin of Error)}$$
$$= \text{(Point Estimate)} \pm \text{(Critical Value)} - \text{(Standard Error)}$$
$$= \bar{x} \pm t_{\alpha/2} \dfrac{s}{\sqrt{n}}$$

Example:

A librarian in Tampa, Florida, conducted a survey to find out the average number of hours a library member spends in the library each week. She took a simple random sample of 91 members who often visited the library and computed a sample mean of 5.4 hours per week with a standard deviation of 1.2 hours. Find a 95% confidence interval for the population mean.

Solution:

First, we note a few things:

- The two conditions above are met ($n > 30$).
- The point estimate is $\bar{x} = 5.4$.
- The confidence level is 95% = 0.95 = $1 - \alpha$, so $\alpha = 0.05$.
- The degrees of freedom are $n - 1 = 90$.
- The critical value is $t_{\alpha/2} = t_{0.05/2} = 1.987$ (area in one tail is 0.025, or area in two tails is 0.05).
- The standard error is $\dfrac{s}{\sqrt{n}} = \dfrac{1.2}{\sqrt{91}} = 0.126$.

Therefore, the confidence interval is:

$$\bar{x} \pm t_{\alpha/2} \dfrac{s}{\sqrt{n}} \;\blacktriangleright\; 5.4 \pm (1.987)(0.126) \;\blacktriangleright\; 5.4 \pm 0.250 \;\blacktriangleright\; (5.15, 5.65)$$

So with 95% confidence, we claim that the average hours per week a library user spends in the library each week, as studied by the librarian, is between 5.15 and 5.65 hours.

10.10 Determining Sample Size

In each example concerning confidence interval estimation, the sample size was selected without regard to the width of the resulting confidence interval. In the business world, the calculation of the sample size can become a very complicated procedure, subject to the constraints of budget, time, and ease of selection. But perhaps the most frequently asked question concerning sampling is, "What size sample do I need?" The answer to this question is influenced by a number of factors, including the purpose of the study, population size, the risk of selecting a bad sample, and the allowable sampling error.

Sample size criteria. In addition to the purpose of the study and population size, three criteria usually need to be specified to determine the appropriate sample size:

* The level of precision,
* The level of confidence or risk,
* And the degree of variability in the attributes being measured (Miaoulis and Michener, 1976).

We will also discuss the strategies for determining sample size and look at R to apply these characteristics.

1. The Level of Precision
    The *level of precision*, sometimes called *sampling error*, is the range in which the true value of the population is estimated to fall. This range is often expressed in percentage points (e.g., ±5 percent) in the same way that results for political campaign polls are reported by the media. Thus, if a researcher finds that 60% of farmers in the sample have adopted a recommended practice with a precision rate of ±5%, then he or she can conclude that between 55% and 65% of farmers in the population have adopted the practice.
2. The Confidence Level
    The confidence or risk level is based on ideas encompassed under the *central limit theorem*. The key idea encompassed in the central limit theorem is that when a population is repeatedly sampled, the average value of the attribute obtained by those samples is equal to the true population value. Furthermore, the values obtained by these samples are distributed normally about the true value, with some samples having a higher value and some obtaining a lower score than the true population value. In a normal distribution,

approximately 95% of the sample values are within two standard deviations of the true population value (e.g., mean). In other words, this means that if a 95% confidence level is selected, 95 out of 100 samples will have the true population value within the range of precision specified earlier (figure 10.6). There is always a chance that the sample you obtain does not represent the true population value. Such samples with extreme values are represented by the shaded areas in figure 10.6. This risk is reduced for 99% confidence levels and increased for 90% (or lower) confidence levels.

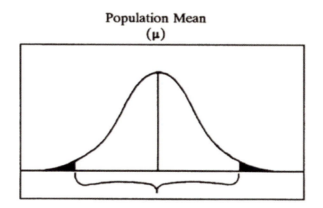

Population Mean
(μ)

95% of sample means
within two standardized deviations

Figure 10.6. Distributions of means for repeated samples.

3. Degree of Variability

The third criterion, the *degree of variability* in the attributes being measured, refers to the distribution of attributes in the population. The more heterogeneous a population, the larger the sample size required to obtain a given level of precision. The less variable (more homogeneous) a population, the smaller the sample size required.

10.11 Strategies for Determining Sample Size

There are several approaches to determining the sample size. These include using a census for small populations, imitating a sample size of similar studies, using published tables, and applying formulas to calculate a sample size.

Determining sample size under margin of error. Clearly, the size of the sample has an impact on the confidence interval, since it affects the margin of error and the point estimate. The question is what sample size should be chosen at the start of the study to give a confidence interval. Often, what statisticians do is decide they want a small margin of error, then find a sample size that gives them that margin of error.

Example:

In the example above, for $\hat{p} = 0.08$ and $\alpha = 0.05$ (i.e., confidence level of 95%), find the sample size n required for the margin of error to be less than 0.02.

Solution:

We want the margin of error to be 0.02.

Also, we know the margin of error is $Z_{\alpha/2}\sqrt{\dfrac{\hat{p}\hat{q}}{n}}$, because this is the amount added and subtracted to the point estimate.

Therefore, figuring out n is as easy as solving the equation $Z_{\alpha/2}\sqrt{\dfrac{\hat{p}\hat{q}}{n}} = 0.02$ for n!

$$Z_{\alpha/2}\sqrt{\frac{\hat{p}\hat{q}}{n}} = 0.02 \Rightarrow 1.96 \cdot \sqrt{\frac{(0.08)(0.92)}{n}} = 0.02 \Rightarrow \sqrt{\frac{0.0736}{n}} = 0.0102 \Rightarrow \frac{0.0736}{n} = 0.00010404 \Rightarrow n = 707.42$$

Thus, we would need a sample size of *at least 708* to get a margin of error that small.

Finding a general formula for sample size. In the general case, we can solve for n as follows (here, E is the desired size of the margin of error):

$$Z_{\alpha/2}\sqrt{\frac{\hat{p}\hat{q}}{n}} = E \Rightarrow \sqrt{\frac{\hat{p}\hat{q}}{n}} = \frac{E}{Z_{\alpha/2}} \Rightarrow \frac{\hat{p}\hat{q}}{n} = \frac{E^2}{Z_{\alpha/2}^2} \Rightarrow \frac{1}{n} = \frac{E^2}{\hat{p}\hat{q}Z_{\alpha/2}^2} \Rightarrow \boxed{n = \hat{p}\hat{q}\frac{Z_{\alpha/2}^2}{E^2}}$$

If the value of $\hat{p}$ is known, the formula is as stated above.

If the value of $\hat{p}$ is *unknown*, then use $\hat{p} = 0.50$.

Effects of sample size and confidence level on confidence intervals. Notice that in all three estimates we discussed (proportion and mean with σ known and unknown), two things were always true:

1. In the margin of error, n appears in the denominator.
2. The larger α gets, the smaller the critical value gets.

This means that if n is increased, the margin of error will get smaller. Also, if the confidence level $1 - \alpha$ is decreased (i.e., α is increased), the margin of error will get smaller. A smaller margin of error means a tighter confidence interval, which means we are saying the range of values for the true population proportion/

mean is much smaller. In general, it is a good thing to have a smaller confidence interval, as long as your degree of confidence is high.

This introduces the idea of a trade-off in the size of a confidence interval:

- For a fixed sample size n, to reduce the size of a confidence interval, we must reduce the confidence level.
- For a fixed confidence level, to reduce the size of a confidence interval, we must increase the sample size.

Thus, to get better confidence intervals, you must either *reduce your level of confidence* or *gather more data*.

How to find the confidence interval for the difference between means or how to choose between Z and t. There are key steps you will need to follow:

a. Identify a sample statistic. Use the difference between sample means to estimate the difference between population means.
b. Select a confidence level. The confidence level describes the uncertainty of a sampling method. Often, researchers choose 90%, 95%, or 99% confidence levels, but any percentage can be used.
c. Find the margin of error. When the sample size is large, you can use a t score or a Z score for the critical value. Since it does not require computing degrees of freedom, the Z score is a little easier. When the sample sizes are small (less than 40), use a t score for the critical value. If you use a t score, you will need to compute degree of freedom (DF). Here's how:

The following formula is appropriate whenever a t score is used to analyze the difference between means. $DF = (s_1^2/n_1 + s_2^2/n_2)^2 / \{ [(s_1^2 / n_1)^2 / (n_1 - 1)] + [(s_2^2 / n_2)^2 / (n_2 - 1)] \}$

If you are working with a pooled standard deviation (see above),

$$DF = n_1 + n_2 - 2.$$

Table 10.2 summarizes the difference between when you use Z and t.

Table 10.2.

If σ is known, and:	If σ is unknown, and:	If:
The population is normally distributed and/or $n \geq 30$	The population is normally distributed and/or $n \geq 30$	The population is *not* normally distributed *and* $n < 30$
Then use Z	Then use t	You have to use other methods

10.12 Working in R

The R code for building confidence intervals for a population:

The mean with σ known using summary statistics: `qnorm`
The mean with σ unknown using summary statistics: `qt`
The mean with σ unknown using raw data: `t.test`
The proportion using summary statistics: `qnorm`

Example:
    Suppose we've collected a random sample of 10 recently graduated students and asked them what their annual salary is. Imagine that these are the data we see:

```
>x <- c(44617, 7066, 17594, 2726, 1178, 18898, 5033, 37151, 4514, 4000
```

Goal: Estimate the mean salary of all recently graduated students. Find a 90% and a 95% confidence interval for the mean.

Setting I: Assume that incomes are normally distributed with unknown mean and SD = $15,000.

a. $(1 - \alpha)100\%$ CI is

```
Xbar +- z(alpha/2) * sigma/sqrt(n)
```
We know $n = 10$, and are given $\sigma = 15000$.
a) 90% CI.

This means $\alpha = .10$
We can get $z(\alpha/2) = z(0.05)$ from R: `> qnorm(.95)`
`[1] 1.644854`
`> qnorm(.05) [1] -1.644854`
And the sample average is just:

```
> mean(x) [1] 14277.7
```

So our margin of error is:

```
> me <- 1.644*(15000/sqrt(10)) > me
[1] 7798.177
```

The lower and upper bounds are:

```
> mean(x) - me [1] 6479.523 > mean(x) + me [1] 22075.88
```

So our 90% CI is ($6479, $22076).

b. For a 95% CI, $\alpha = .05$.

All of the steps are the same, except we replace z(.05) with z(.025):

```
> me <- qnorm(.975)*(15000/sqrt(10))
> me
[1] 9296.925 > mean(x) - me [1] 4980.775 > mean(x) + me
[1] 23574.63
```

The new interval, (9296, 23574) is wider, but we are more confident that it contains the true mean.

Setting II: Same problem, only now we do not know the value for the SD. Therefore, we must estimate it from the data:

```
> sd(x)
[1] 15345.95
```

Now a $(1 - \alpha)100\%$ CI looks like

Xbar +- t(α/2, df) * s/sqrt(n)

We just calculated s = 15345 and *n* = 10 still. Xbar is still 14277.

1. 90% CI, $\alpha = .10$.

All we need is the t-value:

Because the degrees of freedom are $n - 1 = 10 - 1 = 9$:

```
> qt(.95,9)
[1] 1.833113
> me <- qt(.95,9)*sd(x)/sqrt(10)
> me
[1] 8895.76
> mean(x) - me
[1] 5381.94
> mean(x) + me
[1] 23173.46
```

So the 90% CI is: (8896,23173).
Note that this is wider than the last 90% CI.

2. 95% CI, $\alpha = .05$.

```
> me <- qt(.975,9)*sd(x)/sqrt(10) > me
[1] 10977.83
> mean(x) - me
[1] 3299.868 > mean(x) + me [1] 25255.53
(3300,25255)
```

A *bootstrap interval* might be helpful. Here are the steps involved:

1. From our sample of size 10, draw a new sample, with replacement, of size 10.
2. Calculate the sample average, called the *bootstrap estimate*.
3. Store it.
4. Repeat steps 1–3 many times (we'll do 1,000).
5. For a 90% CI, we will use the 5% sample quantile as the lower bound, and the 95% sample quantile as the upper bound. (Because $\alpha = 10\%$, so $\alpha/2 = 5\%$. So chop off that top and bottom 5% of the observations.)

Here's the R code:

```
> bstrap <- c()
> for (i in 1:1000){
+ # First take the sample
+ bsample <- sample(x,10,replace=T)
+ #now calculate the bootstrap estimate + bestimate <-
mean(bsample)
+ bstrap <- c(bstrap,bestimate)}
> #lower bound
> quantile(bstrap,.05)
5% 7413.795
> #upper bound
> quantile(bstrap,.95)
95% 21906.49
```

We use the same output to get the 95% confidence interval:

```
> #lower bound for 95% CI is the 2.5th quantile: >
quantile(bstrap,.025)
2.5% 6357.615
```

```
> quantile(bstrap,.975)
97.5% 23736.75
```

So the 90% CI is (7414,21906) and the 95% is (6358,23737).

Note: this method of using the sample quantiles to find the bootstrap confidence interval is called the *percentile method*. There are other methods that might be more suitable for some situations.

This code could be made much more streamlined:

```
> bstrap <- c()
> for (i in 1:1000){
+ bstrap
<- c(bstrap, mean(sample(x,10,replace=T)))}
```

and then you find the quantiles as before.

You can also write a function that takes a dataset (x), number of bootstrap samples (B) as input:

```
bsci <- function(x,B){
bstrap <- c()
for (i in 1:B){
bstrap <- c(bstrap,mean(sample(x,length(x),replac
e=T)))}}
```

Now to find, say, a 95% CI we need only do:

```
> output <- bsci(x,1000)
> quantile(output,.025)
2.5% 6486.743
> quantile(output,.975) 97.5%
23768.4
```

10.13 Summary

This chapter introduced the subject of confidence interval estimation. We began by stating that *statistical inference* is the process of using a sample to draw conclusions about the characteristics of a population. The purpose of taking a random sample from the population and computing a statistic, such as the mean from the data, is to approximate the mean of the entire population. However, in this process the need to estimate the underlying population value is always an issue. A *confidence interval* addresses this issue because it provides a range of values that is likely to contain the population parameter of interest. We discussed the term confidence intervals and its proportions from one to two populations. We also illustrated the use of confidence intervals to find the population parameter (the population mean, the proportions in the population with a certain characteristics, and so on). We also discussed the confidence interval when the population standard deviation was unknown and known. We looked at the formulas for determining the sample size.

10.14 Glossary

central limit theorem—When a population is repeatedly sampled, the average value of the attribute obtained by those samples is equal to the true population value.

confidence interval—A range of values that is likely to contain the population parameter of interest.

confidence level—The probability that the interval actually covers the true population parameter.

critical value—A value that determines the boundary between those samples resulting in a test statistic that leads to rejecting the null hypothesis and those that lead to a decision not to reject the null hypothesis.

degree of variability—The distribution of attributes in the population.

level of precision—Also called the sampling error; the range in which the true value of the population is estimated to fall.

margin of error—The value added and subtracted from the point estimate to make the interval.

parameter—A number that describes the population.

percentile method—Method of using the sample quantiles to find the bootstrap confidence interval.

point estimate—The sample statistic (this is our best guess at the true parameter value given our sample).

randomization—Selecting a random sample of a population.

standard error—In a sampling distribution, the standard deviation is called the standard error of the mean.

statistic—A number that describes a sample.

statistical inference—A process that makes use of information from a sample to draw conclusions (inferences) about the population from which the sample was taken.

Student-t distribution—Also known as t distribution, the continuous probability family occurring when estimating the mean of a normally distributed population, when the sample size is small and population standard deviation is unknown.

10.15 Reference

Miaoulis, George, and R. D. Michener. 1976. *An Introduction to Sampling.* Dubuque, Iowa: Kendall/Hunt Publishing Company.

CHAPTER 11

Fundamentals of Hypothesis Testing

11.1   Introduction to Hypotheis Testing
11.2   The Objectives of Testing Hypothesis
11.3   The Methodology behind Hypothesis Testing
11.4   Test Statistic
11.5   Level of Significance α
    11.5.1   Type I Error
    11.5.2   Type II Error
11.6   Tails of a Tests
    11.6.1   Two-Tailed Hypothesis
    11.6.2   One-Tailed Hypothesis
11.7   The P-Value
11.8   T Distribution
11.9   When α Is Known and Unknown
11.10   Summary
11.11   Glossary
11.12   References

I have not been able to discover the case of these properties of gravity from phenomena, and I frame no hypothes [hypothese non fingo].

—Newton (1729/1960, p. 547)

11.1 Introduction to Hypothesis Testing

Hypothesis testing refers to the process of choosing between two hypotheses statements about a probability distribution based on observed data from the distribution. It is a core topic in statistics, and indeed is a fundamental part of the language of statistics. The hypotheses statements are derived from the existing body of theory that is tested using the methods of the particular science, according to Lehmann et al. (2005). Hypothesis testing often entails step-by-step methodology that allows you to make inferences about a population parameter by analyzing differences between the results observed (the sample statistic) and the results that can be expected if some underlying hypothesis is actually true. In this chapter, we will examine the methodology behind hypothesis testing, the critical value of test statistics, and the risk in decision making using hypothesis testing methodology.

11.2 The Objectives of Hypothesis Testing

As we discussed in chapters 9 and 10, estimation is based on the value of a population parameter. In comparison, the purpose of hypothesis testing is to determine whether there is enough statistical evidence in favor of a certain belief, or hypothesis, about a parameter. It aims to provide us with a mechanism for making quantitative decisions about a process or processes. The intent of hypothesis testing is to determine whether there is enough evidence to "reject" a conjecture or hypothesis about the process. Hypothesis testing consists of two statements: the null and alternative hypotheses. Under these two statements, we make a claim about a population characteristic, determine how much evidence is needed to reject this claim, obtain data, and make a conclusion about the claim.

11.3 The Methodology behind Hypothesis Testing

The term *hypothesis* derives from the ancient Greek *hypotitenai*, which means "to purpose," according to Cavalier-Smith (2002). Ever since then, the term hypothesis became an essential part of scientific discovery, such as Newton's report on his attempt to establish his hypothesis. The methodology behind hypothesis testing consists of five steps, where each step is essential to finalize the findings:

1. State the null hypothesis.
2. Select the distribution to use.
3. Determine the rejection and non-rejection regions.
4. Calculate the value of the test statistic.
5. Make a decision.

Step 1 State the null hypothesis.

In step 1 you set up two statements to determine the validity of a statistical claim: a null hypothesis and an alternative hypothesis. The null hypothesis is a statement to capture what you aim to examine. It is a statement containing a *null*, or zero, difference. It is the null hypothesis that undergoes the testing procedure, whether it is the original claim or not. The notation for the null hypothesis H_0:

- Represents the status quo or what is assumed to be true.
- Always contains the equal sign.

Examples:

- In a jury trial, the person is assumed innocent.
- The average starting salary of a librarian at a state university in Georgia was $53,000 last year (m = $53,000).

The alternative statement must be true if the null hypothesis is false. An alternative hypothesis H_1:

- Is the opposite of the null and is what you wish to support.
- Never contains the equal sign.

Examples:

- In a jury trial, the person is guilty.
- The average starting salary of a librarian at a state university in Georgia was not $53,000 last year (m ≠ $53,000).

We will set up our hypothesis testing around the population we want to measure.

Example:

Our first step to establish a working hypothesis about the population parameter is to establish our hypothesis statement about our population, for example, popularity among Facebook library users in Tampa, Florida. Our null hypothesis is denoted by the symbol H_0. The value specified in the null hypothesis often holds a historical value, a claim, or a production specification. In our case, according to a recent Pew Research Center study (2013), Facebook followers are between the ages of 18 and 29. We want to examine if promoting the library services among Facebook users will bring back library users between the ages of 18 and 29 (in this case $\mu = 23.5$). Any hypothesis that differs from the null hypothesis in this case will be called an *alternative hypothesis*. In this example, we assume that the distribution is normally distributed, and as result, we can claim that 23.5 is the average age among Facebook users for our own testing.

Result:

H_0 = 23.5 – the null hypothesis
H_1 ≠ 23.5 – the alternative hypothesis

When testing a hypothesis, we often refer to test statistic and level of significance. We begin with test statists.

Step 2 Select the distribution to use.
The logic of hypothesis testing is rooted in an understanding of the sampling distribution around the mean. The characteristics of the mean regarding the population allow us to examine the hypothesis in the following manner.

a. The sample mean is an unbiased estimator of the population mean. On average, a randomly selected sample will have a mean equal to the mean of the population. In hypothesis testing, we use the mean indictor to calculate if our null hypothesis is true or false.
b. The sampling distributions of the sample and the population in this chapter count for normal distribution. Assuming that the distribution is normally distributed, we can therefore state an alternative hypothesis to locate the probability of obtaining a sample mean with less than a 5% chance of being selected if the value in the null hypothesis is true. We will discuss this in more detail in two-tailed selection (section 11.6.1).

To locate the probability of obtaining a sample mean in a sampling distribution we must know: (1) the population mean and (2) the standard error. Each value is entered in the test statistic formula computed in step 3. Table 11.1 summarizes the notation used for the mean, variance, and standard deviation for a sample, population, and sampling distributions.

Table 11.1.

Characteristics	Population	Sample	Sample Distribution
Mean	μ	$\bar{x}$	$\mu x = \mu$
Variance	σ^2	s^2	$\sigma^2 n = \sigma^2 / n$
Standard deviation	σ	S	$\sigma n = \sigma / \sqrt{n}$

Step 3 Determine the rejection and non-rejection regions.
The signifiance level is discussed below.

Step 4 Calculate the value of the test statistic.
The test statistic is discussed below.

11.4 Test Statistic

We use a *test statistic* to determine the likelihood of rejecting or accepting the null hypothesis. Specifically, a test statistic tells us how far, or how many standard deviations, a sample mean is from the population mean. The larger the value of the test statistic, the farther the distance, or number of standard deviations, a sample mean is from the population mean stated in the null hypothesis. For example, suppose we measure a sample of five users who found out about the library activities from Facebook; the mean of their age is equal to 29 years. To make a decision, we need to evaluate how likely this sample outcome is, if the population's mean stated by the null hypothesis (23.5) is true.

A test statistic is a quantity calculated from our sample of data. Its value is used to decide whether or not the null hypothesis should be rejected in our hypothesis test.

The choice of a test statistic will depend on the assumed probability model and the hypotheses under question.

A sample statistic or value based upon a sample population is the data used in deciding the validity of a given hypothesis.

In our example, a Pew Research Center study (2013) found that Facebook followers are between the ages of 18 and 29. This data will be used in deciding and comparing our sample regarding our given hypothesis.

However, the test statistic begins with the assumption that x has a normal distribution with the mean μ and standard deviation σ. Given that it has a normal distribution with known mean, our formula will consists of:

$$Z = \frac{\bar{x} - \sigma}{\sigma_{\bar{x}}} = \frac{\bar{x} - \sigma}{\frac{\sigma}{\sqrt{n}}}$$

Where
x = mean of a sample random sample
μ = value stated in H_0
n = sample size

Example:

Suppose we want to show that only high school students spend more time in the library than the population average. It is known that the mean time spent in the library at all ages is 190 minutes. We set up to test 100 high school students to find out that

x = 198 and the standard deviation of the population is 15.

We employ the test statistic to find out if we can accept or reject the null hypothesis.

$$Z = \frac{\overline{x} - \mu}{\frac{\sigma}{\sqrt{n}}} = \frac{198 - 190}{\frac{15}{\sqrt{100}}} = 5.33$$

Since z is so high, the probability that H_0 is true is so small that we decide to reject H_0 and accept H_1. Therefore, we can conclude that only high school students spend more time in the library than the national average.

11.5 Level of Significance α

The level of significance α is the probability of rejecting H_0, when it is true. This is the probability of a Type I error. The second type of error, also known as a Type II error, occurs when rejecting the null hypothesis when it is false.

11.5.1 TYPE I ERROR

A Type I error occurs when H_0 is actually true but it just happens that we draw a sample and make a mistake with our calculation and as a result we wrongfully reject the null hypothesis H_0. The value of α, called the significance level of the test, represents the probability of making a Type I error. In other words, α is the probability of rejecting the null hypothesis, H_0, when in fact it is true. The Type I formula is:

$$\alpha = P \frac{H_0 \ is \ rejected}{H_0 \ is \ true}$$

The size of the rejection in a statistics problem to test a hypothesis depends on a value assigned to α. In one approach to test a hypothesis, we assign a value to α before making the test. Although any value can be assigned to α, we often do not exceed .01, 0.05, and 0.10.

11.5.2 TYPE II ERROR

However, we also often encounter another error, Type II (β). This case occurs when the null hypothesis H_0 is actually false but we do not reject the null hypothesis. The formula is:

$$\beta = P(\frac{H_0 \text{ is not rejected}}{H_0 \text{ is false}})$$

Table 11.2.

		True State	
H_0 True (No Effect)		H_0 False (H_1 True)	
Decision	Do not reject H_0	Correct	Type II Error
	Reject H_0	Type I Error	Correct

The error probabilities are:

$\alpha = P(\text{Type I error})$
$\beta = P(\text{Type II Error})$

11.6 Tails of a Test

After we have considered the distribution of our sample testing given by the null hypothesis, the tails test aims to determine whether or not the null hypothesis should be rejected in favor of the alternative hypothesis. There are two different types of tests that can be performed. A one-tailed test looks for an increase or decrease in the parameter, whereas a two-tailed test looks for any change in the parameter (which can be any change—increase or decrease). However, it is often recommended to use the two-tailed as preferred methodology to test the hypothesis. We will start with the two-tailed hypothesis.

11.6.1 TWO-TAILED HYPOTHESIS

A hypothesis test where the rejection region is divided equally between two critical values at the extremities of the distribution is two-tailed. A two-tailed test is applied when an alternative hypothesis (H$_1$) equals a given quantity (H$_1$ = x).

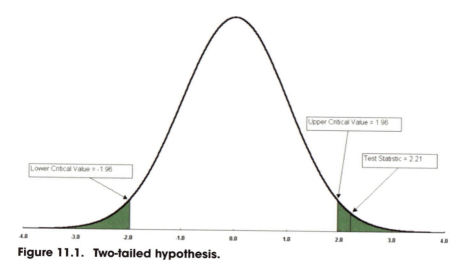

Figure 11.1. Two-tailed hypothesis.

11.6.2 ONE-TAILED HYPOTHESIS

In a one-tailed test, the critical region will have just one part. If our sample value lies in this region, we reject the null hypothesis in favor of the alternative. One-tailed hypotheses hold right- and left-tailed hypotheses.

Right-Tailed Hypothesis. A hypothesis test where the rejection region is located to the extreme right of the distribution is right-tailed. A right-tailed test is conducted when the alternative hypothesis (H$_A$) contains the condition H$_1$ > x (greater than a given quantity).

Left-Tailed Hypothesis. A hypothesis test where the rejection region is located to the extreme left of the distribution is left-tailed. A left-tailed test is conducted when the alternative hypothesis (H$_1$) contains the condition H$_1$ < x (less than a given quantity).

Example:
   In this example, we will test the parameter of *p* of a binomial distribution at a significance level of 10%. We will use the old example of tossing a coin.

Suppose a coin is tossed 10 times and we get 7 heads. We want to test whether or not the coin is fair. If the coin is fair, $p = 0.5$. Put this as the null hypothesis:

H_0: $p = 0.5$
H_1: $p \neq$ (doesn't equal) 0.5

Now, because the test is two-tailed, the critical region has two parts. Half of the critical region is to the right and half is to the left. So the critical region contains both the top 5% of the distribution and the bottom 5% of the distribution (since we are testing at the 10% level). If H_0 is true, X ~ Bin(10, 0.5).

If the null hypothesis is true, what is the probability that x is 7 or above?

$$P(X \geq 7) = 1 - P(X < 7) = 1 - P(X \leq 6) = 1 - 0.8281 = 0.1719$$

Is this in the critical region? No—because the probability that x is at least 7 is not less than 0.05 (5%), which is what we need it to be.

Many statistical tests used paired data samples to draw conclusions about the difference between two population means. We will cover two tests: the p-value and T distribution.

11.7 The P-Value

Another quantitative measure for reporting the result of a test of hypothesis is the *p-value*. It is also called the probability of chance in order to test. The lower the p-value the greater likelihood of obtaining the same result. And as a result, a low p-value is a good indication that the results are not due to random chance alone. P-value = the probability of obtaining a test statistic equal to or more extreme than the observed value if H_0 is true.

We then compare the p-value with α:

1. If p-value $< \alpha$, reject H_0.
2. If p-value $>= \alpha$, do not reject H_0.
3. "If p-value is low, then H_0 must go."

There is an important distinction between what are called *one-* and *two-tailed* statistical hypothesis tests.

There is no direct way to calculate the p-value through R. The easiest way to calculate the p-value through R is to use T distribution.

11.8 t Distribution

The t distribution (aka, Student's t-distribution) is a probability distribution that is used to estimate population parameters when the sample size is small and/or when the population variance is unknown (σ is unknown). William Gosset, who published under the pseudonym Student, was the first to study this distribution. In this book, we will not examine the proof of the t distribution; you will find in on our website.

We use the t distribution when sample sizes are sometimes small, and often we do not know the standard deviation of the population. When either of these problems occurs, statisticians rely on the distribution of the t statistic whose values are given by:

$$t = \frac{\bar{x} - \mu}{s_x}$$

Where x is the sample mean, μ is the population mean, and s is the standard deviation of the sample.

There are actually many different t distributions. The particular form of the t distribution is determined by its *degrees of freedom*. The degrees of freedom refer to the number of independent observations in a set of data. The definition of degree of freedom is the number of values that can vary after certain restrictions have been imposed on all values.

t distribution has the following properties:

1. The mean of the distribution is equal to 0.
2. The variance is equal to $v / (v - 2)$, where v is the degrees of freedom (see previous section) and $v \geq 2$.

The variance is always greater than 1, although it is close to 1 when there are many degrees of freedom. With infinite degrees of freedom, the t distribution is the same as the standard normal deviation.

When do we use t distribution? Here are four conditions in which we often employ t distribution:

a. The population distribution is normal.
b. The sampling distribution is symmetric without extreme values and the sample size is less than 15.
c. The sampling distribution is moderate, without outliers, and the sample size is between 16 and 40.
d. The sample size is greater than 40, without outliers.

However, as a general rule, t distribution should *not* be used with small samples from populations that are not approximately normal.

When a sample of size n is drawn from a population having a normal (or nearly normal) distribution, the sample mean can be transformed into a t score using the same equation as stated above.

There are two ways to calculate T distribution. The first method is using the t distribution table; the second is to calculate the t distribution using R. In this book, we selected the second option.

In R:

We will demonstrate in this example the use of dnorm function. This function provides a set of values that returns the height of the probability distribution at each point. If you only give the points, it assumes you want to use a mean of zero and standard deviation of one. There are options to use different values for the mean and standard deviation.

We will set two values, X and Y:

```
> x = rnorm(10)
> y = rnorm(10)
> t.test(x,y)
```

Welch two sample t-test:

```
data: x and y
t = 1.4896, df = 15.481, p-value = 0.1564
alternative hypothesis: true difference in means is not equal to 0
95 percent confidence interval:
 -0.3221869 1.8310421
Sample estimates:
 mean of x mean of y
 0.1944866 –0.5599410
```

The power of R:

The results provide us with a t-test result of 1.4896, degree of freedom of 15.481, and p-value of 0.1564.

R also gives us results that compare the estimate mean of x and y.

Before we can use this function in a simulation, we need to find out how to extract the t-statistic (or some other quantity of interest) from the output of the t.test function. For this function, the R help page has a detailed list of what the object returned by the function contains. A general method for a situation like this is to use the class and names functions to find where the quantity of interest is. In addition, for some hypothesis tests, you may need to pass the object from the hypothesis test to the summary function and examine its contents. For t.test it's easy to figure out what we want:

```
> ttest = t.test(x,y)
> names(ttest)
[1] "statistic" "parameter" "p.value" "conf.int"
"estimate"
[6] "null.value" "alternative" "method" "data.name"
```

The value we want is named "statistic." To extract it, we can use the dollar sign notation, or double square brackets:

```
> ttest = t.test(x,y)
> names(ttest)
[1] "statistic" "parameter" "p.value" "conf.int"
"estimate"
[6] "null.value" "alternative" "method" "data.name"
```

The value we want is named "statistic." To extract it, we can use the dollar sign notation, or double square brackets:

```
> ttest$statistic/
t
1.489560

> ttest[['statistic']]
t
1.489560
```

Of course, just one value doesn't let us do very much—we need to generate many such statistics before we can look at their properties. In R, the replicate function makes this very simple. The first argument to replicate is the number of samples you want, and the second argument is an expression (not a function name or definition!) that will generate one of the samples you want. To generate 1,000 t-statistics from testing two groups of 10 standard random normal numbers, we can use:

```
> ts = replicate(1000,t.test(rnorm(10),rnorm(10))$stati
stic)
```

Under the assumptions of normality and equal variance, we're assuming that the statistic will have a t-distribution with 10 + 10 − 2 = 18 degrees of freedom. (Each observation contributes a degree of freedom, but we lose two because we have to estimate the mean of each group.)

How can we test if that is true?

One way is to plot the theoretical density of the t-statistic we should be seeing and superimpose the density of our sample on top of it. To get an idea of what range of x values we should use for the theoretical density, we can view the range of our simulated data:

```
> range(ts)
> range(ts)
[1] -4.564359 4.111245
```

Since the distribution is supposed to be symmetric, we'll use a range from −4.5 to 4.5. We can generate equally spaced x-values in this range with seq:

```
> pts = seq(-4.5,4.5,length=100)
> plot(pts,dt(pts,df=18),col='red',type='l')
```

Now we can add a line to the plot showing the density for our simulated sample:

```
> lines(density(ts))
```

The plot appears here.

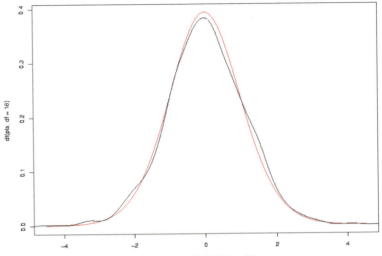

Figure 11.2. Plot X and Y under T distribution.

11.9 When σ Is Known and Unknown

When testing a claim about the value of a population mean, the test statistic will depend on whether the population standard deviation is known or unknown. This situation is identical to finding a confidence interval for a mean and is resolved in exactly the same way.

Testing a single mean with known population standard deviation. If σ is known, then for a large enough sample, the distribution of sample means will be approximately normal. When testing a single mean with unknown population standard deviation, there are also two cases for which a hypothesis test of a mean can be done when σ is unknown. In these cases, for a large enough sample, the distribution of sample mean will follow a t-distribution. Or more specifically, we can expect a t-distribution in the following two cases.

The most common way to divide between known and unknown is looking at the formulas of Z and t distribution.

Z test Statistic (σ Known)   **t Distribution (σ not known)**

$$Z = \frac{\overline{X} - \mu}{\frac{\sigma}{\sqrt{n}}}$$ $$t = \frac{\overline{X} - \mu}{\frac{s}{\sqrt{n}}}$$

Where $\bar{X}$ is the sample mean and μ is population mean *under the null hypothesis*

If the population standard deviation (σ) is *known*, we use the Z test statistic.

Otherwise we use the *t* test statistic and the sample standard deviation (*s*); the *t* statistic has degrees of freedom (*df*) = $n - 1$.

Example:

Suppose we took a sample of 150 visitors to the library who agreed to be interviewed for our study. We asked those volunteers how many times they visited the library in the past year. We conducted this type of study every two years, where we looked back to records to find that the average number of visits was 12.44. We wanted to know if the mean number of visits has changed. We collected 150, where the mean remains the same at 13.71. The standard deviation also remains the same at 2.65. Using the 2% significance rejection regions, we would like to know if we can conclude that the mean amount of all visits this year is different from 12.44.

Solution:

Let μ be the mean amount of all visits to the library based on the past studies and x be the corresponding mean for our sample this year:

$n = 150$, $x = 13.71$ and $\sigma = 2.65$ minutes.

We are to test whether or not the mean amount of all visits to the library is different from 12.44 minutes. The significance level α is 0.02. This is the probability of rejecting the null hypothesis as a Type I error. We will perform the test of hypothesis using the five steps that follow:

1. *State the null hypothesis.*

   We aimed to find out whether or not the mean amount of visits of all current library visitors is different from 12.44 minutes per year.

   Our hypothesis:

   H_0: $\mu = 12.44$
   H_1: $\mu \neq 12.44$

2. *Select the distribution to use.*

   Here, the population standard deviation σ is known and sample size is large ($n > 30$). As a result, the sampling distribution of x is normal with its mean equal to μ and the standard deviation equal to $\sigma_{\bar{x}} = \dfrac{\sigma}{\sqrt{n}}$. We will use the normal distribution to perform the test of this example.

3. *Determine the rejection and non-rejection regions.*

   The significance level is 0.2. The $\neq$ sign in the alternative hypothesis indicates that the test is two-tailed with two rejection regions, one in each tail of the normal distribution curve of x. Because the total area of both rejections is 0.02 (the significance level), the area of the rejection in each tail is 0.01.

   Area in each tail = $\alpha/2 = 0.02 / 2 = 0.01$

4. *Calculate the value of the test statistic.*

   The decision to reject or not reject the null hypothesis will depend on whether the evidence from the sample falls in the rejection or the non-rejection region. If the value of x falls in either of the two rejection regions, we reject H_0. Otherwise, we do not reject H_0. The value of x is equal to 13.71 on the sampling distribution. We first calculate the Z value of the test statistic with the two critical values of the test statistic. Then, we compare the value of the test statistic with the two critical values of Z, -2.33 and 2.33. If the value of the test statistic result is between -2.33 and 2.33, we do not reject H_0. If the value of the test statistic is either greater than 2.33 or less than −2.33, we reject the H_0.

The value of x from the sample is 13.71. We calculate the Z value using the following formula:

$$\sigma_x = \frac{\sigma}{\sqrt{n}} = \frac{2.65}{\sqrt{150}} = 0.2163$$

Then, in the second stage we will use the Z formula

$$Z = \frac{\overline{x} - \mu}{\sigma_{\overline{x}}} = \frac{13.71 - 12.44}{0.2163} = 5.87$$

The value of μ in the calculation of the Z value is substituted from the null hypothesis. The value z = 5.87.

5. *Make a decision.*

In the final step we make a decision based on the location of the value of the statistic Z score we calculated in step 4. The value of Z = 5.87 is greater than the critical value of Z = 2.33, and, as a result, we reject the null hypothesis. By rejecting the hull hypothesis, we are stating that the difference between the sample mean, x = 13.71 minutes, and the hypothesized value of the population mean, μ = 12.44 minutes, is too large and may not have occurred because of the chance of sampling error alone. In order to address this concern, we will employ the p-value: in this case, the test is two-tailed.

The p-value is equal to twice the area under the sampling distribution of x to the right of x = 13.71. By looking at the Z table, we can see the value of 5.87 is zero, and, as we discussed before, we can reject the null hypothesis for any significance level α that is greater than the p-value that allows us to reject the null hypothesis: 0.02 > 0 – the value of 5.87 according to the Z table (see Z table). We conclude that we can reject the null hypothesis and report on our findings.

For this sample, the sample mean was 13.71 and standard deviation is 2.65. We set out to test the hypothesis that the mean amount of visits to the library is 80, setting α = 0.05 (and using a two-tailed test).

H_0: μ = 80
H_1: $\mu \neq 80$

Because we do not know the population standard deviation, we use the t statistic:

$$t = \frac{\overline{X} - \mu}{\frac{s}{\sqrt{n}}} = \frac{75 - 80}{100/\sqrt{25}} = \frac{5}{20} = 2.5$$

Since $n = 25$, our t statistic has $n - 1 = 24$ degrees of freedom.

It is often the case that one wants to calculate the size of a sample needed to obtain a certain level of confidence in survey results. Unfortunately, this calculation requires prior knowledge of the population standard deviation (σ). When σ is unknown, the preliminary sample will be conducted so that a reasonable estimate of this critical population parameter can be made. If such a preliminary sample is not made, but confidence intervals for the population mean are to be constructed using an unknown, then the *Student t distribution* can be used.

Using R, we find that, for $t = 2.5$, $df = 24$, and a two-tailed test, the *p*-value is $p = 0.0197$.

Since $p < \alpha$ (i.e., $0.0197 < 0.05$), we reject H_0.

Conclusion: We reject the null hypothesis that $\mu = 800g$ as implausible. The results support (but do not prove) the alternative hypothesis that $\mu \neq 80$.

11.10 Summary

In this chapter, we discussed hypothesis testing as the process of choosing between competing hypotheses about a probability distribution based on observed data from the normal distribution. We outlined the five steps to calculate the hypothesis testing: state the null and alternative hypothesis; select the distribution to use; determine the rejection and non-rejection regions; calculate the value of statistic; and make a decision. In those five steps, we cover the level of significance α, the test statistic, the p-value, and T distribution.

11.11 Glossary

alternative hypothesis—A claim about a population parameter that will be true if the full hypothesis is false. This is the statement you will adopt if the evidence is so strong that you reject the null hypothesis.

null hypothesis—A claim or statement about a population parameter that is assumed to be true until it is declared false. Usually the null hypothesis represents a statement of "no effect" and "no difference."

one-sided test—A statistical hypothesis test in which the values for which we can reject the null hypothesis, H_0, are located entirely in one tail of the probability distribution. The one-sided test is also referred to as a one-tailed test of significance.

p-value—The probability of obtaining a test statistic value equal to or more extreme than that actually observed given that the null hypothesis H_0 is true.

parameter—The measurable characteristic of a population. It is a value, usually unknown (and which therefore has to be estimated), used to represent a certain population characteristic.

T distribution—A probability distribution that is used to estimate population parameters when the sample size is small and/or when the population variance is unknown.

test statistic—A mathematical formula that allows researchers to determine the likelihood of obtaining sample outcomes if the null hypothesis were true. The value of the test statistic is used to make a decision regarding the null hypothesis.

Type I error—Is committed by rejecting a true null hypothesis.

Type II error—Is committed when a researcher fails to reject a false null hypothesis.

two-sided test—A statistical hypothesis test in which the values for which we can reject the null hypothesis, H_0, are located in both tails of the probability distribution. The two-sided test is also referred to as a two-tailed test of significance.

11.11 References

Cavalier-Smith, T. 2002. "The Phagotrophic Origin of Eukaryotes and Phylogenetic Classification of Protozoa." *International Journal of Systematic and Evolutionary Microbiology* 52: 297–354.

Lehmann, E. L. and J. P. Romano. 2005. *Testing Statistical Hypotheses*. 3rd ed. New York: Springer Publications.

## CHAPTER 12

Correlation and Regression

12.1 Introduction
12.2 Correlation
12.3 What Is the Difference between Correlation and Regression?
12.4 Correlation Coefficient
12.5 The Pearson Product-Moment Correlation Coefficient
12.6 The Measure of Correlation
12.7 Introduction to Regression Analysis
12.8 Least Square Regression
12.9 Prediction
12.10 Summary
12.11 Glossary

12.1 Introduction

This chapter introduces methods of analyzing the relationship between two quantitative variables. The calculation and interpretation of a sample through the correlation coefficient and the linear regression equation are discussed and illustrated. Common misuses of the techniques are also considered. The chapter illustrates the use of R to conduct correlation and regression analyses.

12.2 Correlation

Correlation analysis assesses the simultaneous variability of a collection of variables. Thus, this relationship is not directional and our interest is not on how some variables respond to others, but on how they are mutually associated. Some confusion may occur between *correlation* and *regression analysis*. Both analyses often refer to the examination of the relationship that exists between two variables, X and Y, in the case where each particular value of X_i is paired with one particular value of Y. The difference is that regression analysis is a statistical technique that allows the scientist to examine the existence and extent of this relationship. Regression shows that, given a population, if the researcher can either examine the entire population or perform a random sample of sufficient size, it is possible to mathematically recover the parameters that describe the relationships between variables. Once the researcher has established such a relationship, he or she can then use these parameters to predict values of a new dependent variable given a new independent variable. Regression does not make any specifications about the way that the independent variables are distributed or measured (discrete, continuous, binary, etc.), and in order for the regression to be determined, the appropriate techniques must be used.

12.3 What Is the Difference between Correlation and Regression?

It is important to recognize that regression analysis is fundamentally different from ascertaining the correlations among different variables. Correlation analysis measures how the values of your variables co-vary, while regression analysis is aimed at making a stronger claim: demonstrating how one variable, your independent variable, causes another variable, your dependent variable. Correlation determines *the strength* of the relationship between variables, while regression attempts *to describe* the relationship between these variables. Next, under correlation analysis, we will review correlation coefficient.

12.4 Correlation Coefficient

The correlation coefficient measures the strength of the *linear association* between variables. The best way to look at the Pearson product-moment correlation is to look at a scatter diagram to see whether a line that best describes the relationship between the values of data pairs is useful. Figure 12.1 illustrates examples of a Pearson product-moment correlation between two variables and under three different conditions.

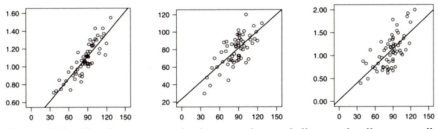

Figure 12.1. The Pearson product-moment correlation under three conditions.

12.5 The Pearson Product-Moment Correlation Coefficient

The *Pearson product-moment correlation coefficient*, often referred to as *Pearson's r*, is a measure of the linear correlation (dependence) between two variables X and Y, given a value between +1 and –1 inclusive, where 1 is total positive correlation, 0 is no correlation, and –1 is total negative correlation. It was developed by Karl Pearson, based on an idea that was introduced by Francis Galton in the 1880s.

There are several formulas that can be used to compute Pearson's correlation. Some formulas make more conceptual sense, whereas others are easier to actually compute. We begin with a conceptual formula.

The correlation coefficient r is a numerical measurement that assesses the strength of a linear relationship between two variables x and y. Its rules are:

1. r is a unitless measurement between –1 and 1. In symbols, $-1 \leq r \leq 1$. If $r = 1$, there is positive linear correlation. If $r = 0$, there is no linear correlation. The closer r is to 1 or –1, the better a line describes the relationship between the two variables x and y.
2. Positive values of r imply that as x increases, y tends to increase. Negative values of r imply that as x increases, y tends to decrease.
3. The value of r is the same regardless of which variable is the explanatory variable and which is the response variable. In other words, the value of r is the same for the pair (x, y) and the corresponding pair (y, x).
4. The value of r does not change when either variable is converted to different units.

The computation conceptual formula for r:

$$r = \frac{\text{covariation of X, Y}}{\text{total variation of X, Y}}$$

Correlation formula:

$$r = \frac{SP}{\sqrt{SS_X SS_Y}}$$

The sum of the products:

SP (sum of products) $= \sum (X - X)(Y - Y)$

$$r = \frac{\sum Z_X Z_y}{n-1}$$

12.6 The Measure of Correlation

The stronger the association of the two variables, the closer the Pearson correlation coefficient, r, will be to either +1 or −1 depending on whether the relationship is positive or negative, respectively. Achieving a value of +1 or −1 means that all your data points are included on the line of best fit—there are no data points that show any variation away from this line. Values for r between +1 and −1 (for example, r = 0.8 or −0.4) indicate that there is variation around the line of best fit. The closer the value of r to 0, the greater the variation around the line of best fit. Different relationships and their correlation coefficients are shown in figure 12.2.

Nitecki and Hernon (2000) studied the subject of cause and effect in library management. They found that saving money was ranked at the top, where the library staff and management associated the term *saving money* with the terms *information resources, staff, space, access, assistance,* and *purpose of use*. Their study did not use correlation analysis methodology. So, we examined their findings in our local library by sending out questionnaires to the library staff. Our premise was to compare the importance of saved money to the effect of information resources. The five subjects ranked the two terms side by side. The possible score was 0 to 100; table 12.1 shows our results:

Table 12.1.

Subject	Money Saved (x)	Information Resources (y)	(X − X̄)	(Y − Ȳ)	(X − X̄)²	(Y − Ȳ)²	(X − X̄)(Y − Ȳ)
A	38	41	(38-58.2) = −20.2	(41-66) = −25	408.04	624	505
B	56	63	(56-58.2) = −2.2	(63-66)= −3	4.84	9	6.6
C	59	70	(59-58.2) = 0.8	(70-66) = 4	0.64	16	3.2
D	64	72	(64-58.2) = 5.8	(72-66) = 6	33.64	36	34.8
E	74	84	(74-58.2) = 15.8	(84-66) = 18	249.64	324	284.4
MEAN	58.2	66			696.8	1010	834
					SSx	SSy	SP

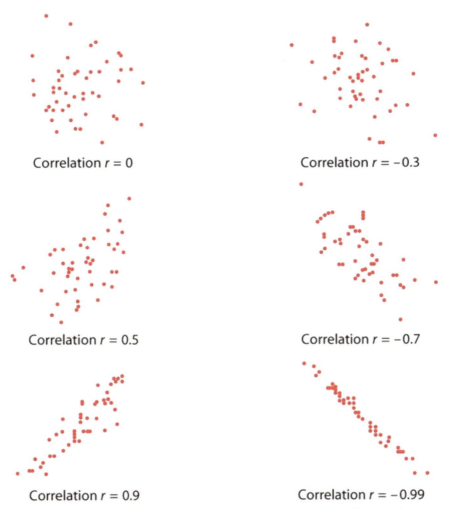

Correlation $r = 0$

Correlation $r = -0.3$

Correlation $r = 0.5$

Correlation $r = -0.7$

Correlation $r = 0.9$

Correlation $r = -0.99$

Figure 12.2. Scatterplots of sample correlations; note positive and negative values.

$$r = \frac{SP}{\sqrt{SS_X SS_Y}} = \frac{834}{696.8 \; x \; 1010}$$

$$= 0.99$$

In R:

```
> x <- c(38,56,59,64,74)
> y <- c(41,63,70, 72, 84)
> cor.test(x,y) Test Pearson's R
Pearson's product-moment correlation
data: x and y
t = 15.9405, df = 3, p-value = 0.0005368
alternative hypothesis: true correlation is not equal
to 0
95 percent confidence interval:
0.910380 0.999633
sample estimates:
cor
0.9941486
```

If we now use the Z score:

- A *Z score* is a way of standardizing the scale of two distributions
- When the scales have been standardized, it is easier to compare scores on one distribution to scores on the other distribution

To calculate the cross-product we will use the Z formula:

$$r = \frac{\sum Z_X Z_y}{n-1}$$

- The product of the Z scores is maximized when the largest z_x is paired with the largest z_y (see table 12.2):

Table 12.2.

	Money Saved X	Information Resources Y	Zx	Zy	ZxZy
A	38	41	−1.53	−1.573	2.406
B	56	63	−0.167	−0.189	0.031
C	59	70	0.061	0.252	0.015
D	64	72	0.439	0.378	0.165
E	74	84	1.197	1.133	1.35
Mean	58.2	66			$\sum = 3.96$
S	13.2	15.59			

The score is 3.96. The Z scale score:

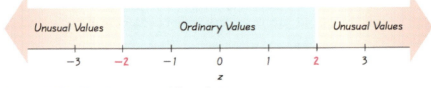

Figure 12.3. The Z score and its values.

In our case, 3.95 is an unusual value and, as a result, provides an indication to unusual values. Now we will need to investigate regression analysis, a tool to help us understand the existence and strength of the relationship between variables.

12.7 Introduction to Regression Analysis

Correlation and regression refer to the relationship that exists between two variables, X and Y, in the case where each particular value of X_i is paired with one particular value of Y_i. For example: the measures of height for individual human subjects, paired with their corresponding measures of weight; the number of hours that individual students in a statistics course spend studying prior to an exam, paired with their corresponding measures of performance on the exam; the amount of class time that individual students in a statistics course spend snoozing and daydreaming prior to an exam, paired with their corresponding measures of performance on the exam; and so on.

Regression analysis is a statistical process for estimating the relationships among variables. It includes many techniques for modeling and analyzing several variables, when the focus is on the relationship between a dependent variable and one or more independent variables. More specifically, regression analysis helps one understand how the typical value of the dependent variable changes when any one of the independent variables is varied, while the other independent variables are held fixed.

Regression analysis gives information on the relationship between a response (dependent) variable and one or more (predictor) independent variables to the extent that information is contained in the data. The goal of regression analysis is to express the response variable as a function of the predictor variables. The duality of fit and the accuracy of conclusion depend on the data used. Thus, for effective use of regression analysis one must:

1. investigate the data collection process,
2. discover any limitations in data collected, and
3. restrict conclusions accordingly.

12.8 Least Square Regression

Least square regression is a method for finding a line that summarizes the relationship between the two variables, at least within the domain of the explanatory variable *x*.

The formula is:

Y= a + bc

$b = r\frac{SD\ y}{SD\ x}$

a = $Y - bx$,

where
 b = the slope of the regression line
 a = the intercept point of the regression line and y axis
 x = Mean of x values
 y = Mean of y values
 SDx = Standard Deviation of x
 SDy = Standard Deviation of y

Figure 12.4. 8 Least Square Regression formula. $r = \dfrac{\Sigma xy - \dfrac{1}{n}(\Sigma x)(\Sigma y)}{(n-1)s_x s_y}$

Example:
 Here is the comparison between high school and college student habits of borrowing books from the local library. Find the least square regression:

Table 12.3.

Student	High School Student= X	College Student
1	2	1.6
2	2.2	2
3	2.6	1.8
4	2.7	2.8
5	2.8	2.1
6	3.1	2
7	2.9	2.6
8	3.2	2.2
9	3.3	2.6
10	3.6	3

We would like to know whether there is a linear relationship between the high school habits and the college habits, and we would like to be able to predict the future college library habits, if we know that the high school rate of another student is, say, 3.4. In the previous section, we came up with a scatterplot for this data:

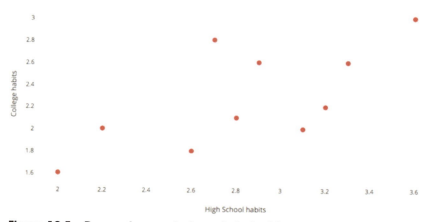

Figure 12.5.   Regression analysis and student borrowing habits.

Now, we want to fit a straight line through these data points in such a way that the line will *fit the data best*:

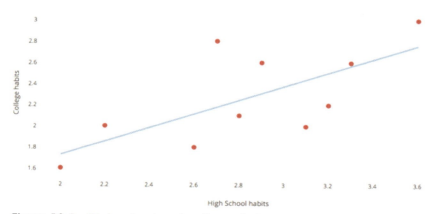

Figure 12.6.   High school and college student habits in use of the library.

In this case we have drawn a line that passes through the data points. It seems clear that no straight line can pass through all data points exactly. So, how can we address this? We find that there is a more statistical way to calculate the *best fit* by using the sum of the squares of the differences to all data points to find which has the smallest possible value. Therefore, the line that fits best in that sense is called *least square fit*, and the process of finding that line is called *least square linear regression*.

Determining the least square regression line manually. Our goal is to determine the equation of the least square regression line. In other words, we want to find the equation of a line (which happens to be the least square regression line). We know from high school that a line has the equation:

$y = m x + b$, where m is the slope of the line, and b is the intersection of the line with the y-axis. For this example, we also recall from high school that lines that go up have a positive slope (figure 12.2 linear interpretation for lines 1, 2, and 3 above), while lines with negative slope go down (figure 12.2, for lines 4, 5, 6).

Example:
Suppose we have four equations of lines as follows:

1. $y = x - 1$
2. $y = 2x - 1$
3. $y = -x + 1$
4. $y = -2x + 1$

Moreover, let's say we have four graphs of lines, as follows:

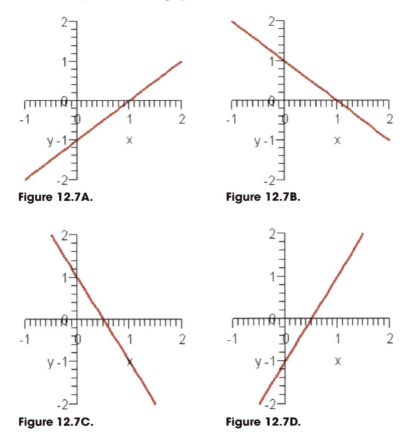

Figure 12.7A.   Figure 12.7B.

Figure 12.7C.   Figure 12.7D.

Which graph matches which equation?

Solution:

According to the equations of the lines, we have the following information:

1. y = x − 1 is a line with slope 1 (going up) and y-intercept −1
2. y = 2x − 1 is a line with slope 2 (going up) and y-intercept −1
3. y = −x + 1 is a line with slope −1 (going down) and y-intercept 1
4. y = −2x + 1 is a line with slope −2 (going down) and y-intercept 1

Graphs A and D show lines going up, so both have positive slope. Both also intersect the y axis at −1, so both have y intercept −1. But the line in graph D is steeper, so it should have a bigger slope. Thus:

- Equation 1 matches graph A.
- Equation 2 matches graph D.

Similarly, both graphs B and C have negative slopes and y intercept at +1, but line C goes down faster and thus has a more negative slope. Therefore:

- Equation 3 matches graph B.
- Equation 4 matches graph C.

In order to determine the least square regression line we must find the slope m and the y-intercept b of the line, then we know the line's equation. As it happens, the slope is related to our quantities S_{xx}, S_{yy}, and S_{xy} that we computed earlier, while the y-intercept is related to the averages (means) of x and y. The formulas are as follows:

- Slope $m = S_{xy} / S_{xx}$
- y-Intercept b = (mean of y) − (mean of x) * m

where
$$S_{xx} = \sum x2 - \frac{(\Sigma x)^2}{n}$$
$$S_{yy} = \sum y2 - \frac{(\Sigma x)^2}{n}$$
$$S_{xy} = \sum xy - \frac{(\Sigma x)(\Sigma y)}{n}$$
The mean of x = (sum of x) / n
The mean of y = (sum of y) / n

Manual solution:

Table 12.4.

Student	High School = X	College = Y	X²	Y²	XY
1	2	1.6	4	2.56	3.2
2	2.2	2	4.84	4	4.4
3	2.6	1.8	6.76	3.24	4.68
4	2.7	2.8	7.29	7.84	7.56
5	2.8	2.1	7.84	4.41	5.88
6	3.1	2	9.61	4	6.2
7	2.9	2.6	8.41	6.76	7.54
8	3.2	2.2	10.24	4.84	7.04
9	3.3	2.6	10.89	6.76	8.58
10	3.6	3	12.96	9	10.8
Total	28.4	22.7	82.84	53.41	65.88

- $S_{xx} = 83.84 - 28.4^2/10 = 2.184$
- $S_{yy} = 54.41 - 22.7^2/10 = 1.881$
- $S_{xy} = 65.88 - 28.4*22.7/10 = 1.412$

We also can quickly compute (since we already know the sums of x and of y):

- The mean of x = 28.4 / 10 = 2.84.
- The mean of y = 22.7 / 10 = 2.27.

But now the difficult work is over, and we can compute the slope and y-intercept, as well as the correlation coefficient, as follows:

- Find the slope:

  $m = S_{xy} / S_{xx} = 1.412 / 2.184 = 0.645$

- Find the y-intercept:

  b = (mean of y) − (mean of x) * m = 2.27 − 2.84 * 0.645 = 1.1360

Finding the correlation coefficient.

  $r = 0.412 / sqrt(2.184 * 1.881) = 0.6966$

Thus, the equation of our least square regression line relating high school (x) and college (y) is:

  y = 0.645 * x + 0.4382

And the correlation coefficient of 1.88 indicates that the relation is superstrong.

Based on the result, we can now use our computed equation to make predictions.

Solution:

First note that x = 3.7 is not one of the original high school scores, but we know the general relationship between x and y (the equation of the least square regression line), which we can use for our prediction:

y = 0.645 * x + 0.4382

So that if x = 3.7, we have for y:

y = 0.645 * 3.7 + 0.4382 = 2.8247

Thus, our prediction is that a high school borrowing rate of 3.7 will result in a college rate of 2.83, approximately. Moreover, because of our correlation coefficient we are relatively confident (but not superconfident) that our prediction is accurate.

In R:

To build our scatterplot, we must first enter the data in R. This is a fairly straightforward task:

```
>highschool <- c(2.0, 2.2, 2.6, 2.7, 2.8, 3.1, 2.9,
3.2, 3.3, 3.6)
>college <-c(1.6, 2.0, 1.8, 2.8, 2.1, 2.0, 2.6, 2.2,
2.6, 3.0)
>plot(college, highschool)
```

Note that the data in figure 12.8 is approximately linear. One could not fit a single line through each and every data point, but one could imagine a line that is fairly close to each data point, with some of the data points appearing above the line, others below for balance. In this next activity, we will calculate and plot the line of best fit, or the *least square regression line*.

We will use R's lm command to compute a "linear model" that fits the data in figure 1. The command lm is a very sophisticated command with a host of options (type ?lm to view a full description), but, in its simplest form, it is quite easy to use.

The syntax college~highschool is called a *model equation* and is a very sophisticated R construct. We are using its simplest form here. The symbol sepa-

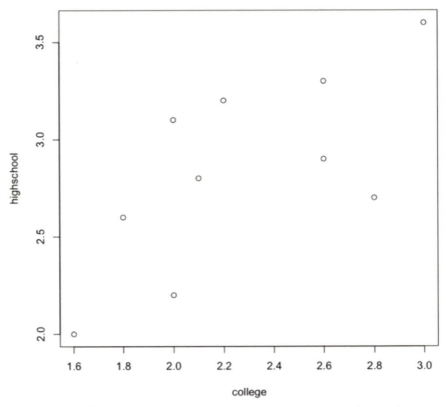

Figure 12.8. R scatterplot of high school vs. college library borrowing.

rating high school and college, in the syntax college~high school, is a *tilde*. It is located on the key to the immediate left of the #1 key on your keyboard. You must use the shift key to access the tilde.

```
> res=lm(college~highschool)
> res
```

Call:

```
lm(formula = college ~ highschool)
```

Coefficients:

```
(Intercept) highschool
0.4339 0.6465
```

Note the *Coefficients* part of the contents of res. These coefficients are the *intercept* and *slope* of the line of best fit. Essentially, we are being told that the equation of the line of best fit is:

high school = 0.645 college + 0.4339

Note that this result has the form $y = mx + b$, where m is the slope and b is the intercept of the line.

It is a simple matter to superimpose the *line of best fit* provided by the contents of the variable res. The command abline will use the data in res to draw the line of best fit. Determining a line of best fit may help us to make a prediction based on current data.

12.8 Prediction

The term *prediction* is a statement about the way things will happen in the future. In statistics, the term stands for a systematic prediction can be made by using statistical methods. In this section, we look at prediction regarding regression. Now that we have the equation of the line best fit, we can use the equation to make prediction. Suppose, for example, that we wished to estimate the average high school library habits of a college student who borrows 27.5 books per year. One technique would be to enter this value into the equation of the line of best fit:

highschool = 0.635 college + 64.928 = 0.635(27.5) + 64.928 = 82.3905.

We can use R as a simple calculator to perform this calculation:

```
> 0.635*27.5+64.928
[1] 82.3905
```

Result:

Thus, the average college student's library habit is to borrow 27.5 books per year; for high school students, this number is 82.3905 books borrowed.

12.10 Summary

In this chapter, we covered basic correlation and regression. We discussed Pearson's correlation coefficient formulas and the result of the analysis. Then we examined regression, where we looked at least square regression. We employed different formulas to find the r. In each case, we learned how to employ R to find the solutions.

12.11 Glossary

correlation analysis—Measures the simultaneous variability of a collection of variables.

least square regression—The smallest possible value for the sum of the squares of the residuals.

Pearson product-moment correlation coefficient—A measure of the strength of a linear association between two variables, is denoted by r.

prediction—A forecast about the future.

## CHAPTER 13

Analysis of Variances and Chi-Square Test

13.1   Introduction
13.2   Point and Interval Estimate
    13.2.1   Confidence Intervals
    13.2.2   Confidence Levels
13.3   The Degrees of Freedom
13.4   The F Distribution
13.5   Introduction to ANOVA under One Variable
13.6   More than Two Groups: One-Way ANOVA
13.7   Introduction to the Chi-Square Test
    13.7.1   The Goodness-of-Fit Test
    13.7.2   Test of Independence under Chi-Square
13.8   Summary
13.9   Glossary
13.10   References

13.1 Introduction

In chapter 11, we discussed the hypothesis testing methodology, where we illustrated how to draw conclusions about possible differences between the two variables we outlined in our hypothesis (x and y). However, frequently, it is necessary to evaluate different parameters of more than two groups. This chapter will introduce the analysis of variance (ANOVA) and its contribution to analyzing more than two groups at a time.

In the field of information science, many researchers have used ANOVA analysis to discover new knowledge. Powell et al. (2002) examined four major professional groups conducting research in the field. The study authors examined the American Library Association (ALA) and the Information Association for the Information Age (ASIS&T) research activities based on questionnaires and analyzed their data based on ANOVA analysis. Their study identified four factors related to practitioners' involvement in research.

In the previous chapter, we first encountered two new concepts that will play a big role in the analysis of variance. The first term is the *degree of freedom* and second term is *F distribution*. We will start by reviewing the idea of estimation as obtained from the population.

13.2 Point and Interval Estimate

In statistics, *estimation* refers to the process by which one makes inferences about a population based on information obtained from a sample. Statisticians use sample statistics to estimate population parameters. For example, sample means are used to estimate population means; sample proportions to estimate population proportions. An estimate of a population parameter may be expressed in two ways:

- *Point estimate.* A point estimate of a sample parameter is a single value, a statistic, of a population. For example, the sample mean x is a point estimate of the population mean μ. Similarly, the sample proportion p is a point estimate of the population proportion P.
- *Interval estimate.* An interval estimate is defined by two numbers between which a population parameter is said to lie. For example, $a < x < b$ is an interval estimate of the population mean μ. It indicates that the population mean is greater than a but less than b.

13.2.1 CONFIDENCE INTERVALS

Statisticians use a *confidence interval* to express the precision and uncertainty associated with a particular sampling method. A confidence interval consists of three parts:

- a confidence level
- a statistic
- a margin of error

The confidence level describes the uncertainty of a sampling method. The statistic and the margin of error define an interval estimate that describes the precision of the method. The interval estimate of a confidence interval is defined by the *sample statistic ± margin of error.*

For example, suppose we compute an interval estimate of a population parameter. We might describe this interval estimate as a 95% confidence interval. This means that if we used the same sampling method to select different samples and compute different interval estimates, the true population parameter would fall within a range defined by the *sample statistic ± margin of error* 95% of the time. Confidence intervals are preferred to point estimates, because confidence intervals indicate (a) the precision of the estimate and (b) the uncertainty of the estimate.

13.2.2 CONFIDENCE LEVELS

The probability part of a confidence interval is called the *confidence level.* The confidence level describes the likelihood that a particular sampling method will produce a confidence interval that includes the true population parameter. Here is how to interpret a confidence level. Suppose we collected all possible samples from a given population and computed confidence intervals for each sample. Some confidence intervals would include the true population parameter; others would not. A 95% confidence level means that 95% of the intervals contain the true population parameter; a 90% confidence level means that 90% of the intervals contain the population parameter; and so on.

Margin of error. In a confidence interval, the range of values above and below the sample statistic is called the *margin of error.* For example, suppose the Association for Library and Education (Alise) conducted an election survey and reported that the independent candidate would receive 30% of the vote. The researchers at Alise stated that the survey had a 5% margin of error and a confidence level of 95%. These findings resulted in the following confidence interval: we are 95% confident that the independent candidate will receive between 25% and 35% of the vote.

Note: Many public opinion surveys report interval estimates, but not confidence intervals. They provide the margin of error, but not the confidence level. To clearly interpret survey results, you need to know both! We are much more likely to accept survey findings if the confidence level is high (say, 95%) than if it is low (say, 50%).

13.3 The Degrees of Freedom

Many information science researchers use the concept of degrees of freedom both in the computation of their data and when locating critical values in the various tables. The term *degrees of freedom*, abbreviated as df, has often been defined as the number of degrees of freedom or how certain we are that our sample population is representative of the entire population. The higher the degrees of freedom, the more certain we can be that we have accurately sampled the entire population. In simple words, df represents the number of independent values in a calculation, minus the number of estimated parameters. The statistical term *degrees of freedom* was introduced in 1922 by Ronald Aylmer Fisher (Zar, 2010) and has been widely used in statistics since then. However, the simple definition of the term can be held as, "The number of values in the final calculation of a statistic that are free to vary."

For example, consider a case of estimating the standard deviation of a population variable from a random sample of N observations. The formula for the standard deviation is:

$$SD = \sqrt{\frac{\Sigma(U - \bar{U})2}{N-1}}$$

SD = the standard deviation estimated in sample
$\sqrt{}$ = square root
Σ = sum
U = sample observation on the population
U = the average score of the sample observation on U
N = sample size

Note that the numerator is divided by $N - 1$ and not by N.

Imagine you have three (3) new books in the library to assign to students. You receive a list of three students from the local high school. The names of the students are A, B, and C. Now you are going to invite the three students to the library. But what would happen if only one (1) student could make it to the library only on the first day; you can take the three children in three days. But how would you pick them?

Here is where degrees of freedom are used.

Day 1, you are *free to make the choice*: you can take child A, B, or C, whomever you like! (Say you picked child A)

Day 2, you are once again *free to make the choice*: you can take either child B or
C to the library. (Imagine you picked child B)

Day 3, you have no choice—you must pick child C to come to the library. There
are no other choices than child C.

So, in this case, we say that you have *no freedom* to make your choice.

In the preceding example, you had three variables—and three chances to make
a (free) choice. But you could only pick (3 − 1) = 2 variables in a free manner.
Once two variables (A&B, B&C, or A&C) are picked, the other variable became
fixed. So our *degrees of freedom was (3 − 1) = 2.*

Consider the following: freely assign values to a dataset containing three
variables (n = 3) and a mean of 10.

Given the variables are X_1, X_2, and X_3, values can be freely assigned only for
two of the above variables. Since we need to satisfy the mean, our third variable
has to be fixed—not free. If you have assigned X_1=10 & X_2=5, the value for X_3
invariably becomes 15 because:

$(X_1+X_2+X_3)/n$ = 10:
$(10+5+X_3)/3$ = 10
X_3 = (30 − 15) = 15 ~ X_3 is fixed by the values of n and mean
Our degrees of freedom hence is, (n − 1) or (3 − 1)

Degrees of freedom in population and sample statistics. Finally, let us consider the
statistical parameter known as the variance (s^2 or σ^2), (the square root of which
is known as the standard deviation (s or σ), and how degrees of freedom are used
when considering population and sample estimates.

The equation for the variance for a population:

$\sigma^2 = \sum(X_i − \mu)^2 /N$
$s^2 = \sum(X_i − X^-)^2 /(n-1)$

Where X_i is i[th] value of X, μ = population mean, N = number of observations
in the population, and n = number of observations in the sample and (n − 1) =
degrees of freedom.

For the ease of our discussion, we split the above equations into two seg-
ments. The expressions above the division mark give us the statistical parameter
known as *sum of squares.*

$SS = \sum(X_i - \mu)^2$ – *population* sum of squares
$ss = \sum(X_i - X^-)^2$ – *sample* sum of squares
$ss = [\ (2.5 - 3.1)^2 + (2.5 - 5.7)^2 + (3.1 - 2.5)^2 + (3.1 - 5.7)^2 + (5.7 - 3.1)^2 + (5.7 - 2.5)^2\ ] / 3$

Here, each datum is compared to each other to bring about the deviation, and it is squared to negate the minus values, which is then averaged with the others at the end. The point is that each datum is compared to the others $(n - 1)$ times.

The degrees of freedom under the group. The degrees of freedom have often been used to determine group differences versus association, which is considered to be part of the process of determining the statistical purpose. The researcher needs to determine the statistical purpose by examining the hypothesis questions and addressing the questions with the intent to compare groups to see if they are significantly different from one another or to see if there is an association between the variables.

Understanding the significance of group difference is important when the researcher wishes to know if one group has more or less of some variables. For example, two groups, women and men, are compared to discover if a higher proportion of either group invests in bonds.

Here is an illustration of a hypothesis: Does the number of new purchases of online books differ among different product platforms? The result is that three different brands (Kindle, Nook, and iBook) are compared to see if the number of products purchased is significantly different.

The *degree of association* assesses the magnitude of the relationship between two or more variables. It is commonly used in research, for example: Is family income related to the number of books and games borrowed from the local library? The degrees of association are the amount of information your data provide that you can "spend" to estimate the values of unknown population parameters, and calculate the variability of these estimates. We will see the degrees of freedom again under *F* distribution, chi-square, and other techniques.

13.4 The *F* Distribution

The *F* distribution has two degrees of freedom: degrees of freedom for the numerator and degrees of freedom for the denominator. The *F* distribution is often used to calculate the sampling distribution derived from the ratio of two sample variances (s^2) estimating identical population variances (σ^2). The distribution of all possible values of the f statistic is called an F distribution, with $v_1 = n_1 - 1$ and $v_2 = n_2 - 1$ degrees of freedom.

When describing an F distribution, the number of degrees of freedom associated with the standard deviation in the numerator of the f statistic is always stated first. Thus, $f(5, 9)$ would refer to an F distribution with $v_1 = 5$ and $v_2 = 9$ degrees of freedom, whereas $f(9, 5)$ would refer to an F distribution with $v_1 = 9$ and $v_2 = 5$ degrees of freedom.

The F distribution has the following properties:

The mean of the distribution is equal to $v_2 / (v_2 - 2)$ for $v_2 > 2$.
The variance is equal to $[2 * v_2^2 * (v_1 + v_1 - 2)] / [v_1 * (v_2 - 2)^2 * (v_2 - 4)]$ for $v_2 > 4$.

Cumulative probability and the F distribution. Every f statistic can be associated with a unique cumulative probability. This cumulative probability represents the likelihood that the f statistic is less than or equal to a specified value. Statisticians use $f\alpha$ to represent the value of an f statistic having a cumulative probability of $(1 - \alpha)$. For example, suppose we were interested in the f statistic having a cumulative probability of 0.95. We would refer to that f statistic as $f_{0.05}$, since $(1 - 0.95) = 0.05$.

Of course, to find the value of $f\alpha$, we would need to know the degrees of freedom, v_1 and v_2. The degrees of freedom appear in parentheses as follows: $f\alpha(v_1, v_2)$. Thus, $f_{0.05}(5, 7)$ refers to value of the f statistic having a cumulative probability of 0.95, $v_1 = 5$ degrees of freedom and $v_2 = 7$ degrees of freedom.

13.5 Introduction to ANOVA under One Variable

Analysis of variance (ANOVA) is a hypothesis test that evaluates the significance of mean differences. The goal of using ANOVA is to determine whether the mean differences that are found in sample data are greater than can be reasonably explained by chance alone. ANOVA can be used to evaluate differences between two or more treatments (or populations).

ANOVA test of independence. The one-way ANOVA is used with one categorical independent variable and one continuous variable. The independent variable can consist of any number of groups (levels).

The chi-square formula:

$$\sqrt{\frac{\sum(U - \bar{U})2}{N-1}}$$

The computation for the expected frequency for each cell:

$$\chi^2 = \sum \frac{(0-E)^2}{E}$$

Where = the sum is equal to the value of 0, which is equal observed frequency, E. The value of E is equal to expected frequency, and degrees of freedom (df) is equal to the number of rows – 1 times number of columns –1.

Calculating the value of the test statistics

$$F = \frac{Variance\ between\ samples}{Variance\ within\ sample} \text{ or } \frac{MSB}{MSW}$$

Between group variation. The variation due to the interaction between the samples is denoted SS(B) for sum of squares between groups. If the sample means are close to each other (and therefore the grand mean), this will be small. There are k samples involved with one data value for each sample (the sample mean), so there are $k-1$ degrees of freedom.

Within group variation. The variation due to differences within individual samples is denoted SS(W), for sum of squares within groups. Each sample is considered independently; no interaction between samples is involved. The degrees of freedom are equal to the sum of the individual degrees of freedom for each sample. Since each sample has degrees of freedom equal to one less than their sample sizes, and there are k samples, the total degrees of freedom is k less than the total sample size: df = N – k.

The variance due to the differences within individual samples is denoted MS(W) for mean square within groups. This is the within group variation divided by its degrees of freedom. It is also denoted by Sw^2. It is the weighted average of the variances (weighted with the degrees of freedom).

Table 13.1. Summary Table

	SS	df	MS
Between	SS(B)	k – 1	SS(B)/(K – 1)
Within	SS(W)	N – K	SS(W) / (N – k)
Total	SS(W) + SS(B)	N – 1	

Notice that each mean square is just the sum of squares divided by its degrees of freedom, and the F value is the ratio of the mean squares. Do not put the largest variance in the numerator; always divide the between variance by the within variance. If the between variance is smaller than the within variance, then the means are really close to each other and you will fail to reject the claim that they are all equal. The degrees of freedom of the F test are in the same order they appear in the table.

Example:

A manager in the library wished to determine whether the mean times required to complete a certain task differed for the three levels of employee training. He randomly selected 10 employees with each of the three levels of training (Beginner, Intermediate, and Advanced). Does the data provide sufficient evidence to indicate that the mean times required to complete a certain task differ for at least two of the three levels of training? The data is summarized in the *contingency table* (table 13.2).

Introduction to the contingency table. Often we may have information on more than one variable for each element; this can be summarized and presented using a two-way classification table also known as a *cross-tabulation table*. In the example above:

Table 13.2.

	n		S^2
Advanced	10	24.2	21.54
Intermediate	10	27.1	18.65
Beginner	10	30.2	17.76

Using R to produce the contingency table:

```
> value<- c("Advanced," "Intermediate," "Beginner")
> x <- c(24.2, 27.1, 30.2)
> n <- c(10, 10,10)
> table (value, x, n)
```

Value	24.2	27.1	30.2	x
Advanced	1	0	0	10
Beginner	0	0	1	10
Intermediate	0	1	0	10

Table 13.3.

Value	24.2	27.1	30.2	x
Advanced	1	0	0	10
Beginner	0	0	1	10
Intermediate	0	1	0	10

Our hypothesis is:

H_0: The mean times required to complete a certain task does not differ for at least two of the three levels of training.

H_1: The mean times required to complete a certain task differs for the three levels of training.

Our assumptions:

The samples were drawn independently and randomly from the three populations. The time required to complete the task is normally distributed for each of the three levels of training. The populations have equal variances.

Test Statistics: $F = \frac{MST}{MSE}$

df numerator = p − 1 and df denominator = n − p

$\alpha = 0.05$

Calculations:

$$SST = (= 10(24.2 - 27.16...)^2 + 10(27.1 - 27.16...)^2 + 10(30.2 - 27.16...)^2$$
$$= 180.066...$$

$$MST = \frac{SST}{p-1} = \frac{180.066}{2} = 90.033$$

$$SSE = (n_i - 1) = 9(21.54) + 9(18.64) + 9(17.76)$$
$$= 521.46$$

$$MSE = \frac{SSE}{n-p} = \frac{521.46}{27} = 19.313$$

$$F = \frac{MST}{MSE} = \frac{90.033}{19.313} = 4.662$$

Table summary of our result:

Table 13.4.

Source	Df	SS	MS	F
Treatments	2	180.067	90.033	4.662
Error	27	521.46	19.313	
Total	29	702.527		

Decision: We will reject H_0.
Rationale: There is sufficient evidence to indicate that the mean times required to complete a certain task differ for at least two of the three levels of training.

13.6 More than Two Groups: One-Way ANOVA

In this section, we examine a second approach to testing two means for equality. The logic of this approach extends directly to one-way analysis of variance with k groups. We can use our data to calculate two independent estimates of the population variance: one is the pooled variance of scores within groups, and the other is based on the observed variance between group means. These two estimates are expected to be equal if the population means are equal for all k groups (H_0: $\mu_1 = \mu_2 = \ldots = \mu_k$), but the estimates are expected to differ if the population means are not all the same.

Within-groups estimate. Our single best estimate of the population variance is the pooled within groups variance, s_y^2 from Formula 2. In our example $s_y^2 = 18$, with df = 10. In ANOVA terminology, the numerator of Formula 2 is called the sum of squares within groups, or SS_{WG}, and the denominator is called the degrees of freedom within groups, or df_{WG}. The estimate of the population variance from Formula 2, SS_{WG}/df_{WG}, is called the mean square within groups, or MS_{WG}. Formula 3 is an equivalent way to express and compute MS_{WG}.

$$\text{Within-groups estimate of } \sigma_y^2 = \frac{\sum_{ij}\left(y_{ij} - \bar{y}_j\right)^2}{\sum_j\left(n_j - 1\right)} = \frac{SS_{WG}}{df_{WG}} = MS_{WG}$$

$$= \frac{100+80}{5+5} = \frac{180}{10} = 18.00$$

Between-groups estimate. If the null hypothesis ($\mu_1 = \mu_2$) is true and the assumptions are valid (random, independent sampling from normally distributed populations with equal variances), then a second independent estimate of the population variance can be calculated. As stated by the central limit theorem, if independent samples of size n are drawn from some population with variance = σ_y^2, then the variance of all possible such sample means $\sigma_{\bar{y}}^2$ is σ_y^2/n. We can use our observed sample means to calculate an unbiased estimate of the variance for the distribution of all possible sample means (for samples of size n). Our estimate of the variance of means is not very stable because it is based on only two scores, $\bar{y}_1 = 97$ and $\bar{y}_2 = 105$, but nonetheless it is an unbiased estimate of $\sigma_{\bar{y}}^2$. With our data, $est\sigma_{\bar{y}}^2 = s_{\bar{y}}^2 = 32$ and df = 1.

$$est\sigma_{\bar{y}}^2 = s_{\bar{y}}^2 = \frac{\sum_j \left(\bar{y}_j - \bar{y}..\right)^2}{k-1}$$

$$= \frac{(97-101)^2 + (105-101)^2}{(2-1)} = \frac{(-4)^2 + (4)^2}{} = 16 + 16 = 32.$$

Because $\sigma_{\bar{y}}^2 = \sigma_y^2/n$, it follows that $\sigma_y^2 = n\sigma_{\bar{y}}^2$. Now we can estimate the variance of the population based on the observed variance of 32 for the sample means. With our data, where $n = 6$ for each sample, we find $s_y^2 = (n)(s_{\bar{y}}^2) = (6)(32) = 192$. This tells us that if we draw samples of size $n_j = 6$ from a population where $\sigma_y^2 = 192$, the expected variance of sample means is $\sigma_{\bar{y}}^2 = \sigma_y^2/n = 192/6 = 32$. Thus, if the groups in the population have equal means and variances, we can estimate this common population variance to be 192 because that would account for the observed variance of 32 between our sample means.

Calculation of this second estimate of the population variance using ANOVA analysis. The MS_{BG} is our best estimate of the population variance based only on knowledge of the variance among the sample means.

$$\text{Between-groups estimate of } \sigma_y^2 = \frac{\sum_j n_j\left(\bar{y}_j - \bar{y}..\right)^2}{(k-1)} = \frac{SS_{BG}}{df_{BG}} = MS_{BG}$$

$$\frac{\sum_j n_j\left(\bar{y}_j - \bar{y}..\right)^2}{(k-1)} = \frac{6(97-101)^2 + 6(105-101)^2}{2-1} = \frac{6(16) + 6(16)}{1} = 192$$

Comparing the two estimates of population variance. The estimate of the population variance based on the variability between sample means ($MS_{BG} = 192$) is considerably larger than the estimate based on variability within samples (MS_{WG} = 18). We would like to know how likely it is that two estimates of the same population variance would differ so widely if all of our assumptions are valid and ($\mu_1 = \mu_2$). The F ratio is designed to test this question (H_0: $\sigma_1^2 = \sigma_2^2$)

$$F(df_{BG}, df_{WG}) = \frac{Between\ Groups\ estimate\ of\ \sigma_y^2}{Within\ Groups\ estimate\ of\ \sigma_y^2} = \frac{MS_{WG}}{MS_{BG}}$$

$$F(1,10) = 192\ /\ 18 = 10.67\ (p = .0085)$$

The degrees of freedom for the two estimates of variance in Formula 6 are df_{BG} = k – 1 = 2 – 1 = 1, and df_{WG} = ($n_1 + n_2 - k$) = (6 + 6 – 2) = 10.

If the null hypothesis and assumptions were true, such that independent random samples were drawn from two normally distributed populations with equal means and equal variances, then it would be very surprising indeed ($p<.01$) to find that these two estimates of the common population variance would differ so widely.

We conclude that the null hypothesis and assumptions are not likely all to be true. If we are confident that our assumptions are OK, then we reject the null hypothesis (H_0: $\mu_1 = \mu_2 = ...= \mu_k$).

Assumptions of the test. We can expect our calculated level of statistical significance (the p value from the F distribution) to be accurate only if the assumptions required for the test procedure have been satisfied. Recall the assumptions:

1. observations were randomly and independently chosen from the population;
2. population distributions are normal for each group; and
3. population variances are equal for all groups.

If the sampling was not independent and random, the results of the F test may be completely spurious. No statistical procedure will allow strong generalizations to a population if random sampling is not used. Fortunately, the sampling procedure is generally under the control of the researcher, so faulty sampling as an explanation for a surprisingly large F usually can be ruled out.

Perhaps the best approach to identify serious departures from normality in the shape of the population distributions is to plot the sample distributions and apply the "intraocular trauma test." Extreme departures from normality, especially strong skew or outliers, will be apparent. Admittedly, some practice is needed to calibrate your eyes, but a plot is likely to be more useful than summary statistics alone for identifying problems in your data. Distributions with isolated extreme scores (e.g., three or more standard deviations away from the mean) typically cause more serious problems than smoothly skewed distributions.

There are several ways to deal with extreme scores. Transformations may be useful to reduce the effects of extreme scores (and reduce skew). Sometimes an outlier is caused by an error in coding that can be corrected. Be especially alert for missing data codes that accidentally are used as legitimate data. Sometimes outliers are legitimate scores from cases that are qualitatively different from the population of interest. Such cases should be removed and treated separately. They may be very interesting and important cases, so they should not routinely be ignored. Recent years have seen the development of a number of *robust* methods that are less sensitive to extreme scores. With Winsorized data, some number (g) of scores in each tail of the distribution are set equal to the next most extreme score (the g + 1st score from the end). With trimmed data, some proportion of the scores from each tail are discarded. A popular level of trimming is 15% from each end. Hampel and biweight procedures retain all data but give less weight to scores farther from the mean.

Equality of variance can be tested, but there are compelling arguments against using the test to decide whether or not to use ANOVA. First, ANOVA is little affected by small to moderate departures from homogeneity of variance, especially if the sample sizes are equal or nearly equal. Second, the tests of homogeneity are more powerful for larger samples than for smaller samples, but ANOVA is less affected by heterogeneity when the samples are larger. This leads to the awkward situation where the tests of homogeneity are most likely to detect a violation of homogeneity when it least matters. Third, several of the most commonly used tests of homogeneity are inaccurate for non-normal distributions. One example of a homogeneity test is Levene's test, known for its being less sensitive to departures from normality. Box (1953) characterized testing for homogeneity before using ANOVA as sending a rowboat out into the ocean to see if it is calm enough for an ocean liner.

Unequal within-group variances for the different populations is a problem for ANOVA (and the t-test) only when three conditions simultaneously exist:

1. the variances are quite unequal (say a 2:1 ratio or greater);
2. the samples are quite unequal in size (say a 2:1 ratio or greater); and
3. at least one sample is small (say 10 or fewer cases).

In this situation, ANOVA is too liberal (gives false significance) when the smallest samples are taken from the populations with the largest variance. Conversely, ANOVA is too conservative (fails to detect differences among means) when the smallest samples are taken from the populations with the smallest variance. Many statistical packages, including Statistical Package for the Social Science, also known as SPSS, provide tests of equality of variance in ANOVA and also ANOVA tests that do not assume equal variance.

If you suspect that an assumption of ANOVA has been violated in a way that compromises the test, it is prudent to supplement the regular analyses with procedures that are robust to the suspected violation of the assumption. If both approaches yield the same conclusions, report the results from the standard test and note that the results were confirmed with the robust procedure. If the results differ, considerable caution is warranted, and the more conservative test is probably appropriate. Last, the statistical significance.

Statistical significance, practical significance, and non-significance.
In recent years, the practice of significance testing of null hypotheses has come under severe criticism. For now, keep in mind that failure to reject the null hypothesis does not mean that the null hypothesis is true (it almost certainly is false). On the other hand, if we reject the null hypothesis, we have not necessarily found a practical or important effect. It is important to examine plots of the data and to report means and variances, not just p values from significance tests.

ANOVA with R

Example:

```
value <- c(1,1,2,3,1,3,2,4,1,2,6,5,1,3,5,1,2,3,4)
group <- c(0,0,0,0,0,0,0,0,0,0,0,1,1,1,1,1,1,1,1,1)
data <- data.frame(group, value)
```

F test in R:

```
af.test(data[data["group"]==0,2],
data[data['group']==1,2])
### F test to compare two variances and result:
data: data[data["group"] == 0, 2] and data[data["group"]
== 1, 2]
F = 0.3419, num df = 9, denom df = 8, p-value = 0.1306
alternative hypothesis: true ratio of variances is not
equal to 1
95 percent confidence interval:
0.07846272 1.40237802
sample estimates:
ratio of variances:
0.3418803
```

As you can see here, you have two dfs (degrees of freedom; DOFs): the df for the numerator and df for the denominator. The F test is using the ratio of the variances, which is also shown as "ration of variances." This is why you have two dfs. And it is exactly the same as the F value. In this example, the p value is 0.13, so our F value is not extreme enough to say that we have a difference in the two variances.

13.7 Introduction to the Chi-Square Test

The chi-square test is a statistical test that can be used to determine whether observed frequencies are significantly different from expected frequencies. The chi-square test is used to examine differences with categorical variables. There are a number of features of the social world that we characterize through categorical variables—religion, political preference. In library science, we are familiar with different categorical variables used to organize knowledge. The chi-square test is used in two similar but distinct circumstances:

- For estimating how closely an observed distribution matches an expected distribution—we'll refer to this as the *goodness-of-fit test*
- For estimating whether two random variables are independent

13.7.1 THE GOODNESS-OF-FIT TEST

The chi-square goodness-of-fit test is a single-sample nonparametric test, also referred to as the one-sample goodness-of-fit test or Pearson's chi-square goodness-of-fit test. It is used to determine whether the distribution of cases (e.g., participants) in a single categorical variable (e.g., "gender," consisting of two groups: "males" and "females") follows a known or hypothesized distribution (e.g., a distribution that is "known," such as the proportion of males and females in a country; or a distribution that is "hypothesized," such as the proportion of males versus females that we anticipate voting for a particular political party in the next elections). The proportion of cases expected in each group of the categorical variable can be equal or unequal (e.g., we may anticipate an "equal" proportion of males and females reading books about baking, or an "unequal" proportion, with 70% of those books' readers being male and only 30% female).

Under the goodness-of-fit test, the degrees of freedom are:

dk = $k - 1$, where k denotes the number of possible outcomes (or categories) for the experiment.

The procedure to make a goodness-of-fit test involves the following formula:

$$\chi^2 = \sum \frac{(O-E)^2}{E}$$

Where O = observed frequency for a category
E = expected frequency for a category = np

Example:

New Library inserted a Talking Machine that allows the library to provide users a way to return their books in their own time. The manager of the library wanted to investigate if the numbers of transactions made by the Talking Machine were the same for each day (Monday through Friday) of the week. The information she obtained is given in the following table, where the number of users represents the number of transactions on the Talking Machine on these days.

Table 13.5.

Day	Monday	Tuesday	Wednesday	Thursday	Friday
Number of users	253	197	204	279	267

At the 1% level of significance, can we reject the null hypothesis that the number of users who use this Talking Machine each of the five days of the week is the same? Assume that this week is typical of all weeks in regard to the use of the Talking Machine.

Solution:

Step 1.

State the null hypothesis and alterative hypothesis.

Because there are five categories (days) listed in the table, the number of Talking Machine users will be the same each of these five days if 20% of all users use the Talking Machine each day. The null and alternative hypothesis are as follow:

H_0: The number of users using the Talking Machine is the same for all five days of the week.

H_1: The number of users using the Talking Machine is not the same for all five days of the week.

If the number of people using the Talking Machine is the same for all five days of the week, then let p5 be the proportion of users who use this machine on

Monday, Tuesday, Wednesday, Thursday, and Friday. Then, the null and alternative hypothesis can also be written as:

H_0: = p1 = p2 = p3 = p4 = p5 = 0.20
H_1 = At least two of the five proportions are not equal to 0.20

Step 2.
    Select the distribution to use.
    Because there are five categories (i.e., days on which the Talking Machine is used), this is a multinomial experiment. Consequently, we use the chi-square distribution to make this test.

Step 3.
    Determine the rejection and non-rejection regions.
    The significance level is given as 0.01, the degrees of freedom are calculated as follows:

K = number of categories = 5
Df = K – 1 = 5 – 1 = 4

From the chi-square distribution (table VI of appendix C), the critical value of χ^2 for df = 4 and 0.01 will be 13.277.

Step 4.
    Calculate the value of the test statistic.

Table 13.6.

Category (day)	Observed Frequency (O)	P	Expected Frequency E = np	(O – E)	(O – E)²	$\frac{(O – E)^2}{E}$
Monday	253	0.2	1200(0.20) = 240	13	169	0.704
Tuesday	197	0.2	1200(0.20) = 240	–43	1849	7.704
Wednesday	204	0.2	1200(0.20) = 240	–36	1296	5.4
Thursday	279	0.2	1200(0.20) = 240	39	1521	6.338
Friday	267	0.2	1200(0.20) = 240	27	729	3.038
N = 1200 Sum = 23.184						

The calculations made in table 13.6 are explained next.

1. The first two columns of table 13.6 list the five categories (days) and the observed frequencies for the sample of 1,200 users who used the Talking Machine during each of the five days of the selected week. The third column contains the probabilities for the five categories assuming that the null hypothesis is true.

2. The fourth column contains the expected frequencies. These frequencies are obtained by multiplying the sample size ($n = 1,200$) by the probabilities listed in the third column. If the null hypothesis is true (i.e., the Talking Machine users are equally distributed over all five days), then we will expect 240 out of 1,200 users to use the Talking Machine each day. Consequently, each category in the fourth column has the same expected frequency.
3. The fifth column lists the differences between the observed and expected frequencies, that is, $O - E$. These values are squared and recorded in the sixth column.
4. Finally, we divide the squared differences (that appear in the sixth column) by the corresponding expected frequencies (listed in the fourth column) and write the resulting numbers in the seventh column.
5. The sum of the seventh column gives the value of the test statistics χ^2:

$$\chi^2 = \sum \frac{(O-E)^2}{E} = 23.184$$

13.7.2 TEST OF INDEPENDENCE UNDER CHI-SQUARE

In a test of independence for a contingency table, we test the null hypothesis that the two attributes (characteristics) of the elements of a given population are not related. For example, we want to test if there is an association between a man or a woman and having a preference for reading books found in the library.

The definition of degrees of freedom for a test of independence involves a test of the null hypothesis that two attributes of a population are not related. The degrees of freedom for a test of independence are:

$$df = (R - 1)(C - 1)$$

where R and C are the number of rows and the number of columns found in a given contingency table.

The value of test statistic χ^2 in a test of independence is obtained using the same formula as the goodness-of-fit test discussed in section 13.7.1.

The test of independence formula:
The value of the test statistics χ^2 for a test of independence is calculated as

$$\chi^2 = \sum \frac{(O-E)^2}{E}$$

where O and E are the observed and expected frequencies for a cell.

The null hypothesis in a test of independence always holds two attributes that are not related. The alternative hypothesis is that the two attributes of the two characteristics are related.

Example:

The increase in access to technology and decline in library funding caused the decline in public attendance at the library. A random sample of 300 adults was selected, and these adults were asked if they were in favor of closing the library in their local community. The two-way classification of the responses of these adults is presented in the following table.

Table 13.7.

	In Favor of Closing the Local Library	Against	No Opinion
Men (M)	93	70	12
Women (W)	87	32	6

Calculate the expected frequencies for this table, assuming that the two characteristics (gender and opinions) are independent.

Solution:

Table 13.8.

	In Favor of Closing the Local Library	Against	No Opinion	Total
Men (M)	70	93	12	175
Women (W)	32	87	32	125
Total	102	180	18	300

As stated earlier, the null hypothesis in a test of independence is that the two characteristics are independent (gender and opinion). In an independent test of the hypothesis, first we assume that the null hypothesis is true and that the two attributes are independent. Assuming that the null hypothesis is true and the gender and opinions are not related in this example, we calculate the expected frequency for the cell that corresponds to the Men and In Favor.

P (a person is a Man) = P(M) = 175/300
P (a person is in favor) = P(F) = 180/300

Because we are assuming that M and F are independent (by assuming that the null hypothesis is true), the joint probability of these two events is:

$$P(M \text{ and } F) = P(M) \times P(F) = \frac{175}{300} \times \frac{180}{300}$$

Then, assuming that M and F are independent, the number of persons expected to be a Man and In Favor in a sample of 300 is:

$$= 300 \times \frac{175}{300} \times \frac{180}{300} = \frac{175 \times 180}{300} = \frac{(Row\ total)(Column\ total)}{Sample\ size}$$

Thus, the rule for obtaining the expected frequency for a cell is to divide the product of corresponding row and column totals by the sample size.

Expected Frequencies for a Test of Independence

$$E = \frac{(Row\ total)(Column\ total)}{Sample\ size}$$

Using this rule, we calculate the expected frequencies of the six cells:

Men and In favor cell E $= \dfrac{(102)(180)}{300} = 59.00$

Men and Against cell E $= \dfrac{(175)(180)}{300} = 105$

E for Men and No opinion $= \dfrac{(175)(18)}{300} = 10.50$

E for Women and In Favor cell $= \dfrac{(125)(102)}{300} = 42.50$

E for Woman and Against cell $= \dfrac{(125)(180)}{300} = 75.00$

E for Woman and No opinion cell $= \dfrac{(125)(18)}{300} = 7.5$

Table 13.9.

	In Favor of Closing the Local Library	Against	No Opinion	Total
Men (M)	70	93	12	175
	−59.5	−105	−10.5	
Women (W)	32	87	32	125
	−42.5	−75	−7.5	
Total	102	180	18	300

As a result, like a goodness-of-fit test, a test of independence is *always right-tailed*. To apply a chi-square test of independence, the sample size should be large enough so that the expected frequency for each cell is at least equal to 5. If the expected frequency for a cell is not at least 5, we either increase the sample size or combine the categories.

So, does the sample we examined provide sufficient evidence to conclude that the two characteristics, gender and opinions, of adults are dependent using 1% significance level? In order to pursue this question, we follow five steps.

Step 1.
    State the null and alternative hypothesis.

H_0: Gender and opinions of adults are independent
H_1: Gender and opinions of adults are dependent

Step 2.
    Select the distribution to use.
    We use the chi-square distribution to make a test of independence for a contingency table.

Step 3.
    Determine the rejection and non-rejection regions.
    The significance level is 1%. The contingency table contains two rows (Men and Women) and three columns (In Favor, Against, No opinion). Note that we do not count the row and column of totals. The degrees of freedom are:

$$df = (R - 1)(C - 1) = (2 - 1)(3 - 1) = 2$$

To test the value of the test statistics χ^2 for a test of independence, we will use the following formula:

$$\chi^2 = \sum \frac{(O-E)^2}{E}$$

$$= \frac{(70-59.50)^2}{59.50} + \frac{(93-105)^2}{105} + \frac{(12-10.5)^2}{10.50} + \frac{(32-42.5)^2}{42.5} + \frac{(97-75)^2}{75} + \frac{(32-42.50)^2}{42.5}$$

$$= 1.371 + 1.853 + 0.214 + 1.920 + 2.594 + 0.300 = 8.252$$

So, the value of χ^2 is equal to 8.252, less than the critical value of $\chi^2 = 9.210$, and it falls in the non-rejection region. Here, we fail to reject the null hypothesis and state that there is not enough evidence from the sample to conclude that the two characteristics, gender and opinion of adults, are dependent for this issue.

Conducting chi-square in R

The code in R for chi-square is

```
chisq.test(x, y = NULL, correct = TRUE,
p = rep(1/length(x), length(x)), rescale.p = FALSE,
simulate.p.value = FALSE, B = 2000)
```

This function is used for both the goodness-of-fit test and the test of independence, and it does depend upon what kind of data you feed it. If "x" is a numerical vector or a one-dimensional table of numerical values, a goodness-of-fit test will be done (or attempted), treating "x" as a vector of observed frequencies. If "x" is a 2-D table, array, or matrix, then it is assumed to be a contingency table of frequencies, and a test of independence will be done.

Example:
Professor Smith takes a random sample of students enrolled in statistics in Library 101 at ABC University. He finds the following: there are 25 freshman, 32 sophomores, 18 juniors, and 20 seniors. Test the null hypothesis that freshman, sophomores, juniors, and seniors are equally represented among students signed up for Stat in Library 101.

This is a goodness-of-fit test with equal expected frequencies. The "p" vector does not need to be specified, since equal frequencies is the default:

```
> chisq.test(c(25,32,18,20))
```

Chi-square test for given probabilities:

```
data: c(25, 32, 18, 20)
X-squared = 4.9158, df = 3, p-value = 0.1781
```

You could also have begun by assigning the observed frequencies to a vector and then named the vector "x":

```
> ofs <- c(25,32,18,20)
> chisq.test(ofs)
```

Chi-square test for given probabilities:

```
data: ofs
X-squared = 4.9158, df = 3, p-value = 0.1781
```

Either way, the null hypothesis cannot be rejected at α = .05.

The University Administration argues that Professor Smith is wrong, and that the number of freshman and sophomores enrolled is twice the number of juniors and the number of seniors. Test the Administration's hypothesis from these same data.

Now the expected frequencies are no longer equal, so a "p" vector must be specified. A little algebra leads us to the expected probabilities of 1/3, 1/3, 1/6, and 1/6. Since these numbers are awkward to enter as decimal numbers, they are best entered as fractions, letting R do the arithmetic for us:

```
  null.probs <- c(1/3,1/3,1/6,1/6)
> chisq.test(ofs, p=null.probs)
```

Chi-square test for given probabilities:

```
data: ofs
X-squared = 2.8, df = 3, p-value = 0.4235
```

A warning: since R does not expect the "p" vector to come second inside the chisq.test( ) function, it must be given its correct name, "p=." It doesn't appear that we can reject the Administration's null hypothesis either.

The chi-square distribution is a continuous probability distribution which is being used here as an approximation to the discrete case. To be an accurate approximation, the expected frequencies must be sufficiently large. R will issue a warning message if any of the EFs fall below 5, but it's good practice to check them nevertheless. This leads us to a device we will use often in future tutorials—storing the output of an R procedure to a data object and then extracting the information we want. Usually, the printed output of an R procedure is only a small part of what R has calculated. Here's how to see more:

```
> chisq.test(ofs, p=null.probs) -> results
> results
```

Chi-square test for given probabilities:

```
data: ofs
X-squared = 2.8, df = 3, p-value = 0.4235
> results$expected
[1] 31.66667 31.66667 15.83333 15.83333
> results$residuals
[1] -1.18469776 0.05923489 0.54451008 1.04713477
```

The "results" object now contains a list of the stuff R has calculated. To see what is in the list, see the section headed "Value" on the help page for the `chisq.test( )` function. The query `results$expected` showed the expected frequencies under the null hypothesis. The query `results$residuals` showed the unsquared chi values in each cell, allowing us to see where the biggest deviations are from frequencies the null predicted.

Data.frame. A typical dataset contains data of different modes. A data.frame is a list of variables of the same numbers of rows with unique row names, given class "data.frame."

Data.frames can be created in R with the `data.frame()` function by passing in an arbitrary number of same-length vectors as arguments. For example, score and gender are two datasets that the `data.frame` can join them together.

```
> score <- c("M", "M", "F", "F", "F")
>gender <- c(47, 83, 98, 76, 39)
>info <- data.frame(gender.score)
> info
  score gender
1 47    M
2 83    M
3 98    F
4 76    F
5 39    F
```

In the following example, we use the package called MASS that will provide us with a built-in dataset.

To install the package, type:

```
> install.packages("MASS").
```

To open the package library, type:

> library(MASS).

If a data.frame contains categorical data in one variable, it can be extracted into a 1-D frequency table using the `table( )` function:

```
> data(survey,package="MASS")
> str(survey)
'data.frame': 237 obs. of 12 variables:
$ Sex : Factor w/ 2 levels "Female", "Male": 1 2 2 2 2
1 2 1 2 2 ...
$ Wr.Hnd: num 18.5 19.5 18 18.8 20 18 17.7 17 20 18.5
...
$ NW.Hnd: num 18 20.5 13.3 18.9 20 17.7 17.7 17.3 19.5
18.5 ...
$ W.Hnd : Factor w/ 2 levels "Left","Right": 2 1 2 2 2
2 2 2 2 2 ...
$ Fold : Factor w/ 3 levels "L on R","Neither",..: 3 3
1 3 2 1 1 3 3 3 ...
$ Pulse : int 92 104 87 NA 35 64 83 74 72 90 ...
$ Clap : Factor w/ 3 levels "Left","Neither",..: 1 1 2
2 3 3 3 3 3 3 ...
$ Exer : Factor w/ 3 levels "Freq","None",..: 3 2 2 2 3
3 1 1 3 3 ...
$ Smoke : Factor w/ 4 levels "Heavy","Never",..: 2 4 3
2 2 2 2 2 2 2 ...
$ Height: num 173 178 NA 160 165 ...
$ M.I : Factor w/ 2 levels "Imperial","Metric": 2 1 NA
2 2 1 1 2 2 2 ...
$ Age : num 18.2 17.6 16.9 20.3 23.7 ...
> table(survey$Smoke)
Heavy Never Occas Regul
11 189 19 17
> table(survey$Smoke)->smokers
> smokers
Heavy Never Occas Regul
11 189 19 17
```

These are the responses of 237 statistics students at the University of Adelaide to a number of questions. The "Smoke" variable contains their responses to a question about smoking habits and resulted in each student being classified into one of four categories: Never, Occasional, Regular, and Heavy. We have extracted these data and have placed them into a 1-D table of frequencies called "smokers." This table can now be subjected to any reasonable (or even unreasonable) goodness-of-fit test. For example, we can test the null hypothesis that 70% of statistics students are nonsmokers and that the other 30% are divided equally among the remaining categories. The only thing we have to be careful of is that our null probabilities are given in the same order as the frequencies are given in the "smokers" table:

```
> chisq.test(smokers, p=c(.1, .7, .1, .1))
chi-square test for given probabilities
data: smokers
X-squared = 12.8983, df = 3, p-value = 0.004862
> chisq.test(smokers, p=c(.1, .7, .1, .1))$resid
Heavy Never Occas Regul
-2.593669 1.851706 -0.946895 -1.358588
```

The hypothesis is rejected. It appears in particular that we have very much overestimated the percentage of "Heavy" smokers. Now, there are two more things. One, the last part of this example shows that we do not need to store the output of the procedure to request residuals. All we need to do is attach $resid on the end of the command. We could have done the same with $expected or any other element of the outputted results. Also demonstrated is the convenient fact that, if we are too lazy to type the entire word "residuals," we can use just enough of it that R is able to recognize what we are asking.

13.8 Summary

We began with a review of the difference between the point estimate and the interval estimate and its connection to sampling statistics. We also introduced several other terminologies including degree of freedom and the F distribution. Then, we looked closely at one-way and two-way ANOVA. We also explored the two uses of chi-square with regard to goodness-of-fit and test for independence. We saw that the chi-square is based on the difference between the observed and expected frequencies.

13.9 Glossary

ANOVA—The analysis of variance.

confidence interval—Used to express the precision and uncertainty associated with a particular sampling method, the confidence interval consists of the confidence level, the statistic, and a margin of error.

confidence level—A term to describe the uncertainty of a sampling method.

contingency table—Data that is presented, sorted, and organized in a matrix format.

degree of association—Amount of information provided by the researcher to assess the magnitude of the relationship between two or more variables.

degree of freedom—Representation of the number of independent values in a calculation, minus the number of estimated parameters.

estimation—Process by which one makes inferences about a population based on information obtained from a sample.

_F_ distribution—The distribution of all possible values of the _f_ statistic.

F test—Statistical assessment in which the _test statistic_ has an _F_ distribution under the null hypothesis.

goodness-of-fit test—Trial to show how well your random data fits within the distribution you have selected.

interval estimate—Range of values, defined by two numbers, between which a population parameter is said to lie, as $a < x < b$.

margin of error—Representation, usually in a confidence interval, of the range of values above and below the sample statistic that may contain the correct values.

MS(W)—Mean square within groups.

point estimate—A single value, a statistic, of a sample parameter such as a population.

SS(B)—Sum of squares between groups.

SS(W)—Sum of squares within groups.

sum of squares—A value calculated when each datum first is compared to the others through the value of the mean to reveal its deviation from the mean; second, this deviation is then squared to negate the minus values, then finally all of these values are totaled together.

13.10 References

Box, G. E. P. 1953. "Non-normality and Tests on Variances." *Biometrika* 40: 318–35.

Fisher, R. A. 1922. "On the Mathematical Foundations of Theoretical Statistics." *Philosophical Transactions of the Royal Society of London. Series A, Containing Papers of a Mathematical or Physical Character.* 309–68. "New Data on the Genesis of Twins." *Eugen. Rev.* 14, 115–17.

Powell, R. R., L. M. Baker, and J. J. Mika. 2002. "Library and Information Science Practitioners and Research." *Library & Information Science Research* 24: 49–72.

Zar, J. H. 2010) *Biostatistical Analysis.* 5th ed. Upper Saddle River, NJ: Prentice-Hall.

CHAPTER 14

Time Series and Predictive Analysis

14.1 Introduction to Time Series
14.2 The Goal of Time Series Analysis
14.3 Identifying Data Patterns in Time Series
    14.3.1 Systematic Patterns and Random Noise
    14.3.2 Two General Aspects of Time Series Patterns
    14.3.3 Trend Analysis
    14.3.4 Smoothing
14.4 Least Square Method
14.5 Forecast Using Time Series Models
    14.5.1 Introduction
    14.5.2 Time Series and Forecasting
    14.5.3 Forecasting Method
    14.5.4 Forecasting Errors
    14.5.5 Power System Load Forecasting
    14.5.6 Time Series Model
    14.5.7 Linear Regression Method
14.6 Summary
14.7 Glossary
14.8 Reference

14.1 Introduction to Time Series

Time series models have been the basis for any study of a behavior or metrics over a period of time. In decisions that involve a factor of uncertainty about the future, time series models have been found to be one of the most effective methods of forecasting. We often encounter different time series models in sales forecasting, weather forecasting, inventory studies, and so on. In the field of information science, Jeong and Kim (2010) reviewed a selected annotated bibliography of core books in order to conduct a time series analysis. Based on their analysis, they developed a strategy of scholarly resources. They then classified each category into subfields in order to develop future techniques to support teaching and conducting research by librarians, students, and faculty. In their study, they employed the exponential *trend* model. In this chapter, we will cover different methods and applications. We will use R to help us illustrate those models.

In order to fully understand the essence of the time series, we will first illustrate its impact. Often the first step in a time series analysis is to plot the data and observe any patterns that might occur over time by using a plot. This helps us to determine whether there appears to be a long-term upward or downward movement or whether the series seems to vary around a horizontal line over time. The following scenario will show how the plot illustrates the direction of data. In this example, we follow the number of books borrowed from the library from 1982 to 2014 as found in the public library log in New York City.

In R:

The spreadsheet for this dataset is located on the book website (www. statisticsforlis.org). You will need to download the file located in the library for chapter 14 found on the book website. The title of the file is: library_borrowing.csv.

Then, you will need to import the file to your R:

```
> library_borrowing <-read.csv("C:/library.borrowing",
header=T, dec=",",
sep=";")
```

Note that paths use slashes "/" instead of backslashes.

Future options within this command include **header** and **dec**, which specify if the dataset has the first row containing column-names (**header=T**, but in case one does not have a naming row, one would use **header=F** instead). The option **dec** sets the decimal separator used in case it differs from a point (in the file above, a comma is used as a decimal separator).

Next, the library_borrowing is stored as a matrix-object with the name *library_borrowing*. In order to access particular elements of objects, square

Table 14.1.

	Year	Number of Books Borrowed from the Library
1	1982	1558
2	1983	1564
3	1984	1407
4	1985	1309
5	1986	1424
6	1987	1321
7	1988	1543
8	1989	1321
9	1990	1488
10	1991	1562
11	1992	1618
12	1993	1686
13	1994	1840
14	1995	1865
15	1996	1636
16	1997	1652
17	1998	1453
18	1999	1698
19	2000	1523
20	2001	1437
21	2002	1387
22	2003	1312
23	2004	1212
24	2005	1201
25	2006	1012
26	2007	1009
27	2008	1001
28	2009	999
29	2010	1764
30	2011	1675
31	2012	1218
30	2013	1212
33	2014	1200
Sum		47101

brackets ([]) are used. Rows and columns of matrices can be accessed with object {rowm colum].

A chart with closing values can be created using the plot command:

```
> plot(library_borrowing[, 5], type= "1")
```

The `plot` () command allows for a number of optional arguments, one of which is `type="1,"` which sets the plot type to "lines." Graphic comments allow for a variety of additional options, for example:

```
plot(library_borrowing[, 5], type="1", lowd=2,
col="red", xlab=Years", ylab="Number of books",
main="Number of books borrowed from the library" xl)
```

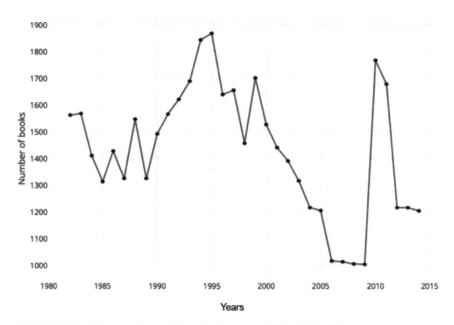

Figure 14.1. The number of books borrowed from the library.

As we can see, this illustration provides an indication and direction of the decline of book borrowing from the library. This trend started in 2000 and stopped in 2010.

Decline and growth are often used in illustrations of time series plots. The subject of long-term growth movement and downward movement is illustrated more clearly in figure 14.2 and figure 14.1. In figure 14.2, the long growth movement is illustrated. All the plots show growth.

In comparison, downward movement provides the opposite direction of the growth we saw in the previous plot. In this case, more than one plot shows the downward fall.

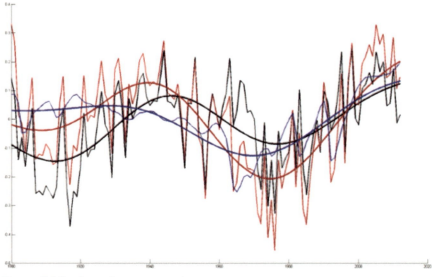

Figure 14.2. Long-term upward.

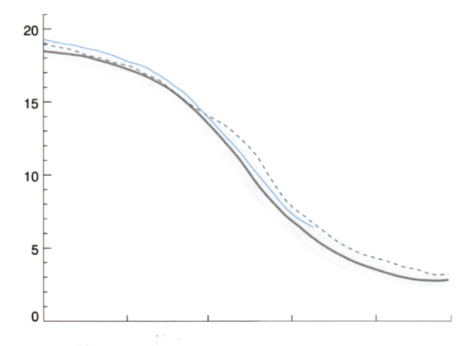

Figure 14.3. Downward movement.

The definition of time series is a collection of data obtained by observing a response variable at periodic points in time.

14.2 The Goal of Time Series Analysis

The goal of the time series can simply be classified as five major objectives:

1. Descriptive: identifying patterns in correlated data—trends and seasonal variations
2. Explanation: understanding and modeling the data
3. Forecasting: prediction of short-term trends from previous patterns
4. Intervention analysis: discovering if a single event changes the time series
5. Quality control: deviations of a specified size indicate a problem

Time series are analyzed in order to understand the underlying structure and function that produce the observations. Understanding the mechanisms of a time series allows a mathematical model to be developed that explains the data in such a way that prediction, monitoring, or control can occur. An example is prediction/forecasting, which is widely used in economics and business. Monitoring of ambient conditions, or of an input or an output, is common in science and industry. Quality control is used in computer science, communications, and industry.

The dataset inside the time series is often assumed to have at least one systematic pattern. The most common patterns are trends and seasonality. Trends are generally linear or quadratic. To find trends, regression analysis is often used. Seasonality is a trend that repeats itself systematically over time. A second assumption is that the data exhibit enough of a random process so that it is hard to identify the systematic patterns within the data. Time series analysis techniques often employ some type of filter to the data in order to dampen the error. Other potential patterns have to do with lingering effects of earlier observations or earlier random errors.

The type of variables used in time analysis can be either discrete or continuous. Both types of variables/observations can be equally spaced, unequally spaced, or have missing data. Discrete measurements can be recorded at any time interval, but are most often taken at evenly spaced intervals. Continuous measurements can be spaced randomly in time, such as measuring how often users borrow books from the library; can entail constant measurement of this phenomenon such as temperature in the library building; or a process such as visiting the library catalog or Facebook.

Time series are also very complex, because each observation is somewhat dependent upon the previous observation and often is influenced by more than one previous observation. As a result, random error is also influential from one observation to another. These influences are called *autocorrelation*—dependent relationships between successive observations of the same variable. The challenge of time series analysis is to extract the autocorrelation elements of the data, either to understand the trend itself or to model the underlying mechanisms.

14.3 Identifying Data Patterns in Time Series

As we observed in our example of the book borrowing patterns across time as illustrated in figure 14.1, we identified four types of data patterns. Those patterns include: (1) systematic pattern and random noise, (2) two general aspects of time series patterns (seasonal and cyclical), (3) trends, and (4) smoothing.

14.3.1 SYSTEMATIC PATTERNS AND RANDOM NOISE

Under this data pattern, the formula is:

$$Y_t = (\text{systematic})_t + (\text{random})_t$$
Yt, where t represents time

As in most other analyses, in time series analysis it is assumed that the data consists of a systematic pattern (usually a set of identifiable components) and random noise (error), which usually makes the pattern difficult to identify. Most time series analysis techniques involve some form of filtering out of noise in order to make the pattern more salient.

14.3.2 TWO GENERAL ASPECTS OF TIME SERIES PATTERNS

Under two general aspects of time series, four patterns are included that have often been discussed: trend, seasonal, cyclical, and random. The formula representing this is:

$$Y_t = (\text{Trend})_t + (\text{Seasonal})_t + (\text{cyclical})_t + (\text{random})_t$$

Most time series patterns can be described in terms of two basic classes of components: trend and seasonality. The former represents a general systematic linear or (most often) nonlinear component that changes over time and does not repeat or at least does not repeat within the time range captured by the data (e.g., a plateau followed by a period of exponential growth). The latter may have a formally similar nature (e.g., a plateau followed by a period of exponential growth); however, it repeats itself in systematic intervals over time. Those two general classes of time series components may coexist in real-life data. For example, in the business world, sales of a company can rapidly grow over the years, but still follow consistent seasonal patterns, for example, as much as 25% of yearly sales each year are made in December, whereas only 4% in August.

14.3.3 TREND ANALYSIS

The term *trend* is a long-term movement in a time series. It is the underlying direction (an upward or downward tendency) and rate of change in a time series, when allowance has been made for the other components. A simple way of detecting trends in seasonal data is to take averages over a certain period. If these averages change with time, we can say that there is evidence of a trend in the series. There are also more formal tests to enable detection of trends in time series.

Under trend analysis, there are no proven automatic techniques to identify trend components in the time series data; however, as long as the trend is monotonous, consistently increasing or decreasing, that part of data analysis is typically not very difficult. If the time series data contain considerable error, then the first step in the process of trend identification is smoothing.

14.3.4 SMOOTHING

Smoothing always involves some form of local averaging of data such that the nonsystematic components (variations away from main trend) of individual observations cancel each other out. The most common technique is *moving average* smoothing, which replaces each element of the series by either the simple or weighted average of n surrounding elements, where n is the width of the smoothing "window." All those methods will filter out the noise and convert the data into a smooth curve that is relatively unbiased by outliers.

14.4 Least Square Method

Among the methods for fitting a straight line to a series of data, this is the one used most frequently. The equation of a straight line is $Y = a + bx$ where x is the time period, say year, and Y is the value of the item measured against time, a is the Y intercept, and b is the coefficient of x indicating slope of the trend line.

In order to find a and b, the following two equations are solved:

$$\sum Y = ax + b \sum x$$
$$\sum XY = a \sum x + b \sum x^2$$

Example:

Old number of years:

Table 14.2.

Year	Old Number of Years
1996	270
1997	285
1998	295
1999	315
2000	330

The linear line graph to this data:

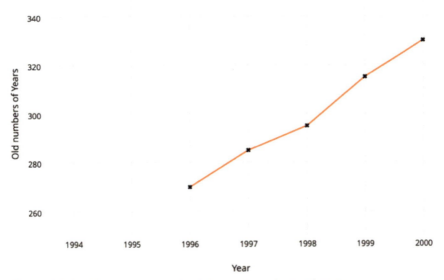

Figure 14.4. Linear line graph of the old numbers of years.

Next, fit a linear trend to these data using the least square method.

Solution:

Table 14.3.

Year	X	Y	XY	χ^2
1996	-2	270	-540	4
1997	-1	285	-285	1
1998	0	295	0	0
1999	1	315	315	1
2000	2	330	-660	4
Total	$0 = \Sigma x$	$1,495 = \Sigma y$	$150 = \Sigma x\,y$	$10 = \Sigma x^2$

Substituting these values in two normal equations, we get

$1495 = 5a + b\,(0)$ (1)
$150 = a\,(0) + b\,(10)$ (2)

Equation (1) gives a = 1,495/5 = 299
Equation (2) gives b = 150/10 = 15
The straight line trend is:

$Y = 299 + 15x$ (origin: year 1998)
                      (x = 1 – year unit)

Let's now examine even number of years:

Table 14.4.

Year	1985	1986	1987	1988	1989	1990
Y	15	14	18	20	17	24

Fit a trend to these data using the least square method.

Solution:

Table 14.5.

Year	X	Y	XY	χ^2
1995	-5	15	-75	25
1996	-3	14	-42	9
1997	-1	18	-18	1
1988	1	20	20	1
1989	3	17	51	9
1990	5	24	120	25
Total	$0 = \Sigma x$	$108 = \Sigma y$	$50 = \Sigma x\,y$	$75 = \Sigma x^2$

Two normal equations are:

$$\Sigma Y = an + b \Sigma x$$
$$\Sigma XY = a\Sigma x + b\Sigma x^2$$

Substituting the values in the two equations, we get

$$108 = 6a + b\ (0) \tag{1}$$
$$56 = a(0) + b\ (70) \tag{2}$$

Solving, we get a = 108/6 = 18

And   b = 56/70 = 0.8

The trend equation is Y = 18 +0.8 x

Origin year: Mid of 1987-88
Unit of X = ½ year

Note: (1) In putting values of x for different years we get values of y, which are trend values (y). (2) For forecasting, calculate the value of x for a given future year and substitute the value of x in the trend equation to get the forecasted value.

Fitting of a parabolic trend by the method of least squares. Let Y_t be the value of the time series at time *t*. Thus Y_t is the independent variable depending on *t*.

Assume a parabolic trend to be of the form $Y_{tc} = a + bt + ct^2$ $\tag{1}$

Note: The values of *a*, *b*, and *c* are estimated from the given time series data by the method of *least squares*.

In this method we have to find out *a*, *b*, and *c* values such that the sum of the squares of the deviations of the actual values Y_t and the computed values Y_{tc} is least.

$$S = \Sigma(Y_t - Y_{tc})^2 \text{ should be least} \tag{1}$$
$$S = \Sigma(Y_t - a - bt - ct^2)^2 \text{ should be least} \tag{2}$$

Now differentiating partially (2) w.r.t. *a* and equating to zero we get:

$$\frac{\partial S}{\partial a} = 2\sum(Y_t - a - bt - ct^2)(-1) = 0$$
$$\Rightarrow \Sigma(Y_t - a - bt - ct^2) = 0$$
$$\Rightarrow \Sigma Y_t = \Sigma a + b\Sigma t - c\Sigma t^2$$
$$\Rightarrow \Sigma Y_t = na + b\Sigma t + c\Sigma t^2 \tag{3}$$

Now differentiating partially (2) w.r.t. b and equating to zero we get:

$$\frac{\partial S}{\partial b} = 2\Sigma(Y_t - a - bt - ct^2) \ (-t) = 0$$
$$\Rightarrow \Sigma t(Y_t - a - bt - ct^2) = 0$$
$$\Rightarrow \Sigma tY_t - a\Sigma t - b\Sigma t^2 - c\Sigma t^3 \qquad\qquad (4)$$

Now differentiating partially (2) w.r.t. c and equating to zero we get

$$\frac{\partial S}{\partial b} = 2\Sigma(Y_t - a - bt - ct^2) \ (-t) = 0$$

$$\Rightarrow \Sigma t(Y_t - a - bt - ct^2) = 0$$
$$\Rightarrow \Sigma t^2 Y_t - a\Sigma t^2 - b\Sigma t^3 - c\Sigma t^4 \qquad\qquad (5)$$

Equations (3), (4) and (5) are called *normal equations.*

Solving these three equations, we get the values of a, b, and c say $\hat{a}$, $\hat{b}$, and $\hat{c}$.

Now putting these three values in equation (1) we get:

$$Ytc = \hat{a} + \hat{b}t + \hat{c}t^2$$

which is the required parabolic trend equation.

Note: The method for assessing the appropriateness of the second-degree equation is the *method of second differences.* If the differences are taken of the first differences and the results are constant (nearly constant), the second-degree equation can be taken to be an appropriate representation of the trend component.

In R:

Based on the first example:

```
> time <- c(1986, 1987, 1988, 1989, 1999)
>number <- c(270, 285, 295, 315, 330)
> res=lm(time~number)
> res=lm(time~number)
> res
```

Call:

```
lm(formula = time ~ number)
```

Coefficients:

(Intercept)   number
1933.293   0.189

14.5 Forecast Using Time Series Models

14.5.1 INTRODUCTION

Predictions of future events and conditions are called *forecasts*, and the act of making such predictions is called *forecasting*. Forecasting is a key element of decision making. Its purpose is to reduce the risk in decision making and reduce unexpected cost in the business world.

Power system load forecasting can be categorized into long-term and short-term functions. Long-term load forecasting usually covers from one to ten years ahead (monthly and yearly values) and is explicitly intended for applications in capacity expansion and long-term capital investment return studies.

The short-term forecast requires knowledge of the load from one hour up to a few days. Information derived from the short-term load forecasts is vital to the system as operations in terms of short-term unit maintenance work; weekly, daily, and hourly load scheduling of generating units; and economic and secure operation of power systems. In this chapter, we will mainly focus on short-term load forecasting with mathematical methods. First, we introduce some basic foundations.

14.5.2 TIME SERIES AND FORECASTING

Time series can be defined as a sequential set of data measured over time, such as the hourly, daily, or weekly peak load. The basic idea of forecasting is to first build a pattern matching available data as accurately as possible, then obtain the forecasted value with respect to time using the established model.

Generally, series are often described as having the following characteristic:

$$X(t) = T(t) + S(t) + R(t) \quad t = \ldots -1, 0, 1, 2, \ldots \tag{1}$$

Here, $T(t)$ is the trend term, $S(t)$ the seasonal term, and $R(t)$ is the irregular or random component. At this moment, we do not consider the cyclic terms since these fluctuations can have a duration from two to ten years or even longer, which is not applicable to short-term load forecasting.

We have made some assumptions to make things a little easier for the moment:

1. The trend is a constant level.
2. The seasonal effect has a period s, that is, it repeats after s time periods, or the sum of the seasonal components over a complete cycle or period is zero.

$$\sum_{j=1}^{s} S(t + j) = 0 \tag{2}$$

14.5.3 FORECASTING METHOD

Until now, many forecasting methods have been utilized, classified into two basic types: *qualitative* and *quantitative* methods.

Qualitative forecasting methods generally use the opinions of experts to predict future loads subjectively. Such methods are useful when historical data are not available or are scarce. These methods include subjective curve fitting, Delphi method, and technological comparisons.

Quantitative methods include regression analysis, decomposition methods, exponential smoothing, and the Box-Jenkins methodology.

14.5.4 FORECASTING ERRORS

Unfortunately, all forecasting situations involve some degree of uncertainty, which makes error unavoidable.

The forecast error for a particular forecast $\hat{X}_t$ with respect to actual value X_t is:

$$e_t = X_t - \hat{X}_t \tag{3}$$

To avoid the offset of positive with negative errors, we need to use the *absolute deviations*.

$$| e_t | = | X_t - \hat{X}_t | \tag{4}$$

Hence, we can define a measure known as the mean absolute deviation (MAD) as follows:

$$MAD = \frac{\sum_{t=1}^{n} |e_t|}{n} = \frac{\sum_{t=1}^{n} |X_t - \hat{X}_t|}{n} \tag{5}$$

Another method is to use the mean squared error (MSE), defined as follows:

$$MSE = \frac{\sum_{i=1}^{n} e_t^2}{n} = \frac{\sum_{i=1}^{n} (X_t - \hat{X}_t)^2}{n} \tag{6}$$

14.5.5 POWER SYSTEM LOAD FORECASTING

The power system load is assumed to be time dependent, evolving according to a probabilistic law. It is common practice to employ a white noise sequence as an input to a linear filter whose output is the power system load. This is an adequate model for predicting the load time series. The noise input is assumed normally distributed with zero mean and some variance σ^2. A number of classes of models exist for characterizing the linear filter.

14.5.6 TIME SERIES MODEL

A time series is a sequence of observations of a random variable. It provides tools for selecting a model that can be used to forecast of future events. Let's take the following example, where we collected the based on years (2010, 2011, 2012, 2013, 1214) and times.

A simple example:

Table 14.6.

Year	1	2	3	4
2010	874	679	616	816
2011	866	700	603	814
2012	843	719	594	819
2013	906	703	634	844
2014	952	745	635	871
Means	888.2	709.2	616.4	832.8

We can average the seasonal values over the series and use these seasonal means, minus the overall mean, as seasonal estimates (overall mean is: 761.65):

$S(1) = 888.2 - 761.65 = 126.55$ $S(2) = 709.2 - 761.65 = -52.4$
$S(3) = 616.4 - 761.65 = -145.25$ $S(4) = 832.8 - 761.65 = 71.15$

After subtraction of these values, the original series removes seasonal effects. It should be noted that this technique works well on series having linear trends with small slopes.

In addition, we can look at the averages for each complete seasonal cycle (the period) since the seasonal effect over an entire period is zero. To avoid losing too much data, a method called *moving average (MA)* is used here, which is simply the series of averages:

$$\frac{1}{s}\sum_{j=0}^{s-1} X_{t+j}, \quad \frac{1}{s}\sum_{j=1}^{s} X_{t+j}, \quad \frac{1}{s}\sum_{j=2}^{s+1} X_{t+j}, \ldots$$

A problem is presented here if the period is even, since the adjusted series values do not correspond to the original ones at time points. To overcome this problem, the *centered moving average (CMA)* is utilized to bring us back to the correct time points. It is shown in table 14.7.

Table 14.7.

Quarter	X(t)	MA	CMA(Order-2)	Difference
1	874			
2	679			
3	616	746.25	745.25	−129.25
4	816	744.25	746.875	69.125
5	866	749.5	747.875	118.125
6	700	746.25	746	−46
7	603	745.75	741.75	−138.75
8	814	737.75	740.125	73.875
9	834	742.5	741.375	92.625
10	719	740.25	740.875	−21.875
11	594	741.5	750.5	−156.5
12	819	759.5	757.5	61.5
13	906	755.5	760.5	145.5
14	703	765.5	768.625	−65.625
15	634	771.75	777.5	−143.5
16	844	783.25	788.5	55.5
17	952	793.75	793.875	158.125
18	745	794	797.375	−52.375
19	635	800.75		
20	871			

Through looking at the differences between CMA and the original series, we can estimate the *k*th seasonal effect simply by averaging the *k*th quarter differences:

$S(1) = 128.954 \quad S(2) = -46.487 \quad S(3) = -142 \quad S(4) = 65$

But the sum of these four values is: 5.107. Recall that we assume the seasonals to sum to zero, so we need to add a correction factor of $-5.107 / 4 = -1.254$ to give:

$$S(1) = 127.34 \quad S(2) = -47.741 \quad S(3) = -143.254 \quad S(4) = 63.746$$

Now the irregular component can be easily calculated by subtracting both the CMA and the seasonal effects.

If we suppose the model (1) is appropriate then we can use it to make predictions. To simplify, we omit the random data, and so all we need to do is predict the trend, say, a linear trend:

$$T(t) = a + bt$$

With the application to the CMA, we have

$$\hat{T}(t) = 713.376 + 3.647t$$

Hence, a prediction is shown in table 14.6:

Table 14.6.

Year	1	2	3	4
2010	874	679	616	816
2011	866	700	603	814
2012	843	719	594	819
2013	906	703	634	844
2014	952	745	635	871
Means	888.2	709.2	616.4	832.8

14.5.7 LINEAR REGRESSION METHOD

This method supposes that the load is affected by some factors such as high and low temperatures, weather condition, and economic growth. This relation can be expressed:

$$y = 0 + \beta_1 x_1 + \beta_2 x_2 + \ldots + \beta_k x_k + \varepsilon \tag{7}$$

where, y is the load, x_i is the affecting factors, β_i is regression parameters with respect to x_i, and ε is an error term.

For this model, we always assume that the error term ε has a mean value equal to zero and constant variance.

Since parameters β_i are unknown, they should be estimated from observations of y and x_i. Let b_i $(i=0,1,2,...k)$ be the estimates in terms of β_i $(i=0,1,2,... k)$. Recall that the error term has a 50% chance of being positive and negative, respectively, and we omit this term in calculating parameters; that means:

$$y = 0 + b_1 x_1 + b_2 x_2 + ... + \beta_k x_k \tag{8}$$

Then, we use the least square estimates method, which minimizes the sum of squared residuals (SSE) to obtain the parameters b_i:

$$\underline{B} = [b_0 \quad b_1 \quad b_2 \quad ... \quad b_k x_k] = (\underline{X}^T \underline{X} - 1) \underline{X}^T \underline{Y} \tag{9}$$

where $\underline{Y}$ and $\underline{X}$ are the following column vector and matrix:

$$\underline{Y} = \begin{bmatrix} y_1 \\ y_2 \\ \vdots \\ y_n \end{bmatrix} \quad and \quad \underline{X} = \begin{bmatrix} 1 & x_{11} & x_{12} \cdots x_{1k} \\ 1 & x_{21} & x_{22} \cdots x_{2k} \\ \vdots & \vdots & \vdots \\ 1 & x_{n1} & x_{n2} \cdots x_{nk} \end{bmatrix} \tag{10}$$

After the parameters are calculated, this model can be used for prediction. It will be accurate in predicting y values if the standard error s is small.

$$s = \sqrt{\frac{SSE}{n-(k+1)}}, \quad SSE = \sum_{i=1}^{n}(y_i - \hat{y}_i)^2, \ y_i : observed, \ \hat{y}_i : estimated \tag{11}$$

There are also some other ways to check the validity of a regression model.

14.6 Summary

In this chapter, we covered what a time series is, and we looked at the goal and data patterns in time series. We looked closely at least square methods that cover a straight line, where $Y = a + bx$. We discussed the fitting trend that least square provides. We also looked at forecasting and its methodologies for the short term.

14.7 Glossary

absolute deviations—Points that show the absolute difference between an element and a given point, which is often a central value such as a mean or a median value.

autocorrelation—Refers to the correlation of a time series with its own past and future values.

centered moving average (CMA)—A calculated value that forecasts predictions of future events and conditions.

forecasting—Indicates to the use of a model to predict future values based on previously observed values.

moving average (MA)—A calculated value that smoothes out differences by averaging a set of points.

time series—A collection of data obtained by observing a response variable at periodic points in time. If repeated observations on a variable produce a time series, the variable is called a time series variable. We use Y_i to denote the value of the variable at time i.

trend—A long-term movement in a time series.

Reference

Jeong, S. H., and S.-T. Kim. 2010. *Core Resources on Time Series Analysis for Academic Libraries: A Selected, Annotated and Bibliography.* Charleston Conference Proceedings. Purdue University Press.

## PART III

VISUALIZATION IN R

CHAPTER 15

Visualization Display

15.1   Introduction to Visualization in R

15.2   What Is Visualization?

15.3   Tufte's Three Important Principles of Visualization

15.4   Colors

15.5   Symbols

15.6   Plotting Symbols

15.7   Pie in R

15.8   Using Custom Colors To Fill the Pie

15.9   Plot in R

15.10   Histograms in R

15.11   Saving Your Plot

15.12   Saving Your File

15.13   Summary

15.14   Glossary

15.15   References

15.1 Introduction to Visualization in R

One of the most engaging things about R is its ability to create powerful visualizations based on its statistical analysis with just a couple of lines of code. This chapter focuses on visualization using R. We will first introduce the subject of visualization and discuss the main milestones in the field. Then, we will move on to how to generate visualization.

15.2 What Is Visualization?

Visualization is the study of representation. According to Segal and Heer (2013), the primary goal of visualization is based on taking statistical analysis and communicating the result of the data clearly and efficiently. Effective visualization representation helps users in reasoning about data and its evidence by making complex data more accessible, understandable, and usable. You can visualize data in many different ways, from simple bar charts to more complex scatterplots, thematic maps, and pyramids.

The history of visualization started before the use of computers and machines. The most famous example of visualization in history is based on the work of Charles Joseph Minard (1781–1870). He captured Napoleon's failure to invade Russia in 1812. One of the leading scholars in the history of visualization, Friendly (2002) reports that in this visualization Minard:

- Forces visual comparisons (the upper lighter band showing the large army going to Moscow versus the narrow dark band showing the small army returning).
- Shows causality (the temperature chart at the bottom).
- Captures multivariate variables including size of army, location, direction, temperature, and time.
- Integrates text and graphics into a coherent whole.
- Illustrates high-quality content (complete and accurate data, presented to support Minard's argument against war).
- Places comparisons adjacent to each other, not sequentially.

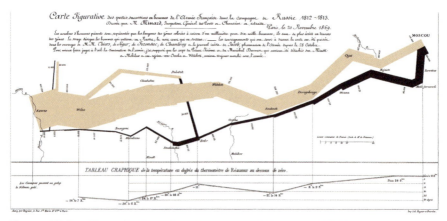

Figure 15.1. Minard's Napoleon invasion of Russia in 1812.

Many scholars have examined Minard's work, including Wainer (2000), Robinson (1967), and Shaw and Tig (1944), however, the scholar who receives the most attention is Edward Tufte (1990 and 1997). He examined Minard's work by looking at the history of visualization, where he called this piece "the best graphic ever produced." In his examination of the history of visualization, Tufte makes a direct connection between qualitative statistics and visualization. "At their best, graphics are instruments for reasoning about quantitative information" (Tufte, 1997). He finds that historical visualization was based on statistical and math analysis that was incorporated into visualization. He later presented the idea of providing more guidelines on how visualization can be displayed. His principles were written primarily for printed graphics (Tufte, 2006). However, many researchers claim that Tufte's guidelines are also valid for computer-generated images (Few, 2009).

15.3 Tufte's Three Important Principles of Visualization

1. 3D vs. 2D
2. Micro/macro reading
3. Layering and separation

The first principle addresses the problem of projecting 3D (or higher) data and objects onto a 2D surface. Tufte (1997) and Few (2013) argue the use of 3D display often creates distractions for the viewer. As a result, the viewer does not pay attention to the details of the visualization.

In the second principle, micro/macro readings, Tufte addresses the issue of information overload and the misconception (in his view) that data must be simplified. As a result, the principle shows how the addition of appropriate detail can enhance understanding and that simpler is not always better. According to Tufte, the key to good data graphics is "maximize the data ink ratio." That is, effective graphics show a lot of data with only a little ink.

The third principle, layering and separation, discusses how the use of color or grey scale and line density can be used to enhance information.

15.4 Colors

The problem of choosing colors for data and information visualization is expressed well by Tufte: "avoiding catastrophe becomes the first principle in bringing color to information: Above all, do no harm" (Tufte, 1997).

Color used well can enhance and clarify a presentation. Color used poorly will obscure, muddle, and confuse. While there is a strong aesthetic component to color, using color well in information and data display is essentially about function: what information are you trying to convey, and how (or whether) color can enhance it.

While we can create visualizations with any visualization software that is available on the market, in R we can create visualizations with just a few lines of code. For example, it takes just one line of code—and a short one at that—to plot two variables in a scatterplot.

Let's use as an example the mtcars dataset installed with R by default. Let's use an an example the mtcars data set installed with the R by default. This dataset was extracted from the 1974 *Motor Trend* US magazine, and comprises fuel consumption and 10 aspects of automobile design and performance for 32 automobiles (1973–74 models). Mtcars data set consist of data frame with 32 observations on 11 variables. To plot the engine displacement column *disp* on the x axis and *mpg* on y:

In R:

```
> plot(mtcars$disp, mtcars$mpg)
```

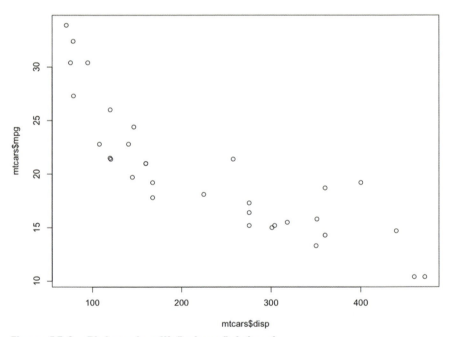

Figure 15.2. Plot made with "mtcars" dataset.

There are three types of colors in R:

1. Hexadecimal colors (#rrggbb)
2. Named colors
3. Integers referring to positions in the current color palette

1. Hexadecimal colors.

Hexadecimal colors are based on a place-value notation method of representing colors by encoding numbers. It uses 16 distinct symbols, most often the symbols *0–9* to represent values 0 to 9, and *A, B, C, D, E, F* (or alternatively *a–f*) to represent values 10 to 15. Hexadecimal numerals are widely used by computer system designers and programmers. Several different notations are used to represent hexadecimal constants in computing languages; the prefix "0x" is widespread due to its use in UNIX and C (and related operating systems and languages). Hexadecimal colors are the three- or six-character codes that are often used in HTML to tell the browser what colors to display. R also uses the hexadecimal codes. These are represented as strings of six characters. Red, green, and blue components are specified as two hexadecimal digits (0–9, A–F), in the form #rrggbb. Specify a hexadecimal color as a parameter by placing the name within quotes, such as `barplot(1, axes=FALSE, col="#4682B4")`.

The hexadecimal for 24-bit contains 256^3 colors = 15,555,216 colors overall. Figure 15.3 represents the hexadecimal color #4682B4. In this example, the color of the barplot takes the form `#rrggbbaa.barplot(Exadecimal colors example col=#FFFF00, axes=FALSE, col="#4682B433")`

In R:

```
> example <- c(5, 6, 5, 9, 11, 13, 14, 21, 9, 5)
> barplot(example, axes=FALSE, col="#4682B4",
main="Hexadecimal colors example col=#4682B4")
```

Hexadecimal colors example col=#4682B4

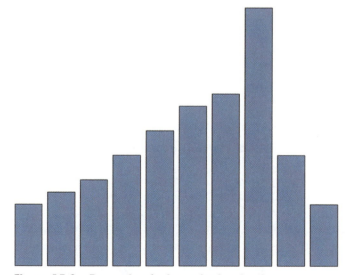

Figure 15.3. Example of a hexadecimal color.

2. Named colors.

R can interpret hundreds of named colors, such as "plum" and "seagreen" as hexadecimal colors. To see the full list of 655 named colors use the command colors(). Here is part of the 655 colors that can be produced under R:

```
> colors()
  [1] "white"              "aliceblue"          "antiquewhite"
  [6] "antiquewhite3"      "antiquewhite4"      "aquamarine"
 [11] "aquamarine3"        "aquamarine4"        "azure"
 [16] "azure3"             "azure4"             "beige"
 [21] "bisque2"            "bisque3"            "bisque4"
 [26] "blue"               "blue1"              "blue2"
 [31] "blueviolet"         "brown"              "brown1"
 [36] "brown4"             "burlywood"          "burlywood1"
 [41] "burlywood4"         "cadetblue"          "cadetblue1"
 [46] "cadetblue4"         "chartreuse"         "chartreuse1"
 [51] "chartreuse4"        "chocolate"          "chocolate1"
 [56] "chocolate4"         "coral"              "coral1"
 [61] "coral4"             "cornflowerblue"     "cornsilk"
 [66] "cornsilk3"          "cornsilk4"          "cyan"
 [71] "cyan3"              "cyan4"              "darkblue"
 [76] "darkgoldenrod1"     "darkgoldenrod2"     "darkgoldenrod3"
 [81] "darkgreen"          "darkgrey"           "darkkhaki"
 [86] "darkolivegreen1"    "darkolivegreen2"    "darkolivegreen3"
 [91] "darkorange1"        "darkorange2"        "darkorange3"
 [96] "darkorchid1"        "darkorchid2"        "darkorchid3"
[101] "darksalmon"         "darkseagreen"       "darkseagreen1"
[106] "darkseagreen4"      "darkslateblue"      "darkslategray"
[111] "darkslategray3"     "darkslategray4"     "darkslategrey"
[116] "deeppink"           "deeppink1"          "deeppink2"
[121] "deepskyblue"        "deepskyblue1"       "deepskyblue2"
[126] "dimgray"            "dimgrey"            "dodgerblue"
[131] "dodgerblue3"        "dodgerblue4"        "firebrick"
[136] "firebrick3"         "firebrick4"         "floralwhite"
[141] "ghostwhite"         "gold"               "gold1"
[146] "gold4"              "goldenrod"          "goldenrod1"
```

Figure 15.4. Part of the list of colors command

3. Integers referring to positions in the current color palette.

The term *palette* in visualization often refers to the range of colors used to fill the graph. Microsoft often uses palettes in its applications. The benefit of using a palette is that you do not need to choose each color in the visualization. The most common palettes in R include rainbow, heat, terrain, and topo.

The following examples will present each palette:

1. *The rainbow palette:*

   In R:

   ```
   >n=20
   > pie(rep(1,n), col=rainbow(n))
   ```

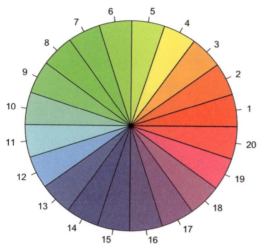

Figure 15.5. The rainbow palette

2. *The heat palette:*

   ```
   > pie(rep(1,n), col=heat(n))
   ```

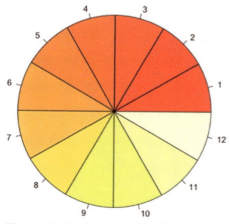

Figure 15.6. The heat palette.

3. *The terrain palette:*

```
> pie(rep(1,n), col=terrain(n))
```

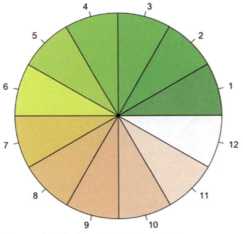

Figure 15.7. The terrain palette.

4. *The topo palette:*

```
> pie(rep(1,n), col= topo (n))
```

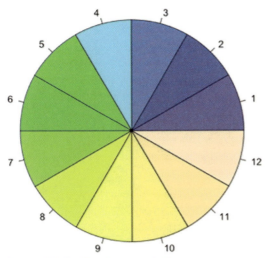

Figure 15.8. The topo palette.

As you can see, each palette consists of different colors. In each palette we can find three different types of colors: primary colors, supporting colors, and accent colors. The primary colors must be used on all materials to ensure that the promotional mark is produced in the proper color combinations. The supporting colors may be used in addition to these primary colors on all materials. The accent colors may be used in small amounts (20% or less) in addition to the primary color palette and other supporting colors.

In the rainbow palette: The accent colors are in the deep blue range and the higher values in the reds. The supporting colors are in the light blue green, yellow, and orange ranges. This palette is used as a default in many visualization systems since it is easy to calculate (it is a linear interpolation between (0,0,255) and (255,0,0) in RGB color space). The primary colors are strong blue, green, and red, and bright colors are visually appealing.

In R you as the creator of the graph have the ability to add different colors to different objects that include points, lines, axes, text, legends, and background. However, we will start with the definition of graphical parameters in R.

The graphical parameters in R consist of code `par`. Parameters can be set by specifying them as arguments to `par` in tag = value form, or by passing them as a list of tagged values.

In R:

Usage:

```
Par() # allows you to view the current setting
opar <- par() # makes a copy of the current settings
Par(col.lab="red") # provides settings for x and y labels in red
hist(mtcars$mpg) # creates a plot with #mpg setting
par(opar) # restores the original settings from the previous settings.
```

15.5 Symbols

The following options can be used to control text and symbol size in graphs:

Table 15.1.

Code	Description
cex	Number indicating the amount by which plotting text and symbols should be scaled relative to the default. 1=default, 1.5 is 50% larger, 0.5 is 50% smaller, etc.
cex.axis	Magnification of axis annotation relative to cex
cex.lab	Magnification of x and y labels relative to cex
cex.main	Magnification of titles relative to cex
cex.sub	Magnification of subtitles relative to cex

15.6 Plotting Symbols

The following are plotting characters or symbols used in R. The following table is PCH symbols used in an R plot. When the PCH is between values 21 and 25, the parameter is "col=" and "bg" should be outlined. The visual representation of this table is presented in figure 4.

Table 15.2.

pch=0, square	pch=13, circle cross
pch=1, circle	pch=14, square and triangle down
pch=2, triangle point up	pch=15, filled square blue
pch=3, plus	pch=16, filled circle blue
pch=4, cross	pch=17, filled triangle point up blue
pch=5, diamond	pch=18, filled diamond blue
pch=6, triangle point down	pch=19, solid circle blue
pch=7, square cross	pch=20, bullet (smaller circle)
pch=8, star	pch=21, filled circle red
pch=9, diamond plus	pch=22, filled square red
pch=10, circle plus	pch=23, filled diamond red
pch=11, triangles up and down	pch=25, filled triangle point down red
pch=12, square plus	

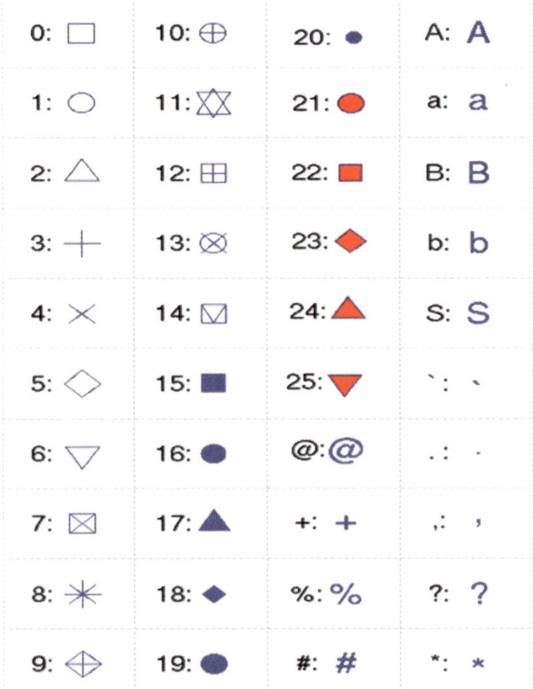

Figure 15.9. R plot pch symbols.

15.7 Pie in R

The most basic plot for descriptive statistics, a pie chart, often called a circle chart, is divided into sections to illustrate the numerical proportion of the data. In a visual pie, the arc length of each section is proportional to the quantity it represents.

In R:
We will start with a simple example where our dataset will consist of four numbers: 40, 30, 20, and 10:

```
>mypie=c(40,30,20,10)
>pie(mypie)
```

The command `pie(mypie)` produces the pie chart shown in figure 15.10.

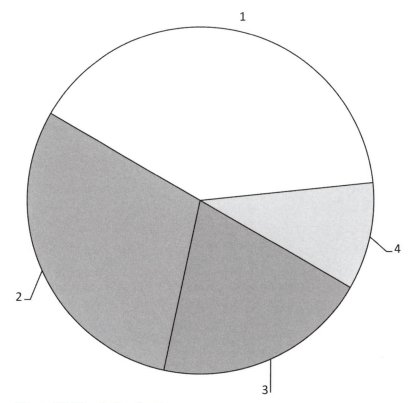

Figure 15.10. A simple pie.

Adding labels to the pie chart.

We can add "names" to the percentages of colored candies favored by children.

```
> names(mypie)=c("Red","Blue","Green","Brown")
```

The **names** command attaches a name to each piece of data. We can see the result of this command by typing the variable name (**mypie**) and hitting the Enter key.

```
>mypie
  Red    Blue    Green    Brown
  40     30       20       10
```

The pie command knows how to apply these names to the pie chart.

```
>pie(mypie)
```

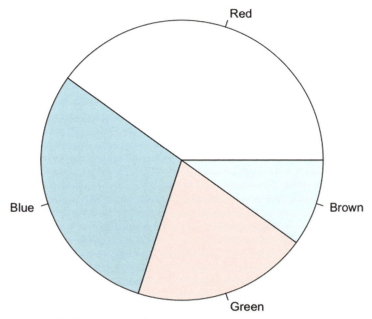

Figure 15.11. A pie with text.

15.8 Using Custom Colors To Fill the Pie

We add our colors and store the corresponding colors under `mycolors`. These colors include "red," "blue," "green," "brown."

In R:

```
> mycolors=c("red","blue","green","brown")
```

The last line in our code will include the pie and color attributes we set up. Plus we will add a title to the pie "My first Pie."

```
>pie(mypie,col="mycolors", main="My first Pie")
```

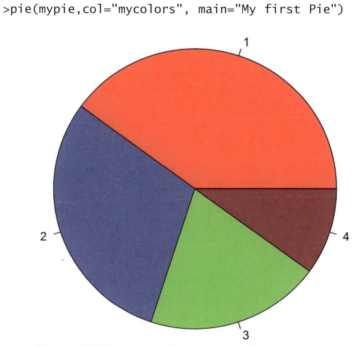

Figure 15.12. A pie with colors and text.

15.9 Plot in R

R has a generic function for the plotting of R objects. The object, plot, takes the arguments (x, y,...), where x is the x-coordinate of the plot and y is the y-coordinate of the plot. The basic structure of the plot consists of `main`, `xlab`, and ylab. The main command will give the title of the plot and the syntax is main="Main title text". The subhead syntax is sub of the overall title of the plot and the syntax is sub="Sub title text". The title for x-axis syntax: xlab="X axis test". The title for y-axis syntax: ylab="Y-axis text".

In the following example, we will use a dataset that is available in all R installations to illustrate the plotting commands. It is called "cars" and contains speed (in miles per hour) and stopping distances (in feet) recorded on cars in the 1920s.

In R, enter the following:

```
> data(cars)
>cars
```

Table 15.3.

	Speed	Dist.
1	4	2
2	4	10
3	7	4
4	7	22
...		
...		
48	24	93
49	24	120
50	25	85

```
>str(cars)
'data.frame': 50 obs. Of 2 variables:
$ speed:  num  4    4   5   5   8   9  10  10  10  11  ...
$ dist:   num  2   10   4  22  16  10  18  26  34  15  ...
>head(cars)
        speed    dist
1         4      2
2         4      10
3         7      4
5         7      22
6         8      16
```

Instead of printing out the entire data frame, it is often desirable to preview it with the **head** function beforehand. We note that "cars" is a data frame with two variables, speed and distance (dist). We first plot using the syntax `plot (x,y)` as displayed in figure 15.13.

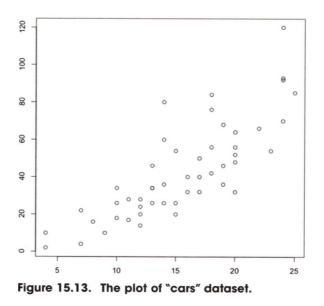

Figure 15.13. The plot of "cars" dataset.

R provides us with different types of plots. Table 15.4 summarizes the types of plots where the function lines (x, y, type=) where x and y are numeric vectors of (x, y) point to connect. Type=can table the following values.

Table 15.4.

Type of Chart	Description
p	points
l	lines
o	overplotted points and lines
b, c	points (empty if "c") joined by lines
s, S	stair steps
h	histogram-like vertical lines
n	does not produce any points or lines

In R:

```
> plot(cars, type = "h")
```

The result:

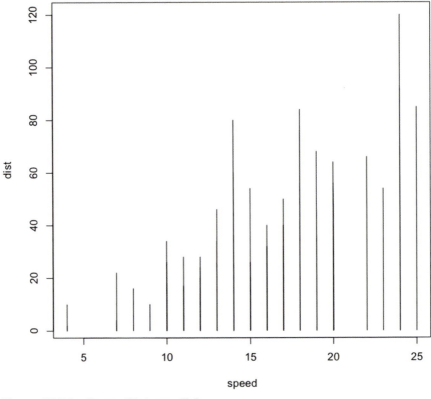

Figure 15.14. Cars with type= "h".

15.10 Histograms in R

Histograms can be used to plot the frequency of different observations, especially with regard to descriptive statistics. In the following example, we will use a data set that is available in all R installations to illustrate the histogram commands. The dataset is called "faithful" and contains "eruption" and "waiting" columns.

We convert this data set to data.frame called "duration."

In R:

```
> duration = faithful$eruptions
```

Next, we closed the interval to the left in order to create the histogram.

```
>hist(duration, right=FALSE)
```

Result:

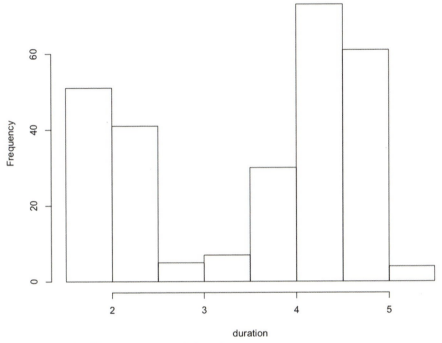

Figure 15.15. The histogram of duration.

In order to add more colors to this histogram, we select a color palette and set it with the colors argument.

The colors we selected are red, yellow, green, black, violet, orange, blue, and cyan.

In R:

```
>colors=c("red", "yellow", "green", "black", "violet",
"orange", "blue", "cyan")
```

Then, when we set up the histogram we add the col=colors, and provided a title for our histogram: Old Faithful Eruptions.

Figure 15.16 represents the color histogram of duration:

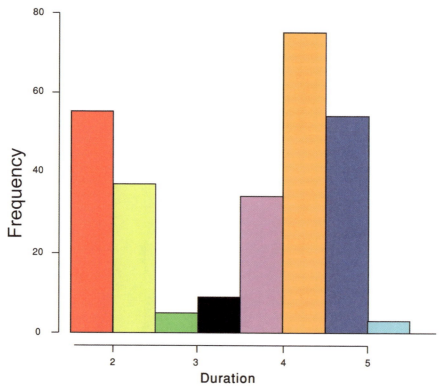

Figure 15.16. Using colors.

15.11 Saving Your Plot

R provides different options for saving the plot. First, what is the purpose of your plot: is it a term paper? for a web presentation? maybe for publication? Depending on your purpose, saving your file format also depends on the machine you are running: PC, Mac, or maybe Linux.

For a PC running Word for Windows, use the bmp file format. This is a bitmapped file format created using the `bmp()` command.
On the web using the jpg file format. This is a compressed bitmapping file format created via the following command: `jpwg()`.
LATEX is a Postscript document system with its own document markup language. Save your plot for this format via the following command: `postscript()`
For PDF. This file format is created via `pdf()`

The bmp file format and jpg file format share several arguments and are therefore described together.

15.12 Saving Your File

Here is a general method of saving the file regardless of operating system or the way that you are connecting:

- Choose the format that you want to use. In this example, our car plot will be saved as a jpg file.
- Save the file in the right directory. The only argument that the device drivers need is the name of the file that you will use to save your graph. The plot will be stored relative to the current directory. You can find the current directory by typing getwd() at the R prompt. You may want to make adjustments to the size of the plot before saving it. Consult the help file for your selected driver to learn how.
- Now enter your plotting commands as you normally would. You will *not* actually see the plot—the commands are being saved to a file instead.
- When you're done with your plotting commands, enter the dev.off() command. This is very important—without it you'll get a partial plot or nothing at all.

To save our cars plot, we would name the file "cars.jpg" containing a plot of cars:

```
> jpeg("car.jpg")
> plot(cars)
> dev.off()
```

15.13 Summary

This chapter introduced the subject of visualization. We first explored visualization by looking at the history of visualization. In particular, we looked at the work of Charles Joseph Minard (1781–1870). We review Tufte's three principles: 3D vs. 2D, micro/macro, and layering and separation. We then looked at colors in R and discussed three types of colors: hexadecimal, named, and palette. We also examined how to create a pie, plot, and histogram in R.

15.14 Glossary

color—The visual perceptual property corresponding in humans to the categories called *red*, *blue*, *yellow*, and others.

hexadecimal colors—Colors based on a place-value notation method of representing colors by encoding numbers.

histogram—A graphical representation of the frequency distribution of data, where rectangles with bases on the horizontal axis are given widths equal to the class intervals and heights equal to the corresponding frequencies.

palette—A range of colors used in a particular picture or graph.

pie chart—A circle that is divided into parts to show the size of the different amounts that are a part of a whole amount.

plot chart—A pyramid or triangular shape chart that captures the data.

15.15 References

Chevallier, V. 1871 "Notice nécrologique sur M. Minard, inspecteur général des ponts et chausées, en retraite." *Annales de Ponts et Chausées* 2: 1–22.

Few, S. 2009. "Edge Sometimes We Must Raise Our Voices." *Visual Business Intelligence Newsletter*.

Friendly, M. 2002. "Visions and R-Visions of Charles Joseph Minard." *Journal of Educational and Behavioral Statistics* 27 (1): 31–51.

Robinson, A. H. 1967. "The Thematic Maps of Charles Joseph Minard." *Imago Mundi* 21: 95–108.

Segal, E., and J. Heer. 2010. "Narrative Visualization: Telling Stories with Data." *Transactions on Visualization and Computer Graphics* 6: 1139–48.

Shaw, W. T., and J. Tig. 1994. *Applied Mathematica: Getting Started, Getting It Done.* Reading, MA: Addison-Wesley.

Tufte, E. R. 1990. *The Visual Display of Quantitative Information.* Cheshire, CT: Graphics Press.

Tufte, E. R. 1997. *Visual Explanations: Images and Quantities, Evidence and Narrative.* Cheshire, CT: Graphics Press.

Tufte, E. R. 2006. *Beautiful Evidence.* Cheshire, CT: Graphics Press.

Wainer, H. 2000. *Visual Revelations: Graphical Tales of Fate and Deception from Napoleon Bonaparte to Ross Perot.* Hillsdale, NJ: Lawrence Erlbaum and Associates.

CHAPTER 16

Advanced Visualization Display

16.1   Introduction to Advanced Visualization
16.2   Basic ggplot2
16.3   Inside ggplot2
16.4   Visualizing Descriptive Statistics
    16.4.1   Histogram
    16.4.2   Box Plot
    16.4.3   Scatterplot
    16.4.4   Pareto Chart
16.5   Visualization of Multivariables
    16.5.1   Heat Map
16.6   Maps
16.7   Summary
16.8   Glossary
16.9   References

16.1 Introduction to Advanced Visualization

The term *advanced visualization* often means the use of technology to capture multivariable datasets. In this chapter, advanced visualization will refer to advanced statistics, similar to what we covered in chapters 5–12 by applying visualization. In order to generate visualizations using R, we will use a package called ggplot2. We will cover basic instructions to use ggplot2 by applying the histogram, box plot, and scatterplot matrix. We will review descriptive statistics and how to capture bivariate data. We will end this chapter with how to use

277

a U.S. map as the background to represent our data collected from all of the library and information studies across the United States.

16.2 Basic ggplot2

ggplot2 is a visualization plotting package for R. It provides a powerful model of graphics that makes it easy to produce complex multilayered graphics. The underlying plan of the creator of ggplot2, Hadley Wickham, was based on the idea that the grammar of graphics can be applied to better design visualization. Wickham's outline of the use of grammar of graphics (2009) as the foundation of his visualization package was the creation of a package based on Wilkinson's (2005) attempt to establish grammar in graphics and visualization. The grammar as implemented by the ggplot2 package exploits the low-level and high-level graphical object controls intrinsic to R while using a simplified code syntax. The foundation of ggplot2 consists of number functions that must be present in the code to ensure success in producing the visualization with ggplot2. In this book, we will cover 4 sections that include: layer, aesthetics, geometrics and scale.

In order to install the ggplot2 package, please insert the following code

```
>install.packages("ggplot2")
>library(ggplot2)
```

16.3 Inside ggplot2

Layers

The most important concept of ggplot2 is that graphics are built based on different layers. This includes anything from the data used, the coordinate system, the axis labels, to the plot's title. This layered grammar is perhaps the most powerful feature of ggplot2. It allows us to build complex graphics by adding more and more layers to the basic graphics while each layer is simple enough to construct. Layers can contain one or more components such as data and aesthetic mapping, geometries, statistics, or scaling.

Let's start with an example using layers:

Example:

1. First line activates ggplot2
2. Second line loads the mycars file
3. Third line creates data.frame where *p* is the header

4. Fourth line creates a layer for the `geom_abline` (line to the plot)
5. Fifth line provides more detail to the line graphic outlines

The code:

```
1. >library(ggplot2)
2. >data(mtcars)
3. > p <- qplot(wt, mpg, data = mtcars)
4. > p + geom_abline()
5. >p + geom_abline(intercept=10, colour = "red", size = 2)
6. the geom_abline will hold the alpha, color, linetype, and size.
```

The result:

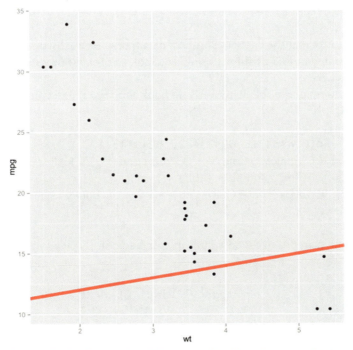

Figure 16.1. Example of line specified by slope and inter-cept.

Aesthetics

Aesthetics are graphic elements mapped to the data. Some of the common aesthetics we usually define are x-y positions, color, size, shape, and line type. An easy way to distinguish these is that you are always trying to assign data to some graphic elements in aesthetics, while in geometries you don't feed in any information on the data.

Plots convey information through various aspects of their `aesthetics` (`aes`). Some aesthetics that plots use are:

- x position
- y position
- size of elements
- shape of elements
- color of elements

ggplot2 comes with its own library. In this example, I will use a dataset called mtcars. The code to pull this dataset is:

```
>data(mtcars)
```

ggplot requires that the dataset consists of data.frame. As we discussed in chapter 4, a data.frame in R is used for storing data tables. It is a list of vectors of equal-length datasets.

For example, the following variable book is a data.frame containing three vectors: n, s, b.

```
> n = c(00433421, 00433422, 00433423)
> s = c("Shakespeare ", " Rousseau ", " Kafka ")
> b = c(TRUE, FALSE, TRUE)
>book = data.frame(n, s, b)        # book is a data.
frame
```

Back to our example. We used a built-in data.frame in R, called mtcars:

```
> mtcars
                  mpg cyl disp  hp drat   wt ...
Mazda RX4        21.0   6  160 110 3.90 2.62 ...
Mazda RX4 Wag    21.0   6  160 110 3.90 2.88 ...
Datsun 710      2 2.8   4  108  93 3.85 2.32 ...
```

The top line of the table, called the *header*, contains the column names. Each horizontal line afterward denotes a *data row*, which begins with the name of the row and is followed by the actual data. Each data member of a row is called a *cell*.

```
> c <- ggplot(mtcars, aes(factor(cyl)))
> c + geom_bar()
```

This example illustrates the **aes** within subgroups that hold color, fill, and α.

The result:

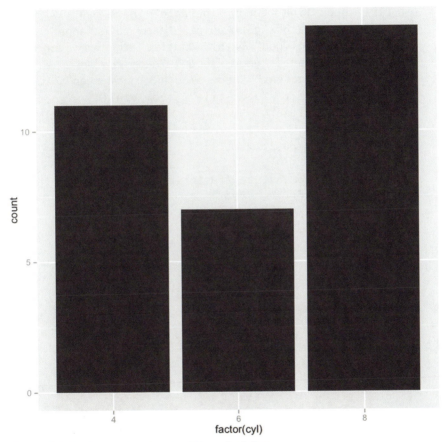

Figure 16.2. Example of color, fill, and alpha.

Geometrics

These are the actual graphic elements used to plot points, lines, and bars. These functions usually start with **geom** and their names. You can also specify color and other graphic elements in these functions, but it will be a single value that's applied to the entire data. Here is a simple way to see what geometric functions are available:

```
> apropos("^geom_")
## [1] "geom_abline" "geom_area" "geom_bar"
## [4] "geom_bin2d" "geom_blank" "geom_boxplot"
## [7] "geom_contour" "geom_crossbar" "geom_density"
## [10] "geom_density2d" "geom_dotplot" "geom_errorbar"
## [13] "geom_errorbarh" "geom_freqpoly" "geom_hex"
## [16] "geom_histogram" "geom_hline" "geom_jitter"
## [19] "geom_line" "geom_linerange" "geom_map"
## [22] "geom_path" "geom_point" "geom_pointrange"
## [25] "geom_polygon" "geom_quantile" "geom_raster"
## [28] "geom_rect" "geom_ribbon" "geom_rug"
## [31] "geom_segment" "geom_smooth" "geom_step"
## [34] "geom_text" "geom_tile" "geom_violin"
## [37] "geom_vline"
```

Example based on the previous example:

```
> c <- ggplot(mtcars, aes(factor(cyl)))
> c + geom_bar(fill = "red")
```

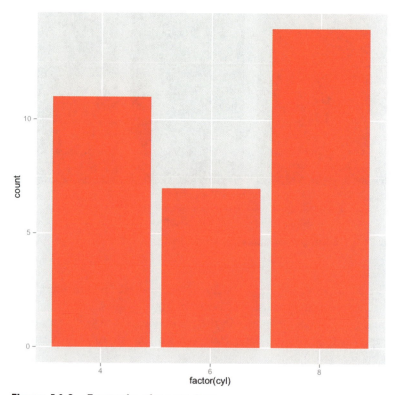

Figure 16.3. Example of geom_bar.

Scale

Another powerful feature to alter the default scale to x-y axes is to do a log transformation instead of the traditional two-step approach of transforming the data first and then plotting it. You can also do more advanced customizations to features like color and fill with these functions. Functions available are:

Table 16.1.

##	[1]	"scale_alpha"	"scale_alpha_continuous"
##	[3]	"scale_alpha_discrete"	"scale_alpha_identity"
##	[5]	"scale_alpha_manual"	"scale_area"
##	[7]	"scale_color_brewer"	"scale_color_continuous"
##	[9]	"scale_color_discrete"	"scale_color_gradient"
##	[11]	"scale_color_gradient2"	"scale_color_gradientn"
##	[13]	"scale_color_grey"	"scale_color_hue"
##	[15]	"scale_color_identity"	"scale_color_manual"
##	[17]	"scale_colour_brewer"	"scale_colour_continuous"
##	[19]	"scale_colour_discrete"	"scale_colour_gradient"
##	[21]	"scale_colour_gradient2"	"scale_colour_gradientn"
##	[23]	"scale_colour_grey"	"scale_colour_hue"
##	[25]	"scale_colour_identity"	"scale_colour_manual"
##	[27]	"scale_fill_brewer"	"scale_fill_continuous"
##	[29]	"scale_fill_discrete"	"scale_fill_gradient"
##	[31]	"scale_fill_gradient2"	"scale_fill_gradientn"
##	[33]	"scale_fill_grey"	"scale_fill_hue"
##	[35]	"scale_fill_identity"	"scale_fill_manual"
##	[37]	"scale_linetype"	"scale_linetype_continuous"
##	[39]	"scale_linetype_discrete"	"scale_linetype_identity"
##	[41]	"scale_linetype_manual"	"scale_shape"
##	[43]	"scale_shape_continuous"	"scale_shape_discrete"
##	[45]	"scale_shape_identity"	"scale_shape_manual"
##	[47]	"scale_size"	"scale_size_area"
##	[49]	"scale_size_continuous"	"scale_size_discrete"
##	[51]	"scale_size_identity"	"scale_size_manual"
##	[53]	"scale_x_continuous"	"scale_x_date"
##	[55]	"scale_x_datetime"	"scale_x_discrete"
##	[57]	"scale_x_log10"	"scale_x_reverse"
##	[59]	"scale_x_sqrt"	"scale_y_continuous"
##	[61]	"scale_y_date"	"scale_y_datetime"
##	[63]	"scale_y_discrete"	"scale_y_log10"
##	[65]	"scale_y_reverse"	"scale_y_sqrt"

Example:

The aesthetic fill also takes different coloring scales.

```
# setting fill equal to a factor variable uses a
discrete color scale
```

```
> k <- ggplot(mtcars, aes(factor(cyl), fill =
factor(vs)))
> k + geom_bar()
```

In this case, we rename the data.frame k and provide the color as vs.

The result:

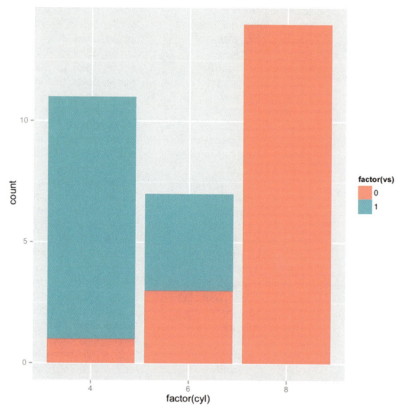

Figure 16.4. Example of different coloring scales.

16.4 Visualizing Descriptive Statistics

Under descriptive statistics we use the following visual patterns: histogram, cumulative percentage polygon, and Pareto diagram.

16.4.1 HISTOGRAM

A histogram is a way of summarizing data that is measured on an interval scale (either discrete or continuous). It is often used in exploratory data analysis to illustrate the major features of the distribution of the data in a convenient form. It divides up the range of possible values in a dataset into classes or groups. For each group, a rectangle is constructed with a base length equal to the range of values in that specific group and an area proportional to the number of observations falling into that group. This means that the rectangles might be drawn of non-uniform height.

Under ggplot2, we will use the aesthetics function where the geom_car will include the X value, α, color fill, linetype, size, and weight. As we illustrated in figures 16.3, 16.4, and 16.5, the use of histograms was based on displaying the dataset on the x axis only. In this example, the display will consist of the y axis. In order to achieve this, the second line consists of +coord_flip().

```
> k <- ggplot(mtcars, aes(factor(cyl), fill =
factor(vs)))
> k + geom_bar()+ coord_flip()
```

The result:

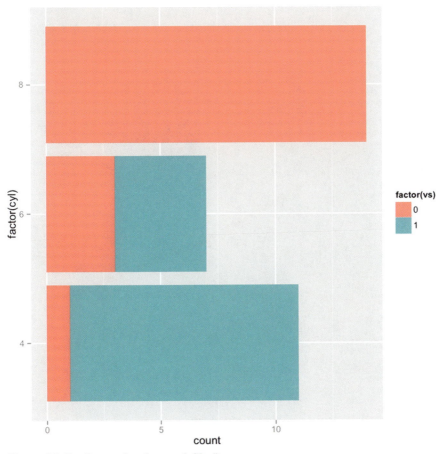

Figure 16.5. Example of coord_flip()

As discussed in chapter 5, the aim of this method is to provide a summary of the data. Under ggplot2, the function of `stat_summary` is to provide the ability to add additional visualization aspects to the statistics summary. Under the `stat_summary` command we provide the ability to add the summarization functionality to the visualization. The `summary` function can either operate on a data.frame (with argument name base.data) or on a vector (base.y, base.y, base.ymax, and others).

Example:

```
tat_sum_single <- function(, geom="point", ...) {
+ stat_summary(base.y=base, colour="red", geom=geom,
size = 3, ...)
+ }
> d + stat_sum_single(mean)
> d + stat_sum_single(mean, geom="line")
```

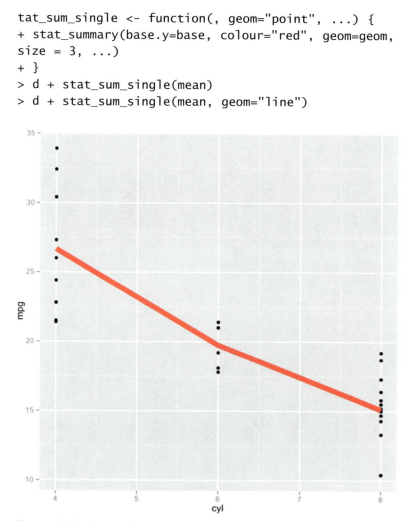

Figure 16.6. Example of stat_summary.

16.4.2 BOX PLOT

A box plot is a representation that splits the dataset into quartiles. According to Wickham and Stryjewski (2011), John Tukey introduced the box and whiskers plot as part of his toolkit for exploratory data analysis (Tukey, 1977). It did not become widely known until a formal publication (Tukey, 1977). The box plot is a compact distributional summary displaying less detail than a histogram or kernel density, but also taking up less space. Box plots use robust summary descriptive statistics that are always located at actual data points, are quickly computable (originally by hand), and have no tuning parameters. They are particularly useful for comparing distributions across groups. The box plot is made up of five components that represent a summary of the distribution of a database:

- The median;
- Two hinges, the upper and lower fourths (quartiles);
- The data values adjacent to the upper and lower fences, which lie 1.5 times the inter-fourth range from the median;
- Two whiskers that connect the hinges to the fences; and
- Outliers, individual points farther away from the median than the extremes.

For R, the box plot consists of all the following aesthetics functions: lower, middle, upper, x, ymax, ymin, α, colour, fill, linetype, shape, size, and weight.

In R:

```
> p <- ggplot(mtcars, aes(factor(cyl), mpg))
>p + geom_boxplot()
```

More advanced box plot with colors:

```
>p + geom_boxplot(aes(fill = factor(cyl)))
```

The result:

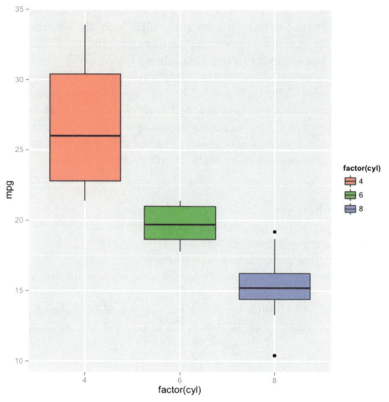

Figure 16.7. Boxplot with colors.

16.4.3 SCATTERPLOT

A scatterplot displays the values for two variables for a set of data. The data is displayed as a collection of points, each having the value of one variable determining the position on the horizontal axis and the value of the other variables that determines the position on the vertical axis. According to Friendly and Denis (2000), Francis Galton (1822–1911) used the scatterplot in his work on correlation and regression. Now, a scatterplot can be presented in 2D and 3D. In ggplot2, the upper whisker extends from the hinge to the highest value that is within 1.5 * IQR of the hinge, where IQR is the inter-quartile range, or distance between the first and third quartiles. The lower whisker extends from the hinge to the lowest value within 1.5 * IQR of the hinge. Data beyond the end of the whiskers are outliers and plotted as points (as specified by Tukey, 1970, 124).

In R:

```
> p <- ggplot(mtcars, aes(wt, mpg))
>qplot(wt, mpg, data = mtcars, colour = I("red"), size
= I(3))
```

The result:

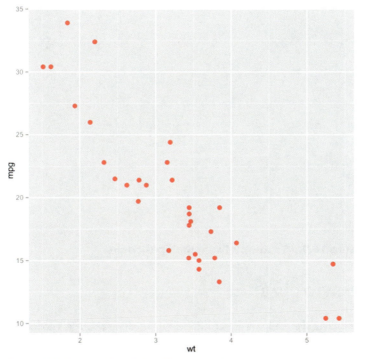

Figure 16.8. Scatterplot with one color.

Next, we employ two colors across the dataset to represent two factors under versus 0 and 1:

```
> d + aes(colour = factor(vs)) + stat_summary(base.y =
mean, geom="line")
```

The result:

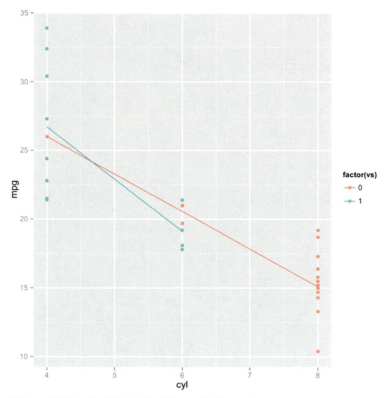

Figure 16.9. Scatterplot with multiple colors.

16.4.4 PARETO CHART

A Pareto chart, also called a Pareto distribution diagram, is a vertical bar graph in which values are plotted in decreasing order of relative frequency from left to right. Pareto charts are extremely useful for analyzing what problems need attention first, because the taller bars on the chart, which represent frequency, clearly illustrate which variables have the greatest cumulative effect on a given system. The creator of the Pareto chart was Vilfredo Federico Damaso Pareto (1848–1923). He studied the history of income and came up with the idea that income can be captured as distribution. In order to communicate this idea, he created the Pareto chart.

In R:

We will use a new package called qcc in order to generate the Pareto chart:

```
>install.packages("qcc")
>library(qcc)
defect <- c(80, 27, 66, 94, 33)
names(defect) <- c("price code", "schedule date",
"supplier code", "contact num.",
"part num.")
pareto.chart(defect, ylab = "Error frequency", col=heat.
colors(length(defect)))
```

The result:

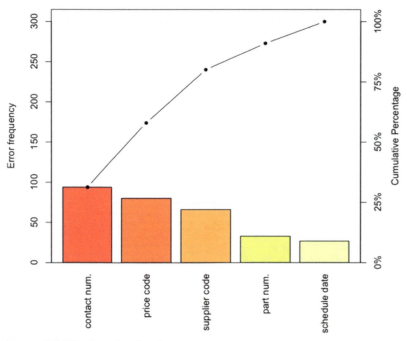

Figure 16.10. Pareto chart.

Just in case, we divided the data into five variables: contact, price, supplier, part, and schedule. We then add another layer, which represents the error frequency. We set up the chart using the heat palette.

16.5 Visualization of Multivariables

Multivariate data consists of the analysis of many variables, numbering from a minimum of six variables to millions. Such data usually includes control variables (factors) and/or characteristics (responses). In order to visualize a dataset that consists of more than five rows of variables, we employ a package called diamonds, also part of the ggplot2 set. The dataset contains the prices and other attributes of 54,000 diamonds.

To download the diamonds dataset to R:

```
>data(diamonds)
```

To review the context of the dataset:

```
> diamonds
```

Table 16.2.

	carat	cut	color	clarity	depth	table	price	x	y	z
1	0.23	Ideal	E	SI2	61.5	55.0	326	3.95	3.98	2.43
2	0.21	Premium	E	SI1	59.8	61.0	326	3.89	3.84	2.31
3	0.23	Good	E	VS1	56.9	65.0	327	4.05	4.07	2.31
4	0.29	Premium	I	VS2	62.4	58.0	334	4.20	4.23	2.63
5	0.31	Good	J	SI2	63.3	58.0	335	4.34	4.35	2.75
6	0.24	Very Good	J	VVS2	62.8	57.0	336	3.94	3.96	2.48
7	0.24	Very Good	I	VVS1	62.3	57.0	336	3.95	3.98	2.47
8	0.26	Very Good	H	SI1	61.9	55.0	337	4.07	4.11	2.53
9	0.22	Fair	E	VS2	65.1	61.0	337	3.87	3.78	2.49
10	0.23	Very Good	H	VS1	59.4	61.0	338	4.00	4.05	2.39

For this example, we will use a 2D rectangular bin:

```
> d <- ggplot(diamonds, aes(carat, depth, z = value))
> d + stat_summary2d()
```

The result:

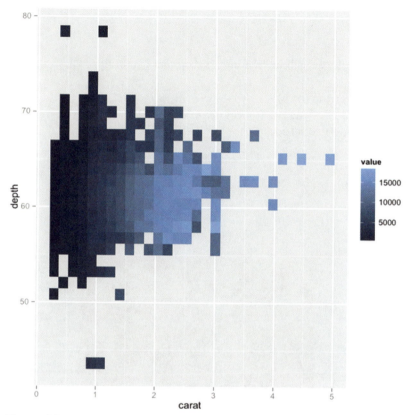

Figure 16.11. Multivariate data in 2D.

In this example we analyze three different variables: depth, carat, and value. ggplot2 allows us to display three layers: depth on the y axis, carat on the x axis, and values rows.

16.5.1 HEAT MAP

A *heat map* is a graphical representation of data where the values contained in the various variables are represented in a color matrix. The term *heat map* was originally coined and trademarked by Cormac Kinney, a software designer, in 1991 to display 2D real-time financial information. Nowadays, many fields and professionals use heat maps. In library science, Khoo et al. (2008) collected survey studies in an academic library. They provided a heat map that aggregated data from 112 seat counts in the library to learn which was the most occupied seating area in the library.

In R:

For this example, we will use the mtcars data that ggplot2 provides:

```
>library(ggplot2)
>mtscaled <- as.matrix(scale(mtcars))
>heatmap(mtscaled, Colv=F, scale='none')
```

The result:

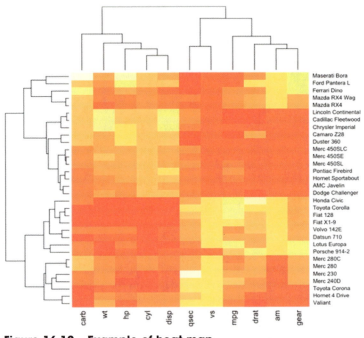

Figure 16.12. Example of heat map.

This heat map clusters both rows and columns. It then reorders the resulting dendrograms according to mean. Setting Colv to false tells it not to reorder the columns, which will come in handy later.

16.6 Maps

A map is a graphic representation or scale model of spatial concepts. It is a means for conveying geographic information. Maps are a universal medium for communication, easily understood and appreciated by most people, regardless of language or culture. Incorporated in a map is the understanding that it is a "snapshot" of an idea, a single picture, a selection of concepts from a constantly changing database of geographic information (Merriam, 1996). Maps became increasingly accurate and factual during the seventeenth, eighteenth, and nineteenth centuries with the application of scientific methods. Many countries undertook national mapping programs. Nonetheless, much of the world was poorly known until the widespread use of aerial photography following World War I. Modern cartography is based on a combination of ground observations and remote sensing.

In R:

Install a new package titled `reshapes2` that will work together with ggplot2 to produce the following maps.

Install a new package titled reshapes2 that will work together with ggplot2 to produce the following maps. In this case, our dataset will consist of USCrime. This data set was reported on the number of arrests for per 100,000 residents who accused of assault, murder, and rape in each of the 50 US states in 1973.

```
>install.packages("reshapes2")
>library(ggplot2)
>crimes <- data.frame(state =
tolower(rownames(USArrests)), USArres
>library(reshape2) # for melt
>crimesm <- melt(crimes, id = 1)
>if (require(maps)) {
states_map <- map_data("state")
ggplot(crimes, aes(map_id = state)) + geom_map(aes(fill
= Murder), map = states_map) + expand_limits(x =
states_map$long, y = states_map$lat)
last_plot() + coord_map()
ggplot(crimesm, aes(map_id = state)) + geom_map(aes(fill
= value), map = states_map) + expand_limits(x = states_
map$long, y = states_map$lat) + facet_wrap( ~ variable)
}
```

The results:

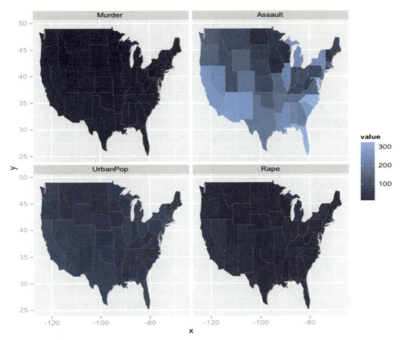

Figure 16.13.   USA Map.

In this case our code comes from the dataset inside ggplot. In this case, the file is *crimes*. It allows us to separate murder, assault, rape, and the urban population (urbanpopl). ggplots2 allows us to display the three types of crime and urban population separately.

Note: If you are interested in using maps, the GADM website provides a database of global administrative areas. You can download the country you like and the format of the file will be in R format (http://www.gadm.org). If you would like to explore the ggplot2 package further, visit http://www.ggplot2.org.

16.7 Summary

In this chapter, we discussed the visualization of data using ggplot2. The big advantage of ggplot2 is its ability to create layers or functions that allow the user to add additional dimensions to the visualization. We discussed the foundations of ggplot2 that includes layer, aesthetics, geometrics, and scale. We illustrated the creation of histograms, scatterplots, box plots, heat maps, and maps.

16.8 Glossary

aesthetics—Graphic elements mapped to the data under ggplot2.

box plot—A graphical rendition of statistical data based on the minimum, first quartile, median, third quartile, and maximum.

ggplot2—Plotting system for R, based on the grammar of graphics, which tries to take the good parts of base and lattice graphics and none of the bad parts.

heat map—A graphical representation of data where the individual values contained in a matrix are represented as colors.

layer—Term used to describe the different levels at which you can place an object or image file under ggplot2.

multivariate data—Dataset that holds more than two variables.

Pareto chart—Chart that contains both bars and a line graph, where individual values are represented in descending order by bars, and the cumulative total is represented by the line.

scatterplot—Graph in which the values of two variables are plotted along two axes, the pattern of the resulting points revealing any correlation present.

16.9 References

Friendly, M., and D. Denis. 2005. "The Early Origins and Development of the Scatterplot." *Journal of the History of the Behavioral Science* 41 (2): 103–30.

Khoo, M., J. Pagano, A. Washington, M. Recker, B. Palmer, and R. Donahue. 2008. "Using Web Metrics to Analyze Digital Libraries." Eighth ACM/IEEE Joint Conference on Digital Libraries (JCDL), Pittsburgh, PA, June 16–20, 2008. Retrieved from http://www.ieee-tcdl.org/Bulletin/v4n1/khoo/khoo.html.

Mandelbrot, B., and R. L. Hudson. 2004. *The (Mis)Behavior of Markets: A Fractal View of Risk, Ruin, and Reward*. New York: Basic Books, p. 153.

Merriam, D. F. 1996. "Kansas 19th Century Geologic Maps." *Kansas Academy of Science, Transactions* 99, 95–114.

Tukey, J. 1977. *Exploratory Data Analysis*. Addison-Wesley.

Wickham, H. 2009. *ggplot2: Elegant Graphics for Data Analysis (Use R)*. London: Springer Publications.

Wickham, H., and L. Stryjewski. 2011. "40 Years of Box Plots." Manuscript submitted for publication. Retrieved from: http://vita.had.co.nz/papers/boxplots.html.

Wilkinson, L. 2005. *The Grammar of Graphics*. New York: Springer Publications.

CHAPTER 17

Applying Visualization to Statistics Analysis

17.1 Introduction
17.2 Visualization and Statistics
17.3 Data Visualization Checklist
    17.3.1 Supporting Text Description
    17.3.2 Arrangement
    17.3.3 Colors
        17.3.3.1 Color Theory
        17.3.3.2 Additive Colors
        17.3.3.3 Subtractive Colors
    17.3.4 Lines
    17.3.5 Overall
17.4 Summary
17.5 Glossary
17.6 References

A picture is worth a thousand words.

—Brisbane (1913)

17.1 Introduction

One of the biggest challenges for visualization creation is the lack of a clear methodology for how to create a good visualization design. In this chapter, we discuss a checklist to use in creating a good visualization. The visualization checklist consists of supporting text description, arrangement, colors, lines, and the visual rationale that the visualization must provide.

17.2 Visualization and Statistics

Graphic symbols are as vital a part of our communication systems as words in the language, numbers, and formulas in statistics. Many scholars discuss the subject of visualization and statistics. They report a similar problem—that visualization, unlike statistics, has no single methodology or single grammar syntax. You can visualize data in many different ways, from simple bar charts to more complex scatterplots or heat maps, based on your experience and your own ability. Adding to the confusion, there is no single comprehensive resource on the subject of data visualization, but rather an extensive array of information consisting of books, journal articles, and online websites.

Another element in the creation of visualization is the meaning we take away from it. Each of us comes from a different background and, as a result, we derive different meanings, or understandings, from the visualizations we encounter. These backgrounds are based in our education, culture, and experiences. Studies have found that each of these backgrounds has an influence on how we interpret and understand visualizations.

In the field of information library science, many researchers have employed and discussed the use of visualization as part of their research. For example, in 2013, the Universal Decimal Classification (UDC) conducted a seminar focused on visualization in knowledge organization, where twenty-four papers were presented. Börner, Chen, and Boyack (2003) addressed the subject of visualizing knowledge by examining different technologies and statistical methods. Their research focused on bibliographic data structure. They discussed the general process for analyzing this of data, its units of analysis, and the layout of different designs and interaction techniques. Friedman (2014) examined the correlation between research methods and visualization by examining one of the leading conference proceedings in our field. He found no correlation between the research methods and the type of visual display the researchers used in their conference papers.

The use of visualization in statistics is intended to help explain, or make clear, the findings based in the statistical analysis. A visual presentation of data should make the main findings easy to observe and understand. Many lists were developed to provide better guidelines for creating a good visualization. Some of these guidelines focused on understanding the audience and the message that one intends to communicate, while others discussed the content of a good visualization with regard to the statistical analysis one has conducted.

17.3 Data Visualization Checklist

In 1983, Edward Tufte introduced the idea of data-ink ratio. It lays out the proportion for the ink that is devoted to a nonredundant display of the data information:

$$\text{Data-ink ratio} = \frac{Data-ink}{Total\ ink\ used\ to\ print\ the\ graphic}$$

The objective of this model is to maximize the proportion of the ink used in the graph that is devoted to the data. Within reasonable limits, non-data-ink and redundant data-ink should be eliminated. Non-data-ink includes aspects of the printed graph that do not relate to the subject of the data as well as grid lines that may be imposed on the graph. However, this ratio has never been examined regarding computer monitors and handheld computer devices.

Evergreen and Emery (2014) provided the following strategy checklist to enhance the user's experience for data visualization. The five key ideas when designing visualizations, according to Evergreen and Emery, consist of (a) supporting text description, (b) arrangement, (c) colors, (d) lines, and (e) overall meaning.

17.3.1 SUPPORTING TEXT DESCRIPTION

Adding a text description to support the visualization may help the user. The idea of adding a text description to the visualization is clarify the graphics:

- Use a six- to twelve-word descriptive title, left-justified in upper corner.
- Add substitle and/or annotations to provide additional information.
- Lay out text horizontally. This includes titles, subtitles, annotations, and data labels. Lines labels and axis labels can deviate from this rule and still receive full points.
- Directly position data labels near the data, rather than in a separate legend (e.g., place them on top of or next to bars or pie slices and next to lines in line charts). Eliminate legends whenever possible, because eye movement back and forth between the legend and the data can interrupt the brain's attempts to interpret the graph.
- Focus attention by removing redundant labels. For example, in line charts, label every other year only, on the axis. Do not label each and every year.

Example:

Figure 17.1 shows a lack of any text description to provide the user with more signals that could enhance the experience.

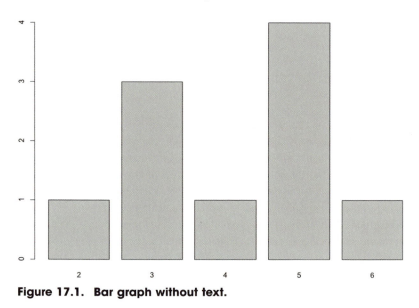

Figure 17.1.   Bar graph without text.

In comparison, figure 17.2 provides more details for interpretation, including the graph title and descriptions of the x and y axes.

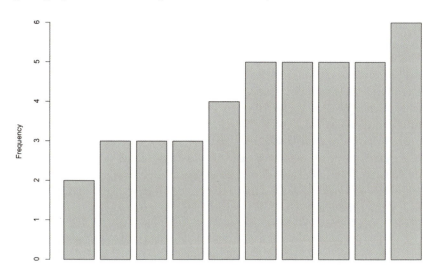

Figure 17.2.   Titled x and y axes.

Figure 17.3 illustrates descriptions such as the title, x and y axes, and a subtitle and annotations.

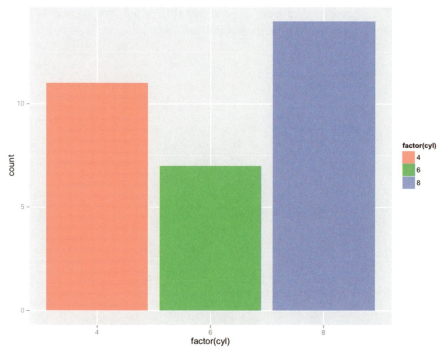

Figure 17.3. Title, annotations, and labels are used sparingly.

17.3.2 ARRANGEMENT

Improper arrangement of graph elements can confuse readers at best and mislead viewers at worst. The goal of the arrangement is getting the viewer to focus on the substance of the visualization rather than on how the visualization was developed. The arrangement needs to take into account the following points:

- A viewer should be able, as a rule, to see that the measure of length or area in the graph matches the relationships indicated by the underlying data.
- Data are ordered intentionally. Data should be displayed in an order that makes logical sense when examined by the viewer. Data may be ordered by reference columns, categories, groups, time periods, or alphabetical order.
- The axis intervals are equidistant. The spaces between axis should reflect the same units, even if every axis interval isn't labeled.
- Graphing in two dimensions is recommend by Few (2012).

- The display is free from decoration. The graph should be free of clip art or other illustrations used solely for decorative purposes.

Figure 17.4 represents data from a set of 3,000 data points displayed in three dimensions. As a result, this graph was not very clear.

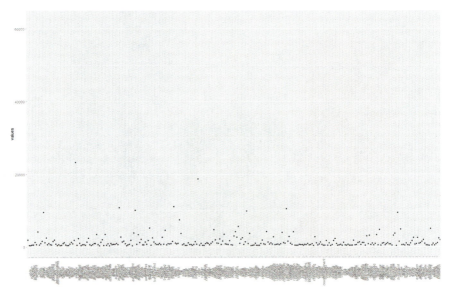

Figure 17.4. This figure holds 3,000 data points based on student's scores.

In order to follow Evergreen and Emery's guidelines, we sort the data and organize them based on a two-dimensional plan: frequency of word use (x axis) and ranking (y axis). The result of our analysis is presented in figure 17.5.

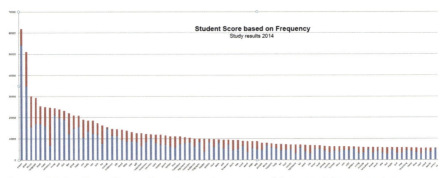

Figure 17.5. Two-dimensional graph arranged by word frequencies.

17.3.3 COLORS

Colors are the visual perceptual properties corresponding in humans to the categories called *red, blue, yellow*, and others. The notion that colors have the power to affect our moods, emotions, and behaviors has its roots in the fourteenth century. Beginning in the days of the Renaissance, artists and architects learned to use colors by mixing them to create visual effects, long before the similar use of color with computers. The work of Isaac Newton's theory of color and the nature of primary colors established new understandings of the notion of color theory.

17.3.4.1 Color Theory

In traditional color theory (used in paint and pigments), primary colors are the three pigment colors that cannot be mixed or formed by any combination of other colors. These three colors are red, yellow, and blue.

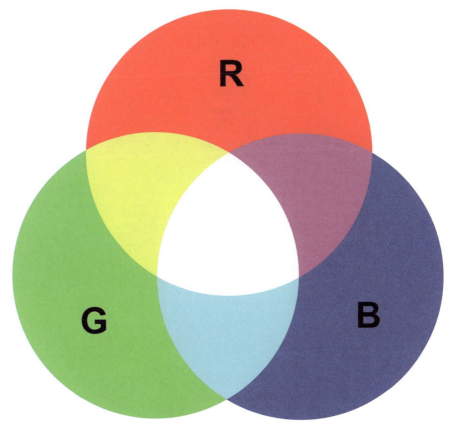

Figure 17.6. The three primary colors.

With the primary colors, another classification exists that categorizes the colors based on their ability to be reproduced. This classification consists of additive and subtractive, also known as reflective colors. We use both categories on a daily basis—the screen you are reading uses additive color to generate all the colors you see, while the book you are reading uses subtractive color for its front design. In simple terms, anything that emits light (such as the sun, a screen, a projector, etc.) uses additive colors, while everything else (which reflects light instead) uses subtractive color.

17.3.3.2 Additive Colors

The additive categories, consisting of red, green, and blue, generate color by beginning with the absence of color, or black, to generate all colors. The three colors are projected onto a screen in various intensities to produce the range of colors. This principle generates color for televisions, computer monitors, and movie screens; that is, all projected color.

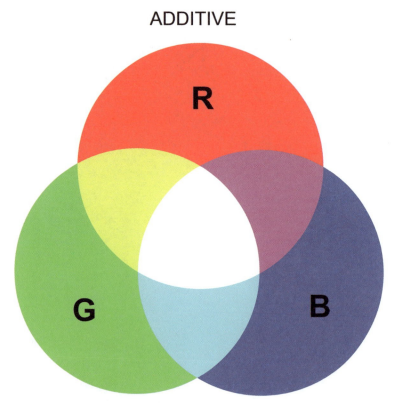

Figure 17.7. Additive colors.

Color on television and monitors is produced from the light of three-color *light guns*, corresponding to each additive primary. These produce color *intensity* based on a voltage level ranging from 0 to 255. Obviously, 0, 0, and 0 will produce black, or the absence of color, and 255, 255, and 255 will produce white, a combination of all colors. Other colors correspondingly relate to a specific voltage combination. Multiply 255 times 255 times 255 and how many color combinations do you get? More than 16.7 million, presuming your monitor is capable of showing that many (most modern monitors are capable of 24-bit or *true color*).

17.3.3.3 Subtractive Colors

Subtractive color synthesis is the creation of color by mixing colors of *pigment*, such as paint or ink, in your computer's printer. This type of color is used in the art and design world. Subtractive color processes work by blocking out parts of the spectrum. The idea of subtractive color is to reduce the amount of undesired color reaching the eye. The additive secondaries become the printers' subtractive primaries, because each of the additive secondaries will reflect two of the additive primaries and absorb one of the additive primaries.

SUBTRACTIVE

Figure 17.8. Subtractive colors.

The use of subtractive pigments allows us to blend colors together.

For example:

Yellow + Cyan = Green
Yellow + Magenta = Red
Cyan + Magenta = Blue

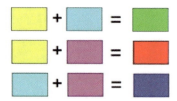

Figure 17.9. Subtractive primaries mixing chart.

According to Evergreen and Emery (2014), we must think of colors in terms of culture; for instance, wearing black is highly associated with high fashion in the United States.

- Color is used to highlight key patterns. Action colors should guide the viewer to key parts of the display. Less important or supporting information should be in muted colors—mix your color arrangement with white or grey, making it less bright.
- Color is legible when printed in black and white. When printed or photo-copied in black and while, the viewer should still be able to see the patterns in the data.
- Color is legible for people with colorblindness. Avoid red-green and yellow-blue combinations when the colors will touch one another.

17.3.4 LINES

Excessive line use—gridlines, border tick marks, and axes can add clutter or noise to a graph, so eliminate them whenever they are not useful for interpreting data.

- Gridlines, if presented, are muted.
- Graphs do not have border lines. A graph should bleed into the surrounding page rather being contained within a border.
- Graphs do not have unnecessary tick marks.
- Graphs must have one horizontal and one vertical axis. Viewers can best interpret one x- and one y-axis, even if one is hidden. Do not add a second y-axis.

Our first example consists of gridlines that, according to Evergreen and Emery, need to be muted.

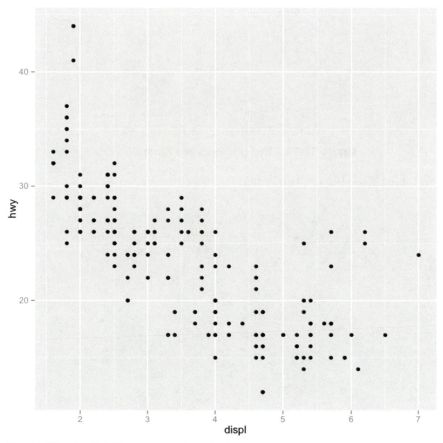

Figure 17.10. Gridlines are not muted.

In Figure 17.11, the gridlines are muted to provide a clear background.

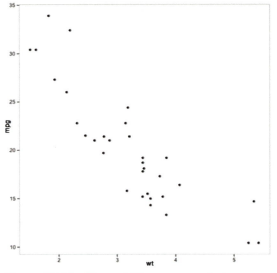

Figure 17.11.   The gridlines are muted.

This third example has a border line.

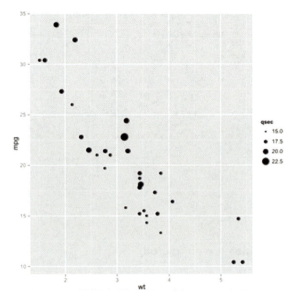

Figure 17.12.   Border.

According to Evergreen and Emery, a good graph should be without any border so it blends into the page. Figure 17.13 captures the same graph without a border.

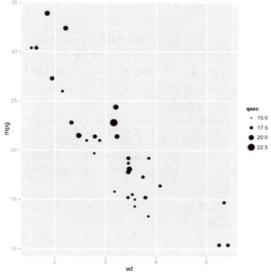

Figure 17.13.   Without border.

According to the recommendation of Evergreen and Emery, it is best to avoid overusing tick marks. Figure 17.14 illustrates where ticks mark are often used.

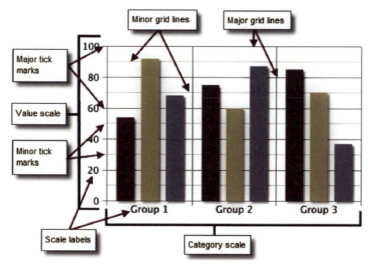

Figure 17.14.   Unnecessary use of too many tick marks.

17.3.5 OVERALL

According to Evergreen and Emery, visualization should catch a viewer's attention so that he or she can visualize the data that need attention.

- Graphs should highlight the significant findings or conclusions.
- The type of graph should be appropriate for the data. Data is displayed effectively when using a graph type suitable for the relationship within the data. For example, a time series should be displayed in a line graph, area chart, or slope graph, but not in a pie chart.
- A graph should provide an appropriate level of precision. When precision is important, choose a type of graph that displays differences through length or points along a line (e.g., bar charts, dot plots). When precision is less important, use a graph that displays differences through angles or area (e.g., pie charts, circle charts, etc.).
- Contextualized or comparison data are present. Comparisons—over time or across programs of subgroups of participants—help viewers understand the significance of the data.
- Individual chart elements work together to reinforce the overarching takeaway message. The choice of graph type, text, arrangement, color, or line should reflect the same end result or message.

17.4 Summary

An important goal of any research scientist is the publication of the results of a completed study. Most academic and professional publications in our field require the researcher to provide a written document, based on their style that entails specifics of data analysis and data collection methods, in order for it to be accepted for their review. Although the written word is still the dominant platform for reporting statistical analysis results and recommendations, visualization has gained recognition. Researchers who employ statistical analyses in their studies often incorporate visualization graphics to help users see the results of the analysis. In this chapter, we looked inside the data visualization checklist created by Evergreen and Emery (2014). We looked at text elements in the graph; the arrangement of elements, color, and lines; and the overall considerations of meaning.

17.5 Glossary

additive color—Color created by mixing light of two or more different colors. Red, green, and blue are additive colors.

color theory—A body of practical guidance for mixing color and the visual effects of a specific color combination.

subtractive color—Mixing colors of paints, dyes, inks, and natural colorants to create colors that absorb some wavelengths of light and reflect others.

17.6 References

Börner, K., C. Chen, and K. Boyack. 2003. "Visualizing Knowledge Domains." *Annual Review of Information Science & Technology 37*: 179–255.

Evergreen, S., and A. K. Emery. 2014. "Introduction to Visualization Checklist." Retrieved from http://stephanieevergreen.com/dataviz-checklist/.

Few, S. 2012. *Show Me the Numbers: Designing Tables and Graphs To Enlighten*. Burlingame, CA: Analytics Press.

Friedman, A. 2014. "The Relationship between Research Methodology and Visual Display: A Study of Conference Proceedings in the Field Knowledge Organization." *Information Research: An International Electronic Journal* 19 (4).

Tufte, E. R. 1983. *The Visual Display of Quantitative Information*. Cheshire, CT: Graphics Press.

APPENDIX A
Statistics Formula Sheet

Statistics formula sheet

Summarizing data

Sample mean:

$$\bar{x} = \frac{1}{n} \sum_{i=1}^{n} x_i.$$

Sample variance:

$$s_x^2 = \frac{1}{n-1} \sum_{i=1}^{n} (x_i - \bar{x})^2 = \frac{1}{n-1} \left(\sum_{i=1}^{n} x_i^2 - n\bar{x}^2 \right).$$

Sample covariance:

$$g = \frac{1}{n-1} \sum_{i=1}^{n} (x_i - \bar{x})(y_i - \bar{y}) = \frac{1}{n-1} \left(\sum_{i=1}^{n} x_i y_i - n\bar{x}\bar{y} \right).$$

Sample correlation:

$$r = \frac{g}{s_x s_y}.$$

Probability

Addition law:

$$P(A \cup B) = P(A) + P(B) - P(A \cap B).$$

Multiplication law:

$$P(A \cap B) = P(A)P(B|A) = P(B)P(A|B).$$

Partition law: For a partition $B_1, B_2, \ldots, B_k$

$$P(A) = \sum_{i=1}^{k} P(A \cap B_i) = \sum_{i=1}^{k} P(A|B_i)P(B_i).$$

Bayes' formula:

$$P(B_i|A) = \frac{P(A|B_i)P(B_i)}{P(A)} = \frac{P(A|B_i)P(B_i)}{\sum_{i=1}^{k} P(A|B_i)P(B_i)}.$$

Discrete distributions

Mean value:

$$E(X) = \mu = \sum_{x_i \in S} x_i p(x_i).$$

Variance:

$$\text{Var}(X) = \sum_{x_i \in S} (x_i - \mu)^2 p(x_i) = \sum_{x_i \in S} x_i^2 p(x_i) - \mu^2.$$

The binomial distribution:

$$p(x) = \binom{n}{x} \theta^x (1-\theta)^{n-x} \text{ for } x = 0, 1, \ldots, n.$$

Appendix A.1.

This has mean $n\theta$ and variance $n\theta(1-\theta)$.
The Poisson distribution:

$$p(x) = \frac{\lambda^x \exp(-\lambda)}{x!} \text{ for } x = 0, 1, 2, \ldots.$$

This has mean λ and variance λ.

Continuous distributions

Distribution function:

$$F(y) = P(X \le y) = \int_{-\infty}^{y} f(x)\,dx.$$

Density function:

$$f(x) = \frac{d}{dx} F(x).$$

Evaluating probabilities:

$$P(a < X \le b) = \int_{a}^{b} f(x)\,dx = F(b) - F(a).$$

Expected value:

$$E(X) = \mu = \int_{-\infty}^{\infty} x f(x)\,dx.$$

Variance:

Summarizing data

$$\text{Var}(X) = \int_{-\infty}^{\infty} (x - \mu)^2 f(x)\,dx = \int_{-\infty}^{\infty} x^2 f(x)\,dx - \mu^2.$$

Hazard function:

$$h(t) = \frac{f(t)}{1 - F(t)}.$$

Normal density with mean μ and variance σ^2:

$$f(x) = \frac{1}{\sqrt{2\pi\sigma^2}} \exp\left\{ -\frac{1}{2} \left(\frac{x - \mu}{\sigma} \right)^2 \right\} \text{ for } x \in [-\infty, \infty].$$

Weibull density:

$$f(t) = \lambda \kappa t^{\kappa-1} \exp(-\lambda t^\kappa) \text{ for } t \ge 0.$$

Exponential density:

$$f(t) = \lambda \exp(-\lambda t) \text{ for } t \ge 0.$$

This has mean λ^{-1} and variance λ^{-2}.

Test for population mean

Data: Single sample of measurements $x_1, \ldots, x_n$.

Hypothesis: $H : \mu = \mu_0$.

Method:
- Calculate $\bar{x}$, s^2, and $t = |\bar{x} - \mu_0|\sqrt{n}/s$.
- Obtain critical value from t-tables, $df = n - 1$.

- **Reject** H at the $100p\%$ level of significance if $|t| > c$, where c is the tabulated value corresponding to column p.

Paired sample t-test

Data: Single sample of n measurements $x_1, \ldots, x_n$ which are the pairwise differences between the two original sets of measurements.

Hypothesis: $H : \mu = 0$.

Method:
- Calculate $\bar{x}$, s^2 and $t = \bar{x}\sqrt{n}/s$.
- Obtain critical value from t-tables, $df = n - 1$.
- **Reject** H at the $100p\%$ level of significance if $|t| > c$, where c is the tabulated value corresponding to column p.

Two sample t-test

Data: Two separate samples of measurements $x_1, \ldots, x_n$ and $y_1, \ldots, y_m$.

Hypothesis: $H : \mu_x = \mu_y$.

Method:
- Calculate $\bar{x}$, s_x^2, $\bar{y}$, and s_y^2.
- Calculate

$$s^2 = \left\{ (n-1)s_x^2 + (m-1)s_y^2 \right\} / (n + m - 2).$$

- Calculate $t = \dfrac{\bar{x} - \bar{y}}{\sqrt{s^2 \left(\dfrac{1}{n} + \dfrac{1}{m} \right)}}$.

- Obtain critical value from t-tables, $df = n + m - 2$.
- **Reject** H at the $100p\%$ level of significance if $|t| > c$, where c is the tabulated value corresponding to column p.

CI for population mean

Data: Sample of measurements $x_1, \ldots, x_n$.

Method:
- Calculate $\bar{x}$, s_x^2.
- Look in t-tables, $df = n - 1$, column p. Let the tabulated value be c say.
- $100(1 - p)\%$ confidence interval for μ is $\bar{x} \pm c s_x / \sqrt{n}$.

CI for difference in population means

Data: Separate samples $x_1, \ldots, x_n$ and $y_1, \ldots, y_m$.

Method:
- Calculate $\bar{x}$, s_x^2, $\bar{y}$, s_y^2.

Appendix A.2.

- Calculate

$$s^2 = \left\{ (n-1)s_x^2 + (m-1)s_y^2 \right\} / (n + m - 2).$$

- Look in t-tables, $df = n + m - 2$, column p. Let the tabulated value be c say.
- $100(1 - p)\%$ confidence interval for the difference in **population** means i.e. $\mu_x - \mu_y$, is

$$(\bar{x} - \bar{y}) \pm c \left\{ \sqrt{s^2 \left(\frac{1}{n} + \frac{1}{m} \right)} \right\}.$$

Regression and correlation

The linear regression model:

$$y_i = \alpha + \beta x_i + z_i.$$

Least squares estimates of α and β:

$$\hat{\beta} = \frac{\sum_{i=1}^{n} x_i y_i - n \bar{x} \bar{y}}{(n-1)s_x^2}, \quad \text{and } \hat{\alpha} = \bar{y} - \hat{\beta} \bar{x}.$$

Confidence interval for β

- Calculate $\hat{\beta}$ as given previously.
- Calculate $s_\varepsilon^2 = s_y^2 - \hat{\beta}^2 s_x^2$.
- Calculate $SE(\hat{\beta}) = \sqrt{\dfrac{s_\varepsilon^2}{(n-2)s_x^2}}$.
- Look in t-tables, $df = n - 2$, column p. Let the tabulated value be c.
- $100(1 - p)\%$ confidence interval for β is $\hat{\beta} \pm c \, SE(\hat{\beta})$.

Test for $\rho = 0$

Hypothesis: $H : \rho = 0$.

- Calculate

$$t = r \left(\frac{n-2}{1-r^2} \right)^{1/2}.$$

- Obtain critical value from t-tables, $df = n - 2$.
- **Reject** H at $100p\%$ level of significance if $|t| > c$, where c is the tabulated value corresponding to column p.

Approximate CI for proportion θ

$$p \pm 1.96 \sqrt{\frac{p(1-p)}{n-1}}$$

where p is the observed proportion in the sample.

Test for a proportion

Hypothesis: $H : \theta = \theta_0$.

- Test statistic $z = \dfrac{p - \theta_0}{\sqrt{\dfrac{\theta_0(1 - \theta_0)}{n}}}$.

- Obtain critical value from normal tables.

Comparison of proportions

Hypothesis: $H : \theta_1 = \theta_2$.

- Calculate
$$p = \frac{n_1 p_1 + n_2 p_2}{n_1 + n_2}.$$

- Calculate
$$z = \frac{p_1 - p_2}{\sqrt{p(1 - p)\left(\dfrac{1}{n_1} + \dfrac{1}{n_2}\right)}}$$

- Obtain appropriate critical value from normal tables.

Goodness of fit

Test statistic
$$\chi^2 = \sum_{i=1}^{m} \frac{(o_i - e_i)^2}{e_i}$$

where m is the number of categories.

Hypothesis $H : F = F_0$.

- Calculate the expected class frequencies under F_0.
- Calculate the χ^2 test statistic given above.
- Determine the degrees of freedom, ν say.
- Obtain critical value from χ^2 tables, $df = \nu$.
- Reject $H : F = F_0$ at the $100p\%$ level of significance if $\chi^2 > c$ where c is the tabulated critical value.

Appendix A.3.

APPENDIX B
Z Score Table

STANDARD NORMAL DISTRIBUTION: Table Values Represent AREA to the LEFT of the Z score.

Z	.00	.01	.02	.03	.04	.05	.06	.07	.08	.09
-3.9	.00005	.00005	.00004	.00004	.00004	.00004	.00004	.00004	.00003	.00003
-3.8	.00007	.00007	.00007	.00006	.00006	.00006	.00006	.00005	.00005	.00005
-3.7	.00011	.00010	.00010	.00010	.00009	.00009	.00008	.00008	.00008	.00008
-3.6	.00016	.00015	.00015	.00014	.00014	.00013	.00013	.00012	.00012	.00011
-3.5	.00023	.00022	.00022	.00021	.00020	.00019	.00019	.00018	.00017	.00017
-3.4	.00034	.00032	.00031	.00030	.00029	.00028	.00027	.00026	.00025	.00024
-3.3	.00048	.00047	.00045	.00043	.00042	.00040	.00039	.00038	.00036	.00035
-3.2	.00069	.00066	.00064	.00062	.00060	.00058	.00056	.00054	.00052	.00050
-3.1	.00097	.00094	.00090	.00087	.00084	.00082	.00079	.00076	.00074	.00071
-3.0	.00135	.00131	.00126	.00122	.00118	.00114	.00111	.00107	.00104	.00100
-2.9	.00187	.00181	.00175	.00169	.00164	.00159	.00154	.00149	.00144	.00139
-2.8	.00256	.00248	.00240	.00233	.00226	.00219	.00212	.00205	.00199	.00193
-2.7	.00347	.00336	.00326	.00317	.00307	.00298	.00289	.00280	.00272	.00264
-2.6	.00466	.00453	.00440	.00427	.00415	.00402	.00391	.00379	.00368	.00357
-2.5	.00621	.00604	.00587	.00570	.00554	.00539	.00523	.00508	.00494	.00480
-2.4	.00820	.00798	.00776	.00755	.00734	.00714	.00695	.00676	.00657	.00639
-2.3	.01072	.01044	.01017	.00990	.00964	.00939	.00914	.00889	.00866	.00842
-2.2	.01390	.01355	.01321	.01287	.01255	.01222	.01191	.01160	.01130	.01101
-2.1	.01786	.01743	.01700	.01659	.01618	.01578	.01539	.01500	.01463	.01426
-2.0	.02275	.02222	.02169	.02118	.02068	.02018	.01970	.01923	.01876	.01831
-1.9	.02872	.02807	.02743	.02680	.02619	.02559	.02500	.02442	.02385	.02330
-1.8	.03593	.03515	.03438	.03362	.03288	.03216	.03144	.03074	.03005	.02938
-1.7	.04457	.04363	.04272	.04182	.04093	.04006	.03920	.03836	.03754	.03673
-1.6	.05480	.05370	.05262	.05155	.05050	.04947	.04846	.04746	.04648	.04551
-1.5	.06681	.06552	.06426	.06301	.06178	.06057	.05938	.05821	.05705	.05592
-1.4	.08076	.07927	.07780	.07636	.07493	.07353	.07215	.07078	.06944	.06811
-1.3	.09680	.09510	.09342	.09176	.09012	.08851	.08691	.08534	.08379	.08226
-1.2	.11507	.11314	.11123	.10935	.10749	.10565	.10383	.10204	.10027	.09853
-1.1	.13567	.13350	.13136	.12924	.12714	.12507	.12302	.12100	.11900	.11702
-1.0	.15866	.15625	.15386	.15151	.14917	.14686	.14457	.14231	.14007	.13786
-0.9	.18406	.18141	.17879	.17619	.17361	.17106	.16853	.16602	.16354	.16109
-0.8	.21186	.20897	.20611	.20327	.20045	.19766	.19489	.19215	.18943	.18673
-0.7	.24196	.23885	.23576	.23270	.22965	.22663	.22363	.22065	.21770	.21476
-0.6	.27425	.27093	.26763	.26435	.26109	.25785	.25463	.25143	.24825	.24510
-0.5	.30854	.30503	.30153	.29806	.29460	.29116	.28774	.28434	.28096	.27760
-0.4	.34458	.34090	.33724	.33360	.32997	.32636	.32276	.31918	.31561	.31207
-0.3	.38209	.37828	.37448	.37070	.36693	.36317	.35942	.35569	.35197	.34827
-0.2	.42074	.41683	.41294	.40905	.40517	.40129	.39743	.39358	.38974	.38591
-0.1	.46017	.45620	.45224	.44828	.44433	.44038	.43644	.43251	.42858	.42465
-0.0	.50000	.49601	.49202	.48803	.48405	.48006	.47608	.47210	.46812	.46414

Appendix B.1.

STANDARD NORMAL DISTRIBUTION: Table Values Represent AREA to the LEFT of the Z score.

Z	.00	.01	.02	.03	.04	.05	.06	.07	.08	.09
0.0	.50000	.50399	.50798	.51197	.51595	.51994	.52392	.52790	.53188	.53586
0.1	.53983	.54380	.54776	.55172	.55567	.55962	.56356	.56749	.57142	.57535
0.2	.57926	.58317	.58706	.59095	.59483	.59871	.60257	.60642	.61026	.61409
0.3	.61791	.62172	.62552	.62930	.63307	.63683	.64058	.64431	.64803	.65173
0.4	.65542	.65910	.66276	.66640	.67003	.67364	.67724	.68082	.68439	.68793
0.5	.69146	.69497	.69847	.70194	.70540	.70884	.71226	.71566	.71904	.72240
0.6	.72575	.72907	.73237	.73565	.73891	.74215	.74537	.74857	.75175	.75490
0.7	.75804	.76115	.76424	.76730	.77035	.77337	.77637	.77935	.78230	.78524
0.8	.78814	.79103	.79389	.79673	.79955	.80234	.80511	.80785	.81057	.81327
0.9	.81594	.81859	.82121	.82381	.82639	.82894	.83147	.83398	.83646	.83891
1.0	.84134	.84375	.84614	.84849	.85083	.85314	.85543	.85769	.85993	.86214
1.1	.86433	.86650	.86864	.87076	.87286	.87493	.87698	.87900	.88100	.88298
1.2	.88493	.88686	.88877	.89065	.89251	.89435	.89617	.89796	.89973	.90147
1.3	.90320	.90490	.90658	.90824	.90988	.91149	.91309	.91466	.91621	.91774
1.4	.91924	.92073	.92220	.92364	.92507	.92647	.92785	.92922	.93056	.93189
1.5	.93319	.93448	.93574	.93699	.93822	.93943	.94062	.94179	.94295	.94408
1.6	.94520	.94630	.94738	.94845	.94950	.95053	.95154	.95254	.95352	.95449
1.7	.95543	.95637	.95728	.95818	.95907	.95994	.96080	.96164	.96246	.96327
1.8	.96407	.96485	.96562	.96638	.96712	.96784	.96856	.96926	.96995	.97062
1.9	.97128	.97193	.97257	.97320	.97381	.97441	.97500	.97558	.97615	.97670
2.0	.97725	.97778	.97831	.97882	.97932	.97982	.98030	.98077	.98124	.98169
2.1	.98214	.98257	.98300	.98341	.98382	.98422	.98461	.98500	.98537	.98574
2.2	.98610	.98645	.98679	.98713	.98745	.98778	.98809	.98840	.98870	.98899
2.3	.98928	.98956	.98983	.99010	.99036	.99061	.99086	.99111	.99134	.99158
2.4	.99180	.99202	.99224	.99245	.99266	.99286	.99305	.99324	.99343	.99361
2.5	.99379	.99396	.99413	.99430	.99446	.99461	.99477	.99492	.99506	.99520
2.6	.99534	.99547	.99560	.99573	.99585	.99598	.99609	.99621	.99632	.99643
2.7	.99653	.99664	.99674	.99683	.99693	.99702	.99711	.99720	.99728	.99736
2.8	.99744	.99752	.99760	.99767	.99774	.99781	.99788	.99795	.99801	.99807
2.9	.99813	.99819	.99825	.99831	.99836	.99841	.99846	.99851	.99856	.99861
3.0	.99865	.99869	.99874	.99878	.99882	.99886	.99889	.99893	.99896	.99900
3.1	.99903	.99906	.99910	.99913	.99916	.99918	.99921	.99924	.99926	.99929
3.2	.99931	.99934	.99936	.99938	.99940	.99942	.99944	.99946	.99948	.99950
3.3	.99952	.99953	.99955	.99957	.99958	.99960	.99961	.99962	.99964	.99965
3.4	.99966	.99968	.99969	.99970	.99971	.99972	.99973	.99974	.99975	.99976
3.5	.99977	.99978	.99978	.99979	.99980	.99981	.99981	.99982	.99983	.99983
3.6	.99984	.99985	.99985	.99986	.99986	.99987	.99987	.99988	.99988	.99989
3.7	.99989	.99990	.99990	.99990	.99991	.99991	.99992	.99992	.99992	.99992
3.8	.99993	.99993	.99993	.99994	.99994	.99994	.99994	.99995	.99995	.99995
3.9	.99995	.99995	.99996	.99996	.99996	.99996	.99996	.99996	.99997	.99997

Appendix B.2.

t Table

cum. prob	$t_{.50}$	$t_{.75}$	$t_{.80}$	$t_{.85}$	$t_{.90}$	$t_{.95}$	$t_{.975}$	$t_{.99}$	$t_{.995}$	$t_{.999}$	$t_{.9995}$
one-tail	0.50	0.25	0.20	0.15	0.10	0.05	0.025	0.01	0.005	0.001	0.0005
two-tails	1.00	0.50	0.40	0.30	0.20	0.10	0.05	0.02	0.01	0.002	0.001
df											
1	0.000	1.000	1.376	1.963	3.078	6.314	12.71	31.82	63.66	318.31	636.62
2	0.000	0.816	1.061	1.386	1.886	2.920	4.303	6.965	9.925	22.327	31.599
3	0.000	0.765	0.978	1.250	1.638	2.353	3.182	4.541	5.841	10.215	12.924
4	0.000	0.741	0.941	1.190	1.533	2.132	2.776	3.747	4.604	7.173	8.610
5	0.000	0.727	0.920	1.156	1.476	2.015	2.571	3.365	4.032	5.893	6.869
6	0.000	0.718	0.906	1.134	1.440	1.943	2.447	3.143	3.707	5.208	5.959
7	0.000	0.711	0.896	1.119	1.415	1.895	2.365	2.998	3.499	4.785	5.408
8	0.000	0.706	0.889	1.108	1.397	1.860	2.306	2.896	3.355	4.501	5.041
9	0.000	0.703	0.883	1.100	1.383	1.833	2.262	2.821	3.250	4.297	4.781
10	0.000	0.700	0.879	1.093	1.372	1.812	2.228	2.764	3.169	4.144	4.587
11	0.000	0.697	0.876	1.088	1.363	1.796	2.201	2.718	3.106	4.025	4.437
12	0.000	0.695	0.873	1.083	1.356	1.782	2.179	2.681	3.055	3.930	4.318
13	0.000	0.694	0.870	1.079	1.350	1.771	2.160	2.650	3.012	3.852	4.221
14	0.000	0.692	0.868	1.076	1.345	1.761	2.145	2.624	2.977	3.787	4.140
15	0.000	0.691	0.866	1.074	1.341	1.753	2.131	2.602	2.947	3.733	4.073
16	0.000	0.690	0.865	1.071	1.337	1.746	2.120	2.583	2.921	3.686	4.015
17	0.000	0.689	0.863	1.069	1.333	1.740	2.110	2.567	2.898	3.646	3.965
18	0.000	0.688	0.862	1.067	1.330	1.734	2.101	2.552	2.878	3.610	3.922
19	0.000	0.688	0.861	1.066	1.328	1.729	2.093	2.539	2.861	3.579	3.883
20	0.000	0.687	0.860	1.064	1.325	1.725	2.086	2.528	2.845	3.552	3.850
21	0.000	0.686	0.859	1.063	1.323	1.721	2.080	2.518	2.831	3.527	3.819
22	0.000	0.686	0.858	1.061	1.321	1.717	2.074	2.508	2.819	3.505	3.792
23	0.000	0.685	0.858	1.060	1.319	1.714	2.069	2.500	2.807	3.485	3.768
24	0.000	0.685	0.857	1.059	1.318	1.711	2.064	2.492	2.797	3.467	3.745
25	0.000	0.684	0.856	1.058	1.316	1.708	2.060	2.485	2.787	3.450	3.725
26	0.000	0.684	0.856	1.058	1.315	1.706	2.056	2.479	2.779	3.435	3.707
27	0.000	0.684	0.855	1.057	1.314	1.703	2.052	2.473	2.771	3.421	3.690
28	0.000	0.683	0.855	1.056	1.313	1.701	2.048	2.467	2.763	3.408	3.674
29	0.000	0.683	0.854	1.055	1.311	1.699	2.045	2.462	2.756	3.396	3.659
30	0.000	0.683	0.854	1.055	1.310	1.697	2.042	2.457	2.750	3.385	3.646
40	0.000	0.681	0.851	1.050	1.303	1.684	2.021	2.423	2.704	3.307	3.551
60	0.000	0.679	0.848	1.045	1.296	1.671	2.000	2.390	2.660	3.232	3.460
80	0.000	0.678	0.846	1.043	1.292	1.664	1.990	2.374	2.639	3.195	3.416
100	0.000	0.677	0.845	1.042	1.290	1.660	1.984	2.364	2.626	3.174	3.390
1000	0.000	0.675	0.842	1.037	1.282	1.646	1.962	2.330	2.581	3.098	3.300
z	0.000	0.674	0.842	1.036	1.282	1.645	1.960	2.326	2.576	3.090	3.291
	0%	50%	60%	70%	80%	90%	95%	98%	99%	99.8%	99.9%
						Confidence Level					

Appendix B.3.

APPENDIX C
Useful R Commands

Command	Purpose
help()	Obtain documentation for a given R command
example()	View some examples on the use of a command
c(), scan()	Enter data manually to a vector in R
seq()	Make arithmetic progression vector
rep()	Make vector of repeated values
data()	Load (often into a data.frame) built-in dataset
View()	View dataset in a spreadsheet-type format
str()	Display internal structure of an R object
read.csv(), read.table()	Load into a data.frame an existing data le
library(), require()	Make available an R add-on package
dim()	See dimensions (# of rows/cols) of data.frame
length()	Give length of a vector
ls()	Lists memory contents
rm()	Removes an item from memory
names()	Lists names of variables in a data.frame
hist()	Command for producing a histogram
histogram()	Lattice command for producing a histogram
stem()	Make a stem plot
table()	List all values of a variable with frequencies
xtabs()	Cross-tabulation tables using formulas
mosaicplot()	Make a mosaic plot
cut()	Groups values of a variable into larger bins
mean(), median()	Identify "center" of distribution
by()	Apply function to a column split by factors
summary()	Display 5-number summary and mean
var(), sd()	Find variance, sd of values in vector
sum()	Add up all values in a vector
quantile()	Find the position of a quantile in a dataset
barplot()	Produces a bar graph
barchart()	Lattice command for producing bar graphs
boxplot()	Produces a boxplot
bwplot()	Lattice command for producing boxplots
plot()	Produces a scatterplot
xyplot()	Lattice command for producing a scatterplot
lm()	Determine the least-squares regression line
anova()	Analysis of variance (can use on results of lm())
predict()	Obtain predicted values from linear model
nls()	Estimate parameters of a nonlinear model
residuals()	Gives (observed - predicted) for a model t to data
sample()	Take a sample from a vector of data
replicate()	Repeat some process a set number of times
cumsum()	produce running total of values for input vector
ecdf()	Builds empirical cumulative distribution function
dbinom(), etc.	Tools for binomial distributions
dpois(), etc.	Tools for Poisson distributions
pnorm(), etc.	Tools for normal distributions
qt(), etc.	Tools for student t distributions
pchisq(), etc.	Tools for chi-square distributions
binom.test()	Hypothesis test and condence interval for 1 proportion
prop.test()	Inference for 1 proportion using normal approx.
chisq.test()	Carries out a chi-square test
fisher.test()	Fisher test for contingency table
t.test()	Student t test for inference on population mean
qqnorm(), qqline()	Tools for checking normality
addmargins()	Adds marginal sums to an existing table
prop.table()	Compute proportions from a contingency table
par()	Query and edit graphical settings
power.t.test()	Power calculations for 1- and 2-sample t
anova()	Compute analysis of variance table for tted model

Appendix C.1.

```
help()
```

```
help(mean)
```

```
example()
```

```
require(lattice)
example(histogram)
```

```
c(), rep() seq()
```

```
> x = c(8, 6, 7, 5, 3, 0, 9)
> x

[1] 8 6 7 5 3 0 9

> names = c("Owen", "Luke", "Anakin", "Leia", "Jacen", "Jaina")
> names

[1] "Owen"   "Luke"   "Anakin" "Leia"   "Jacen"  "Jaina"

> heartDeck = c(rep(1, 13), rep(0, 39))
> heartDeck

 [1] 1 1 1 1 1 1 1 1 1 1 1 1 1 0 0 0 0 0 0 0 0 0 0 0 0 0 0 0 0 0 0 0 0 0 0 0 0 0 0 0 0 0 0 0 0 0 0 0
[49] 0 0 0 0

> y = seq(7, 41, 1.5)
> y

 [1]  7.0  8.5 10.0 11.5 13.0 14.5 16.0 17.5 19.0 20.5 22.0 23.5 25.0 26.5 28.0 29.5 31.0 32.5 34.0
[20] 35.5 37.0 38.5 40.0
```

```
data(), dim(), names(), View(), str()
```

```
> data(iris)
> names(iris)

[1] "Sepal.Length" "Sepal.Width"  "Petal.Length" "Petal.Width"  "Species"

> dim(iris)

[1] 150   5

> str(iris)

'data.frame':      150 obs. of  5 variables:
 $ Sepal.Length: num  5.1 4.9 4.7 4.6 5 5.4 4.6 5 4.4 4.9 ...
 $ Sepal.Width : num  3.5 3 3.2 3.1 3.6 3.9 3.4 3.4 2.9 3.1 ...
 $ Petal.Length: num  1.4 1.4 1.3 1.5 1.4 1.7 1.4 1.5 1.4 1.5 ...
 $ Petal.Width : num  0.2 0.2 0.2 0.2 0.2 0.4 0.3 0.2 0.2 0.1 ...
 $ Species     : Factor w/ 3 levels "setosa","versicolor",..: 1 1 1 1 1 1 1 1 1 1 ...
> View(iris)
```

Appendix C.2.

ls(), rm()

```
> data(iris)
> data(faithful)
> data(Puromycin)
> data(LakeHuron)
> ls()

[1] "faithful"  "heartDeck" "iris"      "LakeHuron" "names"     "Puromycin" "x"         "y"

> newVector = 1:12
> ls()

[1] "faithful"  "heartDeck" "iris"      "LakeHuron" "names"     "newVector" "Puromycin" "x"
[9] "y"

> rm(faithful)
> ls()

[1] "heartDeck" "iris"      "LakeHuron" "names"     "newVector" "Puromycin" "x"         "y"
```

hist()

```
data(faithful)
hist(faithful$eruptions)
hist(faithful$eruptions, n=15)
hist(faithful$eruptions, breaks=seq(1.5,5.25,.25), col="red")
hist(faithful$eruptions, freq=F, n=15, main="Histogram of Old Faithful Eruption Times", xlab="Duration (mins)")
```

Histogram of Old Faithful Eruption Times

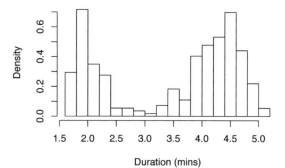

Duration (mins)

Appendix C.3.

library(), require()

```
> library(abd)
> require(lattice)
```

histogram()

```
require(lattice)
data(iris)
histogram(iris$Sepal.Length, breaks=seq(4,8,.25))
histogram(~ Sepal.Length, data=iris, main="Iris Sepals", xlab="Length")
histogram(~ Sepal.Length | Species, data=iris, col="red")
histogram(~ Sepal.Length | Species, data=iris, n=15, layout=c(1,3))
```

read.csv()

```
> As.in.H2O = read.csv("http://www.calvin.edu/~scofield/data/comma/arsenicInWater.csv")
```

read.table()

```
> senate = read.table("http://www.calvin.edu/~scofield/data/tab/rc/senate99.dat", sep="\t", header=T)
```

mean(), median(), summary(), var(), sd(), quantile(),

```
> counties=read.csv("http://www.calvin.edu/~stob/data/counties.csv")
> names(counties)

[1] "County"      "State"       "Population"   "HousingUnits"  "TotalArea"
[6] "WaterArea"   "LandArea"    "DensityPop"   "DensityHousing"

> x = counties$LandArea
> mean(x, na.rm = T)

[1] 1126.214

> median(x, na.rm = T)

[1] 616.48

> summary(x)

    Min.   1st Qu.   Median    Mean   3rd Qu.      Max.
    1.99    431.70   616.50  1126.00   923.20  145900.00

> sd(x, na.rm = T)

[1] 3622.453

> var(x, na.rm = T)

[1] 13122165

> quantile(x, probs=seq(0, 1, .2), na.rm=T)

     0%      20%      40%      60%      80%       100%
   1.99   403.29   554.36   717.94  1043.82  145899.69
```

Appendix C.4.

sum()

```
> firstTwentyIntegers = 1:20
> sum(firstTwentyIntegers)

[1] 210

> die = 1:6
> manyRolls = sample(die, 100, replace=T)
> sixFreq = sum(manyRolls == 6)
> sixFreq / 100

[1] 0.14
```

stem()

```
> monarchs = read.csv("http://www.calvin.edu/~scofield/data/comma/monarchReigns.csv")
> stem(monarchs$years)

  The decimal point is 1 digit(s) to the right of the |

  0 | 0123566799
  1 | 0023333579
  2 | 012224455
  3 | 355589
  4 | 4
  5 | 069
  6 | 3
```

table(), table(), mosaicplot(), cut()

```
> pol = read.csv("http://www.calvin.edu/~stob/data/csbv.csv")
> table(pol$sex)

Female    Male
   133      88

> table(pol$sex, pol$Political04)

        Conservative Far Right Liberal Middle-of-the-road
  Female           67         0      14                 48
  Male             47         7       6                 28

> xtabs(~sex, data=pol)

sex
Female    Male
   133      88

> xtabs(~Political04 + Political07, data=pol)

                   Political07
Political04        Conservative Far Left Far Right Liberal Middle-of-the-road
  Conservative               58        0         2      13                 39
  Far Right                   4        0         3       0                  0
  Liberal                     0        1         1      14                  4
  Middle-of-the-road         20        0         0      22                 32

> mosaicplot(~Political04 + sex, data=pol)
```

Appendix C.5.

pol

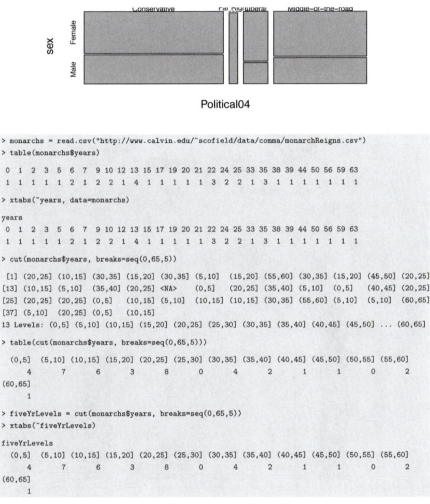

Political04

```
> monarchs = read.csv("http://www.calvin.edu/~scofield/data/comma/monarchReigns.csv")
> table(monarchs$years)

 0  1  2  3  5  6  7  9 10 12 13 15 17 19 20 21 22 24 25 33 35 38 39 44 50 56 59 63
 1  1  1  1  1  2  1  2  2  1  4  1  1  1  1  1  3  2  2  1  3  1  1  1  1  1  1  1

> xtabs(~years, data=monarchs)

years
 0  1  2  3  5  6  7  9 10 12 13 15 17 19 20 21 22 24 25 33 35 38 39 44 50 56 59 63
 1  1  1  1  1  2  1  2  2  1  4  1  1  1  1  1  3  2  2  1  3  1  1  1  1  1  1  1

> cut(monarchs$years, breaks=seq(0,65,5))

 [1] (20,25] (10,15] (30,35] (15,20] (30,35] (5,10]  (15,20] (55,60] (30,35] (15,20] (45,50] (20,25]
[13] (10,15] (5,10]  (35,40] (20,25] <NA>    (0,5]   (20,25] (35,40] (5,10]  (0,5]   (40,45] (20,25]
[25] (20,25] (20,25] (0,5]   (10,15] (5,10]  (10,15] (10,15] (30,35] (55,60] (5,10]  (5,10]  (60,65]
[37] (5,10]  (20,25] (0,5]   (10,15]
13 Levels: (0,5] (5,10] (10,15] (15,20] (20,25] (25,30] (30,35] (35,40] (40,45] (45,50] ... (60,65]

> table(cut(monarchs$years, breaks=seq(0,65,5)))

  (0,5]  (5,10] (10,15] (15,20] (20,25] (25,30] (30,35] (35,40] (40,45] (45,50] (50,55] (55,60]
      4       7       6       3       8       0       4       2       1       1       0       2
(60,65]
      1

> fiveYrLevels = cut(monarchs$years, breaks=seq(0,65,5))
> xtabs(~fiveYrLevels)

fiveYrLevels
  (0,5]  (5,10] (10,15] (15,20] (20,25] (25,30] (30,35] (35,40] (40,45] (45,50] (50,55] (55,60]
      4       7       6       3       8       0       4       2       1       1       0       2
(60,65]
      1
```

Appendix C.6.

`barplot()`

```
pol = read.csv("http://www.calvin.edu/~stob/data/csbv.csv")
barplot(table(pol$Political04), main="Political Leanings, Calvin Freshman 2004")
barplot(table(pol$Political04), horiz=T)
barplot(table(pol$Political04),col=c("red","green","blue","orange"))
barplot(table(pol$Political04),col=c("red","green","blue","orange"),
     names=c("Conservative","Far Right","Liberal","Centrist"))
```

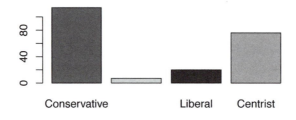

```
barplot(xtabs(~sex + Political04, data=pol), legend=c("Female","Male"), beside=T)
```

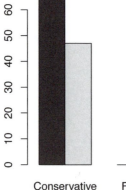

Appendix C.7.

```
boxplot()
```

```
data(iris)
boxplot(iris$Sepal.Length)
boxplot(iris$Sepal.Length, col="yellow")
boxplot(Sepal.Length ~ Species, data=iris)
boxplot(Sepal.Length ~ Species, data=iris, col="yellow", ylab="Sepal length",main="Iris Sepal Length by Species")
```

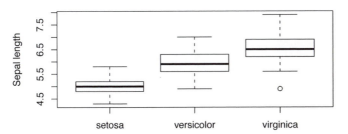

```
plot()
```

```
data(faithful)
plot(waiting~eruptions,data=faithful)
plot(waiting~eruptions,data=faithful,cex=.5)
plot(waiting~eruptions,data=faithful,pch=6)
plot(waiting~eruptions,data=faithful,pch=19)
plot(waiting~eruptions,data=faithful,cex=.5,pch=19,col="blue")
plot(waiting~eruptions, data=faithful, cex=.5, pch=19, col="blue", main="Old Faithful Eruptions",
    ylab="Wait time between eruptions", xlab="Duration of eruption")
```

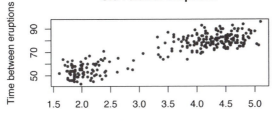

Appendix C.8.

sample()

```
> sample(c("Heads","Tails"), size=1)

[1] "Heads"

> sample(c("Heads","Tails"), size=10, replace=T)

 [1] "Heads" "Heads" "Heads" "Tails" "Tails" "Tails" "Tails" "Tails" "Tails" "Heads"

> sample(c(0, 1), 10, replace=T)

 [1] 1 0 0 1 1 0 0 1 0 0

> sum(sample(1:6, 2, replace=T))

[1] 10

> sample(c(0, 1), prob=c(.25,.75), size=10, replace=T)

 [1] 1 1 1 0 1 1 1 1 1 1

> sample(c(rep(1,13),rep(0,39)), size=5, replace=F)

[1] 0 0 0 0 0
```

replicate()

```
> sample(c("Heads","Tails"), 2, replace=T)

[1] "Tails" "Heads"

> replicate(5, sample(c("Heads","Tails"), 2, replace=T))

     [,1]    [,2]    [,3]    [,4]    [,5]
[1,] "Heads" "Tails" "Heads" "Tails" "Heads"
[2,] "Heads" "Tails" "Heads" "Heads" "Heads"

> ftCount = replicate(100000, sum(sample(c(0, 1), 10, rep=T, prob=c(.6, .4))))
> hist(ftCount, freq=F, breaks=-0.5:10.5, xlab="Free throws made out of 10 attempts",
+      main="Simulated Sampling Dist. for 40% FT Shooter", col="green")
```

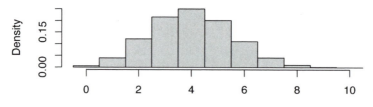

Simulated Sampling Dist. for 40% FT Shooter

Free throws made out of 10 attempts

Appendix C.9.

dbinom(), pbinom(), qbinom(), rbinom(), binom.test(), prop.test()

```
> dbinom(0, 5, .5)      # probability of 0 heads in 5 flips

[1] 0.03125

> dbinom(0:5, 5, .5)    # full probability dist. for 5 flips

[1] 0.03125 0.15625 0.31250 0.31250 0.15625 0.03125

> sum(dbinom(0:2, 5, .5))    # probability of 2 or fewer heads in 5 flips

[1] 0.5

> pbinom(2, 5, .5)    # same as last line

[1] 0.5

> flip5 = replicate(10000, sum(sample(c("H","T"), 5, rep=T)=="H"))
> table(flip5) / 10000   # distribution (simulated) of count of heads in 5 flips

flip5
     0      1      2      3      4      5
0.0310 0.1545 0.3117 0.3166 0.1566 0.0296

> table(rbinom(10000, 5, .5)) / 10000    # shorter version of previous 2 lines

     0      1      2      3      4      5
0.0304 0.1587 0.3087 0.3075 0.1634 0.0313

> qbinom(seq(0,1,.2), 50, .2)    # approx. 0/.2/.4/.6/.8/1-quantiles in Binom(50,.2) distribution

[1]  0  8  9 11 12 50

> binom.test(29, 200, .21)    # inference on sample with 29 successes in 200 trials

        Exact binomial test

data:  29 and 200
number of successes = 29, number of trials = 200, p-value = 0.02374
alternative hypothesis: true probability of success is not equal to 0.21
95 percent confidence interval:
 0.09930862 0.20156150
sample estimates:
probability of success
                 0.145

> prop.test(29, 200, .21)    # inference on same sample, using normal approx. to binomial

        1-sample proportions test with continuity correction

data:  29 out of 200, null probability 0.21
X-squared = 4.7092, df = 1, p-value = 0.03
alternative hypothesis: true p is not equal to 0.21
95 percent confidence interval:
 0.1007793 0.2032735
sample estimates:
    p
0.145
```

Appendix C.10.

pchisq(), qchisq(), chisq.test()

```
> 1 - pchisq(3.1309, 5)    # gives P-value associated with X-squared stat 3.1309 when df=5

[1] 0.679813

> pchisq(3.1309, df=5, lower.tail=F)    # same as above

[1] 0.679813

> qchisq(c(.001,.005,.01,.025,.05,.95,.975,.99,.995,.999), 2)  # gives critical values like Table A

 [1]  0.002001001  0.010025084  0.020100672  0.050635616  0.102586589  5.991464547  7.377758908
 [8]  9.210340372 10.596634733 13.815510558

> qchisq(c(.999,.995,.99,.975,.95,.05,.025,.01,.005,.001), 2, lower.tail=F)  # same as above

 [1]  0.002001001  0.010025084  0.020100672  0.050635616  0.102586589  5.991464547  7.377758908
 [8]  9.210340372 10.596634733 13.815510558

> observedCounts = c(35, 27, 33, 40, 47, 51)
> claimedProbabilities = c(.13, .13, .14, .16, .24, .20)
> chisq.test(observedCounts, p=claimedProbabilities)  # goodness-of-fit test, assumes df = n-1

        Chi-squared test for given probabilities

data:  observedCounts
X-squared = 3.1309, df = 5, p-value = 0.6798
```

addmargins()

```
> blood = read.csv("http://www.calvin.edu/~scofield/data/comma/blood.csv")
> t = table(blood$Rh, blood$type)
> addmargins(t)         # to add both row/column totals

       A  AB   B   O Sum
 Neg   6   1   2   7  16
 Pos  34   3   9  38  84
 Sum  40   4  11  45 100

> addmargins(t, 1)      # to add only column totals

       A AB  B  O
 Neg   6  1  2  7
 Pos  34  3  9 38
 Sum  40  4 11 45

> addmargins(t, 2)      # to add only row totals

       A AB  B  O Sum
 Neg   6  1  2  7  16
 Pos  34  3  9 38  84
```

Appendix C.11.

```
prop.table()
```

```
> smoke = matrix(c(51,43,22,92,28,21,68,22,9),ncol=3,byrow=TRUE)
> colnames(smoke) = c("High","Low","Middle")
> rownames(smoke) = c("current","former","never")
> smoke = as.table(smoke)
> smoke

        High Low Middle
current   51  43     22
former    92  28     21
never     68  22      9

> summary(smoke)

Number of cases in table: 356
Number of factors: 2
Test for independence of all factors:
        Chisq = 18.51, df = 4, p-value = 0.0009808

> prop.table(smoke)

              High        Low      Middle
current 0.14325843 0.12078652 0.06179775
former  0.25842697 0.07865169 0.05898876
never   0.19101124 0.06179775 0.02528090

> prop.table(smoke, 1)

             High       Low    Middle
current 0.4396552 0.3706897 0.1896552
former  0.6524823 0.1985816 0.1489362
never   0.6868687 0.2222222 0.0909091

> barplot(smoke,legend=T,beside=T,main='Smoking Status by SES')
```

Smoking Status by SES

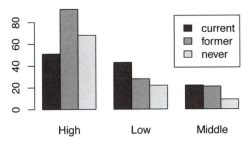

Appendix C.12.

par()

```
> par(mfrow = c(1,2))      # set figure so next two plots appear side-by-side
> poisSamp = rpois(50, 3)   # Draw sample of size 50 from Pois(3)
> maxX = max(poisSamp)      # will help in setting horizontal plotting region
> hist(poisSamp, freq=F, breaks=-.5:(maxX+.5), col="green", xlab="Sampled values")
> plot(0:maxX, dpois(0:maxX, 3), type="h", ylim=c(0,.25), col="blue", main="Probabilities for Pois(3)")
```

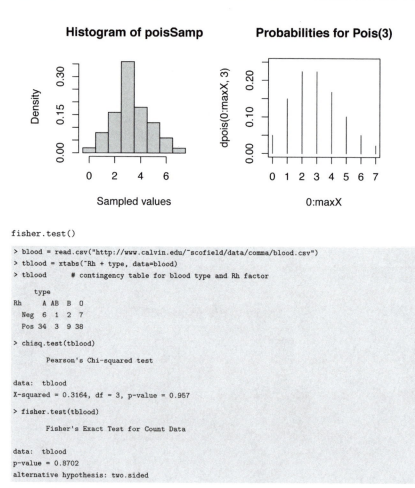

fisher.test()

```
> blood = read.csv("http://www.calvin.edu/~scofield/data/comma/blood.csv")
> tblood = xtabs(~Rh + type, data=blood)
> tblood        # contingency table for blood type and Rh factor

     type
Rh    A AB  B  O
  Neg 6  1  2  7
  Pos 34 3  9 38

> chisq.test(tblood)

        Pearson's Chi-squared test

data:  tblood
X-squared = 0.3164, df = 3, p-value = 0.957

> fisher.test(tblood)

        Fisher's Exact Test for Count Data

data:  tblood
p-value = 0.8702
alternative hypothesis: two.sided
```

Appendix C.13.

dpois(), ppois()

```
> dpois(2:7, 4.2)    # probabilities of 2, 3, 4, 5, 6 or 7 successes in Pois(4.211)

[1] 0.13226099 0.18516538 0.19442365 0.16331587 0.11432111 0.06859266

> ppois(1, 4.2)    # probability of 1 or fewer successes in Pois(4.2); same as sum(dpois(0:1, 4.2))

[1] 0.077977

> 1 - ppois(7, 4.2)    # probability of 8 or more successes in Pois(4.2)

[1] 0.06394334
```

pnorm() qnorm(), rnorm(), dnorm()

```
> pnorm(17, 19, 3)    # gives Prob[X < 17], when X ~ Norm(19, 3)

[1] 0.2524925

> qnorm(c(.95, .975, .995))    # obtain z* critical values for 90, 95, 99% CIs

[1] 1.644854 1.959964 2.575829

> nSamp = rnorm(10000, 7, 1.5)    # draw random sample from Norm(7, 1.5)
> hist(nSamp, freq=F, col="green", main="Sampled values and population density curve")
> xs = seq(2, 12, .05)
> lines(xs, dnorm(xs, 7, 1.5), lwd=2, col="blue")
```

Sampled values and population density curve

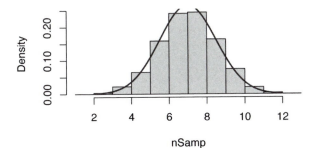

Appendix C.14.

qt(), pt(), rt(), dt()

```
> qt(c(.95, .975, .995), df=9)    # critical values for 90, 95, 99% CIs for means

[1] 1.833113 2.262157 3.249836

> pt(-2.1, 11)       # gives Prob[T < -2.1] when df = 11

[1] 0.02980016

> tSamp = rt(50, 11)    # takes random sample of size 50 from t-dist with 11 dfs
> # code for comparing several t distributions to standard normal distribution
> xs = seq(-5,5,.01)
> plot(xs, dnorm(xs), type="l", lwd=2, col="black", ylab="pdf values",
+     main="Some t dists alongside standard normal curve")
> lines(xs, dt(xs, 1), lwd=2, col="blue")
> lines(xs, dt(xs, 4), lwd=2, col="red")
> lines(xs, dt(xs, 10), lwd=2, col="green")
> legend("topright",col=c("black","blue","red","green"),
+         legend=c("std. normal","t, df=1","t, df=4","t, df=10"), lty=1)
```

Some t dists alongside standard normal curve

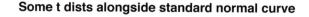

by()

```
> data(warpbreaks)
> by(warpbreaks$breaks, warpbreaks$tension, mean)

warpbreaks$tension: L
[1] 36.38889
-----------------------------------------------------------------------
warpbreaks$tension: M
[1] 26.38889
-----------------------------------------------------------------------
warpbreaks$tension: H
[1] 21.66667
```

Appendix C.15.

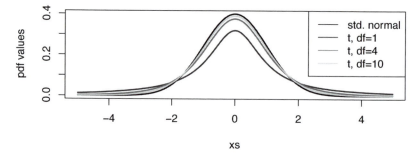

```
t.test()
```

```
> data(sleep)
> t.test(extra ~ group, data=sleep)       # 2-sample t with group id column

        Welch Two Sample t-test

data:  extra by group
t = -1.8608, df = 17.776, p-value = 0.0794
alternative hypothesis: true difference in means is not equal to 0
95 percent confidence interval:
 -3.3654832  0.2054832
sample estimates:
mean in group 1 mean in group 2
          0.75            2.33

> sleepGrp1 = sleep$extra[sleep$group==1]
> sleepGrp2 = sleep$extra[sleep$group==2]
> t.test(sleepGrp1, sleepGrp2, conf.level=.99)        # 2-sample t, data in separate vectors

        Welch Two Sample t-test

data:  sleepGrp1 and sleepGrp2
t = -1.8608, df = 17.776, p-value = 0.0794
alternative hypothesis: true difference in means is not equal to 0
99 percent confidence interval:
 -4.027633  0.867633
sample estimates:
mean of x mean of y
    0.75      2.33
```

```
qqnorm(), qqline()
```

```
> qqnorm(precip, ylab = "Precipitation [in/yr] for 70 US cities", pch=19, cex=.6)
> qqline(precip)    # Is this line helpful?  Is it the one you would eyeball?
```

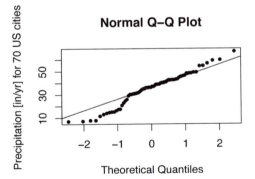

Appendix C.16.

```
power.t.test()
```

```
> power.t.test(n=20, delta=.1, sd=.4, sig.level=.05)   # tells how much power at these settings

    Two-sample t test power calculation

            n = 20
        delta = 0.1
           sd = 0.4
    sig.level = 0.05
        power = 0.1171781
  alternative = two.sided

NOTE: n is number in *each* group

> power.t.test(delta=.1, sd=.4, sig.level=.05, power=.8)   # tells sample size needed for desired power

    Two-sample t test power calculation

            n = 252.1281
        delta = 0.1
           sd = 0.4
    sig.level = 0.05
        power = 0.8
  alternative = two.sided

NOTE: n is number in *each* group
```

```
anova()
```

```
require(lattice)
require(abd)
data(JetLagKnees)
xyplot(shift ~ treatment, JetLagKnees, type=c('p','a'), col="navy", pch=19, cex=.5)
anova( lm( shift ~ treatment, JetLagKnees ) )

Analysis of Variance Table

Response: shift
          Df Sum Sq Mean Sq F value   Pr(>F)
treatment  2 7.2245  3.6122  7.2894 0.004472 **
Residuals 19 9.4153  0.4955
---
Signif. codes:  0 `***' 0.001 `**' 0.01 `*' 0.05 `.' 0.1 ` ' 1
```

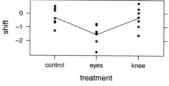

Appendix C.17.

References

Beak, J. Y. 2013. "Public Libraries as Places for STEM Learning. An Exploratory Interview Study with Eight Librarians." StarNetScience-technology Activities and Resources for Libraries. Retrieved from http://www.nc4il.org/images/papers/Baek_Pub lic%20Libraries%20as%20Places%20for%20STEM%20Learning.pdf.

Becker, K. 2012. "24 Hours in the Children's Section: An Observational Study at the Public Library." *Early Childhood Education Journal* 40: 107–14.

Bernoulli, J. 1998. The MacTutor History of Mathematics Archive, School of Mathematics and Statistics, University of St Andrews, UK. Retrieved from http://www-gap .dcs.st-and.ac.uk/~history/Biographies/Bernoulli_Jacob.html.

Borgman, C. L., R. G. Hirsh, V. A. Walter, and A. L. Gallagher. 1995. "Children's Searching Behavior on Browsing and Keyword Online Catalogs: The Science Library Catalog Project." *Journal of the American Society for Information Science* 46: 663–84.

Boulanger, R. 2009. *The Csound Book: Perspectives in Software Synthesis, Sound Design, Signal Processing, & Programming.* Available at http://mitpress.mit.edu/catalog/item/ default.asp?ttype=2&tid=3349.

Börner, K., C. Chen, and K. Boyack. 2003. "Visualizing Knowledge Domains." *Annual Review of Information Science & Technology 37*: 179–255.

Box, G. E. P. 1953. "Non-normality and Tests on Variances." *Biometrika* 40: 318–35.

Cavalier-Smith, T. 2002. "The Phagotrophic Origin of Eukaryotes and Phylogenetic Classification of Protozoa." *International Journal of Systematic and Evolutionary Microbiology* 52: 297–54.

Craft, B., and P. Cairns. 2008. "Directions for Methodological Research in Information Visualization." In E. Banissi, L. Stuart, G. Andrienko, F. T. Marchese, N. Memon, R. Alhajj, and B. Craft, eds. *IV 2008: 12th International Conference on Information Visualization, London, UK 8–11 July, 2008.* Washington, DC: IEEE Computer Society, 44–50.

Creswell, J. W. 2003. *Research Design: Qualitative, Quantitative and Mixed Methods Approaches.* Thousand Oaks, CA: Sage Publications.

Crowley, G. H., et al. 2002. "User Perceptions of the Library's Web Pages: A Focus Group Study at Texas A&M University." *The Journal of Academic Librarianship* 28 (4): 205–10.

Evergreen, S., and A. K. Emery. 2014. "Introduction to Visualization Checklist." Retrieved from http://stephanieevergreen.com/dataviz-checklist/.

Few, S. 2012. *Show Me the Numbers: Designing Tables and Graphs to Enlighten.* Burlingame, CA: Analytics Press.

Fisher, R. A. 1922. "On the Mathematical Foundations of Theoretical Statistics." *Philosophical Transactions of the Royal Society of London. Series A, Containing Papers of a Mathematical or Physical Character.* 309–68.

Friedman, A. 2014. "The Relationship between Research Methodology and Visual Display: A Study of Conference Proceedings in the Field Knowledge Organization." *Information Research: An International Electronic Journal* 19 (4).

Friendly, M. 2002. "Visions and R-Visions of Charles Joseph Minard." *Journal of Educational and Behavioral Statistics* 27 (1): 31–51.

Friendly, M., and D. Denis. 2005. "The Early Origins and Development of the Scatterplot." *Journal of the History of the Behavioral Science* 41 (2): 103–30.

Hodder, I. 1994. *The Interpretation of Documents and Material Culture.* Thousand Oaks, CA: Sage Publications, 155.

Howell, D. C. 2006. *Statistical Methods for Psychology.* 6th ed. London: Thomson.

Huges, A. M. 2011. "The Library as a Preferred Place for Studying: Observation of Students' Use of Physical Spaces." *Evidence Based Library and Information Practice* (EBLIP) 6 (2).

Jeong, S. H., and S.-T. Kim. 2010. *Core Resources on Time Series Analysis for Academic Libraries: A Selected, Annotated and Bibliography. Charleston Conference Proceedings.* Purdue University Press.

Jum, B., and T. Jin 2013. "Incorporating Nonparametric Statistics into Delphi Studies in Library and Information Science." *Information Research* 18 (3). Retrieved from http://www.informationr.net/ir/18-3/paper589.html#.VIcwVIt7VfQ.

Khoo, M., J. Pagano, A. Washington, M. Recker, B. Palmer, and R. Donahue. 2008. "Using Web Metrics to Analyze Digital Libraries." Eighth ACM/IEEE Joint Conference on Digital Libraries (JCDL), Pittsburgh, PA, June 16–20, 2008. Retrieved from http://www.ieee-tcdl.org/Bulletin/v4n1/khoo/khoo.html.

Lehmann, E. L., and J. P. Romano. 2005. *Testing Statistical Hypotheses.* 3rd ed. New York: Springer.

Lynch, B. P., and K. Smith. 2001. "The Changing Nature of Work in Academic Libraries. *College & Research Libraries* 62 (5): 407–20.

Long, Matthew P., and Roger C. Schonfeld 2013. *Ithaka S+R US Library Survey 2013.* Retrieved from http://www.sr.ithaka.org/.../SR_LibraryReport_20140310_0.pdf.

Lynch, B. P., and K. R. Smith. 2001. "The Changing Nature of Work in Academic Libraries." *College & Research Libraries* 62 (5): 407–20.

Mandelbrot, B., and R. L. Hudson. 2004. *The (Mis)Behavior of Markets: A Fractal View of Risk, Ruin, and Reward.* New York: Basic Books, 153.

Merriam, D. F. 1996. "Kansas 19th Century Geologic Maps." *Kansas Academy of Science, Transactions* 99, 95–114.

Miaoulis, G., and R. D. Michener. 1976. *An Introduction to Sampling.* Dubuque, IA: Kendall/Hunt Publishing Company.

Nitecki, D. A., and P. Hernon. 2000. "Measuring Service Quality at Yale University's Libraries." *The Journal of Academic Librarianship* 26 (4): 259–73.

Olson, H. A. 1998. "Mapping beyond Dewey's Boundaries: Constructing Classificatory Space for Marginalized Knowledge Domains." In Geoffrey C. Bowker and Susan Leigh Star, eds., *How Classifications Work: Problems and Challenges in an Electronic Age,* a special issue of *Library Trends* 47 (2): 233–54.

Powell, R. R., L. M. Baker, and J. J. Mika. 2002. "Library and Information Science Practitioners and Research." *Library & Information Science Research* 24: 49–72.

Rao. 2011. "Correlation among Library Facilities: An Analytical Study." *Library Philosophy and Practice* 12 (1).

Rhees, R. 1954. "George Boole as Student and Teacher. By Some of His Friends and Pupils." *Proceedings of the Royal Irish Academy. Section A: Mathematical and Physical Sciences.* Vol. 57. Royal Irish Academy.

Ruthenberg, J. 2013. "Data You Can Believe In, the Obama Campaign's Digital Masterminds Cash In," *New York Times,* June 23. Retrieved from http://www.nytimes.com/2013/06/23/magazine/ the-obama-campaigns-digital-masterminds-cash-in.html.

Savolainen, R. 2010. "Dietary Blogs as Sites of Informational and Emotional Support." *Information Research* 15 (4). Retrieved from http://www.informationr.net/ir/15-4/paper438.html.

Segal, E., and J. Heer. 2010. "Narrative Visualization: Telling Stories with Data." *Transactions on Visualization and Computer Graphics* 6: 1139–48.

Shaw, W. T., and J. Tig. 1994. *Applied Mathematica: Getting Started, Getting it Done.* Reading, MA: Addision-Wesley.

Sproull, N. L. 2002. *Handbook of Research Methods.* 2nd ed. Lanham, MD: Scarecrow Press, Inc.

Swisher, R. 1986. "Focus on Research." *Top of the News* No. 42: 175–77.

Tenopir, C. 2012. "Lib-Value: Measuring Value and Return on Investment of Academic Libraries." *Research Library Issues: A Bimonthly Report from ARL, CNI, and SPARC.*

Trochim, W. 2006. Designing Research Methods Knowledge Base. Retrieved from http://www.socialresearchmethods.net.

Tufte, E. R. 1983. *The Visual Display of Quantitative Information.* Cheshire, CT: Graphics Press.

Tufte, E. R. 1990. *Envisioning Information.* Cheshire, CT: Graphics Press.

Tufte, E. R. 1997. *Visual Explanations: Images and Quantities, Evidence and Narrative.* Cheshire, CT: Graphics Press.

Tufte, E. R. 2006. *Beautiful Evidence.* Cheshire, CT: Graphics Press.

Tukey, J. 1977. *Exploratory Data Analysis.* Addison-Wesley.

Wainer, H. 2000. *Visual Revelations: Graphical Tales of Fate and Deception from Napoleon Bonaparte to Ross Perot.* Hillsdale, NJ: Lawrence Erlbaum and Associates.

Walker, S., J. Hemsley, J. Eckert, R. M. Mason, and K. Nahon. 2013. *SoMe Tools for Social Media Research.* Fort Worth, TX: iConference.

Wang, J. 2009. "An Extensive Study on Automated Dewey Decimal Classification." *Journal of the American Society for Information Science and Technology* (JASIS) 60 (11).

Wattenberg, B. E., ed. 1966. *Statistical History of the United States: From Colonial Times to the Present*. New York: Basic Books.

Wickham, H. (2009). *ggplot2: Elegant Graphics for Data Analysis (Use R)*. London: Springer Publications.

Wickham, H., and L. Stryjewski. 2011. "40 Years of Box Plots." Manuscript submitted for publication. Retrieved from: http://vita.had.co.nz/papers/boxplots.html.

Wilkinson, L. 2005. *The Grammar of Graphics*. New York: Springer Publications.

Zar, J. H. 2010. *Biostatistical Analysis*. 5th ed. Upper Saddle River, NJ: Prentice-Hall.

Zickuhr, K. 2013. "Younger Americans' Reading and Library Habits." Pew Internet & American Life Project. Retrieved from_http://libraries.pewinternet.org/files/legacy -pdf/PIP_ YoungerLibraryPatrons.pdf.

Zuur, A. F., E. N. Lno, and E. H. W. G. Meesters. 2009. *A Beginner's Guide to R*. New York: Springer Publications.

Index

absolute deviations. *See* prediction
alternative testing, 22
analysis. *See also* correlation or regression,
    2, 5, 6, 8, 9, 36–37, 41, 63,
    189–190
    statistical, 5, 8, 16–17, 257
      and visualization, 300, 312
    units of, 5
ANOVA, or *Analysis of Variance*, 211–
    215, 215–220, 231, 232
    and equality of variance, 213
    ANOVA test of independence,
      223–227
    Chi Square, 220
      goodness-of-fit test, 220–223
      multinomial experiments, 222
      test of independence, 223–227
      with categorical variables, 220
    estimating population variance, 223
    one way ANOVA, 211–215
    tests of homogeneity, 218
    unequal within groups variances, 218
    value of test statistics, 223
arguments. See *R, arguments or parameters*
association, 80, 88
    group differences vs. association,
      208–210
    mutual, in correlations, 190

    negative, 80
    no, 80, 82
    positive, 80, 82, 88

Bayesian. *See also* Probability, Bayes
    Theorem, 101
Bell Labs, 9
Bernoulli distribution. *See* distribution,
    discrete
Bernoulli, Jacob, 107
    Beta (β), 23
bias, 24, 39
binomial conditions, 155
bivariate data, 20, 25
bivariate statistics, 79
    correlation analysis, 80
    correlation coefficient, 80
    univariate vs. bivariate. *See* variable
    with Pearson's sample correlation
      coefficient, 80–85
    with Spearman's rank coefficient. *See*
      also Spearman's, 85–86
Bricklin, Daniel, 7
Bureau of Labor Statistics, 30

causality
    statement of, 24
    illustrated in visualizations, 257

causation, 79, 88
Central Limit Theorem, 130–131, 146,
        161, 169, 216
central location. *See* measure of central
        tendency
Chambers, John, 9
character, 44, 63
    variable, 57–58
    string, 52
Chi Square test. *See* ANOVA, Chi Square
cluster sampling. *See* sampling
coding errors and outliers, 218
condition. *See* variable
confidence interval, 151–153, 169, 206–
        207, 232
    difference between means (using Z or
        t), 164
    effects of sample size on, 163
    effects of confidence levels, 161
    estimating a parameter [using *point
        estimate*], 151, 152, 206–207
    margin of error, 152, 162–163,
        206–207
        critical value, 152, 172, 177–179
        standard error (of point estimate),
        154–155
    parts of, 206
    population standard deviation known,
        158–159
    population standard deviation
        unknown,157–158
    Sample size, 163
    t-distribution, 158–159, 170;
confidence level, or *risk level*
    of confidence interval, 151–152, 169,
        206–207
    of population proportion. *See*
        population
    of sample, 159–160, 206–207
    of standard level, 157
    sample size (impact on), 163–164
    vs. certainty, 153, 206–207
Consumer Price Index (CPI), 34
contingency table, 213
continuous variable, 19, 26

correlation, 15, 25, 36, 79, 80, 88, 189–
        190, 297
    correlation coefficient, 80, 88, 190–
        193
    correlation research, 17, 190
    formula, 191
    linear association, 190, 191
    line of best fit. *See* Pearson's r
    measure of, 192–195
    Pearson Product-Moment Correlation
        Coefficient. *See also*
        Pearson's r, 191–192, 204
    perfect, 80, 81, 85
    positive vs. negative, 80
critical value. *See* confidence interval,
        margin of error
cross-sectional study, 33–34, 41

data
    analysis, 9, 15–18, 287, 292, 304
    collection, 30, 34, 35, 36, 37, 312
    correlation, 36
    frame. *See* sampling, frame
    summarizing, 2–13, 284
    univariate vs. bivariate. *See* variable
decision errors. *See* Type I or Type II
        errors
degree of association, 210
degree of variability, 161
degrees of freedom, 157–158, 169, 180,
        188, 210–211, 232
descriptive statistics, 4–5, 11, 67, 13,
        272, 277, 284–291
design(ed) experiment, 30, 31, 36, 41
deviation, 78
    score, 82
Dewey Decimal Classification, 17
discrete variable, 10
distribution, 20
    binomial [discrete random], 111–115,
        119–120, 121
        computing normal distribution,
        118
    mean, 11, 109–110
    standard deviation, 110–111

continuous, 115
converting distribution to standard z
        distribution, 132
critical value. *See* margin of error
        from, 152
discrete, 107–109
    Bernouli, 107
    mean dist., 109–110
    normal dist., 116–119, 173, 174,
        180,
    standard deviation dist., 110–111
    F, 210
    and degrees of freedom, 210
    describing, 210–211
    F statistic format, 210–211
    probability characteristics, 111–112,
        109–113, 139
problems with isolated outliers, 217
sampling distribution, 127–131, 146,
        174, 186
    standard deviation. *See* mean,
        standard error of
standard normal distribution, 6
Student t distribution. *See* probability,
        student-t
Dublin core, 5

estimating a parameter. *See* confidence
        interval
estimating population proportion. *See*
        population
estimation, 206, 231–232
events. *See* probability, events
experiment, 5, 6–8, 3–4, 91, 102, 104
experimental design, 17, 31, 41
extreme scores, methods for, 218

F distribution. *See* distributions, F
F ratio [between two estimates of
        population variances], 217
F test, 217–218
FBI Uniform Crime Rate, 34
factors, 50, 63;
    variables, 58
factual information. *See* survey design

factorials, 113–114
findings, summarizing, or *documenting
        study*, 3, 5, 17, 68
focus group(s), 33, 41
forecasts, forecasting. *See* predictions
fractions, 58–59. *See also* variable,
        fractions
frame. *See* sampling
Frankston, Bob, 7
frequency, 69–70
functions, 49, 50–51, 52–54, 64;
    in R. *See* R, functions
    monotonic functions, 85–86
    of statistics, 2

Galton, Francis, 191
Gates, Bill, 8
General Public License (GPL), 9
Gentleman, Robert, 10
Google, 59, 63

hypothesis, 14, 22–24;
    alternative, 22–23, 27, 172–173, 187
        notation, 185
    deductive, 14
    inductive, 14
    null, 22–23, 27,172–173, 175, 187
        notation, 185
hypothesis testing, 22–24, 26, 172–173,
        187
    and ANOVA. *See* ANOVA
    left-tailed test, 178
    one-sided test, 178
    p-value. *See* probability, p-value
    process, 171, 7–9, 15–16
    right-tailed test, 178
    test statistic, 175–176, 184, 187–188
    two-sided test, or *two-tailed test of
        significance*, 177–178, 188

Ihaka, Ross, 10
inferential statistics, or *inference(s)*, 4–5,
        11, 12, 149, 172
information science, 35–36
instrument, 25–26

integer, 54, 64
  variable, 56–56
interquartile range (IQR), 73–75
inter-rater test, 25
interval estimate, 206
intervention. *See* variable
interview, 31–32, 33, 42

level of precision. *See* sampling, error
library, as a *place* or *field of study (library
        science)*, 2, 4, 7, 9, 10, 2–4,
        6, 8–10, 16, 30–31, 35, 2,
        4, 6–7, 11–12
library, in *statistical programming*, 48, 64,
        4–6
logical value. *See* R, variables
long cross-sectional, or *longitudinal*, study
  time series, 34, 43
  panel, 34–35

machine languages, 48
margin of error. *See* confidence interval
mean or, *arithmetic mean. See also*
        variables, 69, 77, 78, 173
  advantages, 69
  disadvantages, 69
  mean of the sampling distribution,
        138–139
  population mean, 69, 7, 10, 159–161,
        174, 175, 179
    estimating w/standard deviation
        unknown, 157–159
  sample mean, 69, 7–8, 154, 174
  standard error (of the mean), 154, 176
measure, measurement, 7, 2–4, 7, 9,
        16–17, 68, 77
  aggregate, 34
  baseline, 34
  level of, 6
  relative frequency, 128
    and proportion, 138
  repeated, 34–35
measures
  of central tendency. *See also* central
        location, 3, 67, 68, 77, 78;

of position, 76
  of variability, or *dispersion*, 75–76,
median, 70, 78
  advantages, 70
methodology, 2, 9, 11, 15, 22, 30, 32,
        36, 50, 68, 77
Microsoft Excel, 8, 59–60
Minard, Charles Joseph, 258
mode, 70–72, 78
  advantages, 71
  disadvantages, 71
moderately skewed, 72
modules. See *library*
monotonic. See *functions*
MS(B), or *Mean Square between groups*,
        212
MS(W), or *Mean Square within groups*,
        212–213, 232
multivariable data sets
  in visualizations, 258, 292–293
  multivariate analysis. *See also* analysis

negative skewed, 72
nonprobability sampling. *See* sampling,
        non-probability
null hypothesis. *See* hypothesis, null
numeric, or decimal values, 52–53
  variables, 55–56

observation, 1, 17, 26, 35–36, 69
observational research or study, 35
  case studies, 36
  ethnographic studies, 36
  ethological studies, 36
order, 85
open source, 5, 9–11
Open Source Initiative (OSI), 9–11
operator. *See* R
opinions. *See* survey design
outlier, or *extreme value*, 70, 77

P value. *See* probability, P value
panel(s). *See* long cross-sectional study
parameter, 5, 11;
Pearson, Karl, 191

Pearson's r. *See also* Pearson's sample
        correlation coefficient, 80–
        85, 191–192, 204
    line of best fit, 80, 88, 190
point estimate. *See* sample statistic
population, 5–7, 11, 31–32, 33–35, 67,
        68, 77, 155–157, 171
    parameter, 4, 22, 128, 150
    proportion, 155–156, 25, 206
        confidence level, 152–154, 169
        estimation, 152–153
    regression, 189–190
    size, 127, 131, 161
    target, 31–32
    variance, 138, 210, 215
position, 2, 5, 12
positive skewed, 7
power of the test, 23
prediction, or *forecasting,* 34, 203–204,
        236, 247–251, 253
    errors, 248–249
        offset by absolute deviations and
            mean absolute deviations,
            248–249
        offset by mean squared error
            (MSE), 249
    power system load forecasting, 249
    educing decision making risk, 235–
        236
    using the equation of the line of best
        fit, 192
    using time series models, 247–248
        long term (1–10 yrs.), 236, 238
        short term (hrs. to days), 252
probability. *See also* sampling, probability,
        89–90, 171
    addition rules
        addition rule, 97–101
        more than two events, 100
        mutually exclusive events, 93
    Bayes, Rev. Thomas, 101
        Bayes theorem, 101–102, 104
    binomial distribution. *See* distribution,
        binomial
    classical probability rule, 91–93

conditional probability, or *posterior
        probability,* 94, 101–102, 104
cumulative probability, 201
events
    collectively exclusive, 94–95
    dependent, or *conditional,* 95–96
    independent, 7, 94
    mutually exclusive, or *disjoint,* 93,
        101, 104
    random, 90, 97, 104
    joint, 92, 97–98, 104
    marginal, 98, 103, 104
    multiplication rule, 95–96
        independent (intersection)events,
            96, 98
of success. *See* relative frequency
p-value, 146,179, 186, 187, 188
sample space. *See* sample
sampling distribution. *See* sampling,
        distribution
t distribution, or *student-t,* 157–158,
        180–181, 187, 188
    conditions, 180
    vs. standard distribution, 158
theory, 90, 92, 101
values, 90
problem statement. *See* research problem
        statement
proportions, 39, 207, 223
    concept of. *See* relative frequency
    population formula, 138–139
    sample formula, 139–141

qualitative variable, or *categorical,* 9
quantitative variable, or *numeric,* 9–10,
        79, 189
    and visualizations, 259
quartiles, 72–73, 78
quasi-experiment, 17, 26
questionnaire, 32–33, 42, 59
quota sampling. *See* sampling

R
    About, 9–11
    abline, 201

ANOVA, 219
arguments or *parameters,* 53–54, 63, 114
basic functions, 51–52
binomial distribution, 114
Chi Square, 29–32
Central Limit Theorem and R, 135
character string, 52, 54, 64
cluster analysis functions, 125, 146
command line interface, 46, 50
Comprehensive R Archive Network (CRAN), 51
contingency table, 213–214
correlations in. *See also* Pearson, Spearman, 80–84
data container, 49
data frame, 53, 103, 229–230, 278
descriptive statistics, 51
display console, 46–47
first class functions, also called *first class objects,* 63
global environment, 51–52
heatmap, 293–294
histogram, 76, 137; Ch.16 p.
importing data, 59–64
    from Google, 52
    from MS Excel, 59–51
    from the web, 62–63
installing, 46
Least square regression, 201
libraries, common function, 48
lm, 201, 246
logical operator syntax, 49
    arithmetic, 49
    logical, 49
maps. *See also* visualization, 295–296
MASS, 229–230
mean, 69
median, 70
mode, 70–72
model equation, 201
p-value [no direct way in R], 181–182
packages, 9
Pareto chart, or Pareto diagram, 290–291

Pearson's r, 82–84, 194
    using largest z-scores of x and y, 194
    unusual values call for regression analysis, 194
Percentile method [bootstrap confidence level], 168
plotting. *See* R, visualization
programming language of R, 48
random sampling simple sample command, 146
random variables, 105–106
range, 73–74
replace function, 107
res (*Squares Regression Line*) -, 199
return values, 54
runif function, 106
sample function, or *random sample,* 102, 126
scatter plot, 202, 290–291
Spearman's, 85–86
standard deviation, 75–76
standard error, 134
stratified sampling command, 126
summary statistics. *See* central tendency
syntax, 49, 21
systematic sampling command, 126
t distribution, 181–183,
    class and names function, 181–182
time series, 246–247
values, 49, 52, 54–55
variables, types in R, 54–55
variance, 74–75
vectors, 52–53, 103
visualizations, 257
    aesthetics function, 279–280
    color as parameter, 260–265
    color types, 260–265
    ggplot2, 278–289
    graphical parameters, 265
    histogram, 272–274
    pie, 267
        Custom colors, 269
    plot, 269–272

plotting symbols, 266, 9–12
saving your file, 274–275
z scores, 118
randomization, 2
range, 8–9, 11, 13
range of values, 3
regression, 36, 189–190, 195–201, 10
as relationship description, 189–190,
191–194, 196
as statistical process and techniques,
189, 195
cautions, 189
line of best fit, or *least squares
regression*, 196–201, 242–
243
using slope of linear equation,
196–201
relationship description, 195
relationship. *See* variable(s), relationship
reliability, 25, 26
research design, 13–14, 35
research problem statement, 13, 16

S, statistics software language, 8
sample(s), 4–5, 22, 24, 36–41, 124–125,
161
correlation. *See* correlation
regression. *See* regression
selection of, 37, 39–40
size, 24, 37–39, 8, 14–15, 25, 176,
180, 189
factors explained, 15–17
general formula, 17–18
strategies, 16–17
space, 91–93, 94, 103, 104
statistic, or *point estimate*, 151, 152,
153, 159, 169, 172, 175
sampling
advantages of, 33, 34, 35
cluster, 39, 41, 125, 146
confidence levels, 161–162
continuous (random), 115–116
convenience sample, 125, 146
discrete (random), 107–108
distribution, 127–130, 138–140, 146

error, 129, 146, 152, 153, 154
frame, 37, 41, 17
non-probability, 40
non-random, 23, 125
probability, 36–37
quota, 40–41
random, simple, 37–38, 125, 146,
149, 155, 159
sampling variability, 151
snowball, 40
stratified (random), 39, 42, 125, 146
systematic (non-random), 38–39, 42,
125, 146
with replacement, 38, 107
without replacement, 14, 107
significance level. *See* Type 1 error
skewed data, 70
Spearman's Rank coefficient, or
Spearman's rho, 85–86
spread, 73, 77
spreadsheet (applications), 7–8, 11,
59–62
SS(B), or *Sum of Squares between groups*,
216
SS(W), or *Sum of Squares within groups*
[no interaction between
samples], 215–216
Stallman, Richard, 8
standard deviation, 75–76, 154, 157,
169, 174, 184–185, 209
of the sampling distribution of a
statistic. *See* standard error
standard error (of the mean), 129, 134, 154–155
statistics, 1–6, 12
statistic(s) [samples], 2–4, 5, 10, 2, 14,
15, 17, 36, 18, 48–52, 18,
149, 150, 151, 154, 161,
169
applied, 3
defined, 2
descriptive, 3, 8, 2, 13
history of, 3
inference, 5–6, 139–140, 149, 168–
169;

sample. *See* sample statistic
    theoretical, 3
    types, 3
statisticians, 5, 9, 20–21, 163
Student-t. *See* distribution, Student-t
subjects, selection of, 8–9, 15, 16
sum of squares, 9–10, 212
survey design, 31

t distribution. *See* distribution, Student-t
test-retest, 25
theory (statistical), 5, 14, 157, 172,
Thucydides, 3
time series. *See* long cross-sectional study,
        34, 2–8, 14–19
    complexity, 242
    data patterns, 241
    five objectives of, 240
    exponential trend model, 236
    linear regression method, 251
    linear trends, 249
    quality control, 240
    models, 235–236, 249
        Centered Moving Average (CMA),
            250
        Moving Average (MA), 250
    monitoring ambient conditions, 240
    random error and autocorrelation, 240
    time series models, 236
    patterns, 235, 241, 252
    structure and function for prediction,
        240
treatment. *See* variable or independent
        variable, 7–8, 15
trends, 34, 236, 242
    lingering effects, 240
    method of second differences, 246
    random process, 241
    regression analysis, 240
    seasonality, 240
true experiments, 17, 31
Tufte, Edward, 259, 301
two way classification, or *cross-tabulation
        table*, 213

Type I error, *alpha (α)* or *level of
        significance,* 23, 176, 187–
        188
Type II, or *Beta*, error, 23, 177, 187–188

univariate data, 18

validity, 23–25, 27, 31
    construct, 15, 16, 18
    external, 16, 18
    internal, 15, 18
    statistical conclusion, 15, 18
variable(s), 19–20, 105;
    categorical, 19, 55, 58, 63, 220
    conditional, 105, 121
    continuous vs. discrete. *See also*
        random continuous or
        random discrete, 19, 121,
        240–241
    dependent, or *response*, 18, 88, 191,
        195
    fixed, 121
    fractions, 58–59, 63
    independent or *condition, intervention,
        predictor or treatment,* 18, 15
    qualitative vs. quantitative, 19–20
    random, 105–106
        continuous vs. discrete, 121
        mean (discrete random) or
            expected value, 109–110
        standard deviation (discrete
            random),110–111
        binomial (discrete random),
            107
    relationship(s), 79–82, 88
    univariate vs. bivariate data, 20, 25
variance, also *spread* or *dispersion*, 73–75
    attribute(s), 76
    in t-distribution, 180–181
    value(s), 77
vector, 52–53, 64
    index, 54, 64
VisiCalc, 8
visualize, or *visualization*, 9, 76, 258

additive color, 306–307
advanced visualization, 277–278
aesthetics, 278–281, 297
bibliographic data structure and
        visualization, 300
boxplot, 277, 287
checklist, or *guidelines*, 301–313
color, 259–263, 305–306
color theory, 305–308
descriptive statistics
    box plot, 287
    histogram. *See also* R, histogram,
        272–274, 284–285
    scatter plot, 288–290
    pareto diagram, 290–291
generating visualizations. *See also* R,
        visualizations
ggplot2, 278
geometrics, or *graphical elements*,
        281–282
heat map, 293–294

hexadecimal colors, 261
histograms, 272–274
history of, 258
layer, 279, 291
lines, 308–309
maps, 295–296
multivariate data, 292–295
palettes, 262
pie chart, 267–268
plot charts, 260, 269–272
    ggplot2. *See* R, plotting
principles (Tufte), 259
scatterplot, 2, 288–289
statistics, 3
subtractive color, 307–308
visual representation, 258

z, 117, 122, 176
z score, 84, 169, 175–177
z table, or *standard normal z table*, 6–7,
        120–121, 133, 183

About the Author

Alon Friedman is an assistant professor in the School of Information at the University of South Florida. He teaches introduction to visualization and big data, information retrieval, visual communication, and web technologies to undergraduate and graduate students. Previously he taught introductory and advanced statistics as well as research methodologies for ten years across the New York City region. His research interests and expertise focus on statistical classification and visualization using open source R. Dr. Friedman also has worked as a web technologist in New York City and Tel Aviv, Israel.